T0083639

STEPHEN KING'S GOTHIC

SERIES PREFACE

Gothic Literary Studies is dedicated to publishing groundbreaking scholarship on Gothic in literature and film.The Gothic,which has been subjected to a variety of critical and theoretical approaches, is a form which plays an important role in our understanding of literary, intellectual and cultural histories. The series seeks to promote challenging and innovative approaches to Gothic which question any aspect of the Gothic tradition or perceived critical orthodoxy.

Volumes in the series explore how issues such as gender, religion, nation and sexuality have shaped our view of the Gothic tradition. Both academically rigorous and informed by the latest developments in critical theory, the series provides an important focus for scholastic developments in Gothic studies, literary studies, cultural studies and critical theory.The series will be of interest to students of all levels and to scholars and teachers of the Gothic and literary and cultural histories.

SERIES EDITORS

Andrew Smith, University of Glamorgan
Benjamin F. Fisher, University of Mississippi

EDITORIAL BOARD

Stephen King's Gothic

John Sears

UNIVERSITY OF WALES PRESS
CARDIFF
2011

www.uwp.co.uk

British Library CIP Data
A catalogue record for this book is available from the British Library.

ISBN (hardback)   978-0-7083-2345-8
ISBN (paperback)   978-0-7083-2402-8
e-ISBN   978-0-7083-2346-5

Typeset in Wales by Eira Fenn Gaunt, Cardiff
Printed by CPI Antony Rowe, Chippenham, Wiltshire

Contents

ACKNOWLEDGEMENTS

The British Academy generously funded a research visit to the Fogler Library at the University of Maine, Orono, in March 2009. I am grateful to Stephen King for permission to view some of the materials stored there, and to Brenda Steeves and her colleagues at the Special Collections of the Fogler Library for all their assistance with my research.

Early versions of chapters 6, 4 and 8 were delivered at the PCA/ACA conferences in San Francisco in 2008, New Orleans in 2009 and St Louis in 2010. Another version of chapter 4 was delivered at the IGA conference at Lancaster University in 2009. I am grateful to the organisers of all these events for allowing me to present, and to members of the various audiences for their comments and ideas, which were always positive and constructive. In particular I owe much to Mary Findley, Phil Simpson, Tony Magistrale and Patrick McAleer, and to other regular and one-off presenters at the 'Stephen King Area', and to Catherine Spooner and Fred Botting. The anonymous reader for University of Wales Press offered detailed and valuable comments that, in every case, improved this book.

Sue Zlosnik and Berthold Schoene gave important initial encouragement to this project. Patricia Allmer has, as always, supported it from beginning to end, beyond and back.

ABBREVIATIONS

Editions of Stephen King's works used in this book are referred to throughout by the following abbreviations.

BB	*Bag of Bones*, 1998 (London: Hodder & Stoughton)
C	*Carrie*, 1978 (London: New English Library/Hodder & Stoughton)
Ce	*Cell*, 2006 (London: Hodder & Stoughton)
Ch	*Christine*, 1983 (London: Book Club Associates/Hodder & Stoughton)
Cu	*Cujo*, 1981 (London: Hodder/Macdonald & Co.)
DC	*Dolores Claiborne*, 1993 (London: New English Library/ Hodder & Stoughton)
DH	*The Dark Half*, 1989 (London: Hodder & Stoughton)
DK	*Duma Key*, 2008 (London: Hodder & Stoughton)
DM	*Danse Macabre: The Anatomy of Horror*, 1982 (London: Futura Publications)
DS	*Different Seasons*, 1995 (London: Warner Books/Little, Brown)
DZ	*The Dead Zone*, 1992 (London: Warner Books/Little, Brown)
ED	*The Eyes of the Dragon*, 1987 (London: Book Club Associates/Macdonald & Co.)
EE	*Everything's Eventual*, 2002 (London: Book Club Associates/Hodder & Stoughton)
F	*Firestarter*, 1981 (London: Macdonald/Futura Publishers)
FB8	*From a Buick 8*, 2002 (New York: Scribner)
FPM	*Four Past Midnight*, 1991 (London: New English Library/ Hodder & Stoughton)
G	*Gerald's Game*, 1992 (London: Book Club Associates/ Hodder & Stoughton)

GL   *The Girl Who Loved Tom Gordon*, 1999 (London: New English Library/Hodder & Stoughton)
GM   *The Green Mile* (in six parts), 1996 (London: Penguin Books)
HA   *Hearts in Atlantis*, 1999 (London: Hodder & Stoughton)
I   *Insomnia*, 1994 (London: New English Library/Hodder & Stoughton)
It   *It*, 1987 (London: New English Library/Hodder & Stoughton)
LS   *Lisey's Story*, 2006 (London: Hodder & Stoughton)
M   *Misery*, 1988 (London: New English Library/Hodder & Stoughton)
ND   *Nightmares & Dreamscapes*, 1993 (London: New English Library/Hodder & Stoughton)
NS   *Night Shift*, 1979 (London: New English Library/Hodder & Stoughton)
NT   *Needful Things*, 1991 (London: Book Club Associates/Hodder & Stoughton)
OW   *On Writing*, 2000 (London: Hodder & Stoughton)
PS   *Pet Sematary*, 1984 (London: Book Club Associates/Hodder & Stoughton)
RM   *Rose Madder*, 1995 (London: Hodder & Stoughton)
S   *The Shining*, 1980 (London: New English Library/Hodder & Stoughton)
SC   *Skeleton Crew*, 1985 (London: Book Club Associates/Macdonald & Co.)
SL   *'Salem's Lot (Illustrated Edition)*, 2006 (London: Hodder & Stoughton)
St   *The Stand (Complete & Uncut Edition)*, 1990 (London: Book Club Associates/Hodder & Stoughton)
SW   *Secret Windows: Essays and Fiction on the Craft of Writing*, 2000 (New York: Book of the Month Club)
T   *The Tommyknockers*, 1989 (London: New English Library/Hodder & Stoughton)

In memory of
A.G.S. 1933–2009

1

Rereading Stephen King's Gothic

'Does anybody ever reread King? Are his texts susceptible to rereading?'[1]

'Reread too Kings ...'[2]

'If you want to be a writer, you must do two things above all others: read a lot and write a lot.' (OW, 164)

Rereading King

What would it mean to reread Stephen King? What kind of demand would be levied on the rereader? Stephen King's fictions (and those written by the different 'King', Richard Bachman, making two 'Kings' to reread) comprise a vast and ever-increasing number of novels, short stories, screenplays. To reread them (all) would require, above all, time, an extended time of reading that is potentially indefinite as the oeuvre expands within it: in the time of writing this book, King has published three new novels and a collection of short stories. Such a rereading would be, in one sense, simply an exercise in the quantification of reading, in reading as consuming. 'Reading a lot', as King puts it, would also be one result, 'above all others', of rereading King's activity of 'writing a lot'. But 'rereading King' would also be an exercise in the extension of repetition, in the act of rereading an oeuvre already deeply structured (as this book will argue) by its own engagement in the Gothic habit of rereading and, consequent on these rereadings, rewriting what it has read and reread. To reread King would be to enter (to re-enter), and perhaps to become lost within, a labyrinth of intra- and intertextual relations, an immense and complex textual space.

David Punter's question about rereading King is the correct one to ask at the beginning of a discussion of Stephen King's Gothic. The Gothic mode is notoriously predicated on varieties of repetition, on the recycling of narratives and forms, on revisiting older, pre-existent texts, on labyrinthine texts and spaces, and on the seemingly endless resurrection of an apparently dead, outmoded tradition. John Frow writes of 'exhausted genres such as the Gothic romance', which yet 'survive in their modal form'.[3] Fred Botting argues that, with its return to the genre of romance in Francis Ford Coppola's *Bram Stoker's Dracula* (1992), 'Gothic dies, divested of its excesses, of its transgressions, horrors and diabolical laughter [. . .]'. This dying, he suggests, may be a 'prelude to other spectral returns'.[4] In Stephen King's work and in the writings of his contemporaries and younger imitators, Gothic clearly revives or survives, persisting as a remarkably resilient, successful and lucrative mode of popular fiction.

David Punter's questions are, of course, those asked of much popular fiction. For Punter, 'rereading' perhaps implies a mixture of close reading, critical reading and extended theoretical analysis, a different kind of reading from that invited by the initial encounter with the popular fictional text. That encounter of reading is predicated on ostensibly simple meanings: 'popular fiction', Ken Gelder affirms, 'is simple', in opposition to a construction of 'Literature' (with a capital 'L') as 'complex'.[5] Punter's notion of 'rereading' implies a double level of 'complexity', the act of reading as a repetition that nevertheless seeks and perhaps reveals something implicitly missed in the 'first' reading, and geared for the literary critic towards the production of a writing that puts into practice, demonstrates or argues for a (re-) reading. The 'reread' text must demonstrate a 'susceptibility' to repetitive reading strategies (that is, critical analyses) more often associated with the values of the kinds of writing conventionally described as 'Literature'.

Reading and writing – and rereading and rewriting – are insistent activities in King's works. They locate texts and their production and consumption at the moral and political centres of the universes he constructs, and establish writing as crucial to King's constructions of social relations, a pivotal element of his popular appeal. When Ben Mears, the writer-hero of *'Salem's Lot* (1975), is complimented by Susan Norton on one of his books she happens to be reading, he replies 'Thanks. When I take it down and look at it, I wonder how it ever got published' (*SL*, 23). The exchange establishes a social relation through shared but also individual acts of reading and re-reading (and rereading one's own writing), in this case a relation between two people who will become lovers, and one of whom will eventually become radically altered, transformed into a vampire. It indicates the ways in which writers and writing, readers and reading, interact across King's oeuvre to represent different kinds of social relations established initially on the basis of the self's response to the other and in the possibilities contained within that response. These social relations, in turn, are among the things that repeatedly come under threat in King's version of Gothic. At its most extreme, in novels like *The Stand* (1979), this threat is nearly absolute. Here, humanity is virtually eradicated, leaving a small and disparate group of survivors to encounter each other, regroup and learn to live together in reconstructing a new social order in the face of extreme manifestations of monstrous otherness. This structure allows King also to scrutinise in this novel the roles in this social reconstruction of different kinds of reading and writing and of different kinds of text in establishing (or re-establishing) this society. These range from the 'Life History' written by deaf-and-dumb Nick Andros, which finishes with the words 'That was where I learned to read and write', to Harold Lauder's 'ledger', a narrative account that is also 'a solid block of writing, an outpouring of hate' (*St*, 143–4). They include the establishment in chapter 51 of written legal and political constitutions that define some of the rights, privileges and policies of the new society (*St*, 602). *The Stand*, a late 1970s Gothic novel with a strong science fiction element, is itself a product of rereading. It rereads and offers a rewriting of several texts, most notably George R. Stewart's *Earth Abides* (1948) and Terry Nation's TV series *Survivors* (1975–8: remade 2008–10). King cites also 'a book by M. P. Shiel called *The Purple Cloud*', a novel published in 1901 that draws, in turn, on Mary Shelley's *The Last Man* (1826).[6] Such a textual lineage indicates that King's novel deliberately engages with, rereads and extends a long popular fictional tradition that crosses media and genres extending back at least to the Romantic period.

Another version of *The Stand* is offered in *Misery* (1987), where the social world is erased in another way, reduced by Gothic tropes of injury, madness, imprisonment and isolation to a minimal structure of man–woman as writer–reader, in order, again, to enact and examine a struggle over the meanings of texts and over the different kinds of authority exerted by the reader and the writer. *Misery* explores, within claustrophobic constraints of geography and narrative, the horror latent in a world constructed solely of a certain kind of re-reading demanded by a certain kind of rereader who wants only to read the same text repeatedly, who 'wanted Misery, Misery, Misery' (*M*, 31). This is rereading as blank repetition, precisely the kind of rereading without difference that Punter implies might constitute the experience of rereading King. In critiquing this mechanical form of reading-as-consumption, *Misery* enacts a brutal fantasy of punishment and revenge. A degree-zero social relation is established in the novel in order for the male writer to be punished, and for the repetitive female rereader to be exorcised violently in avenging that punishment. The punishment meted out by a repetitive reader who figures, in this context in the mind of the fictional romance writer Paul Sheldon, an indiscriminate and feared social mass of readers, is for producing something different, something outside familiar generic frames. The novel centres its analysis on the tension between difference and repetition, the difference that may be potential in rereading outside the restricted demands of repetition. As I hope to demonstrate, rereading King is, in contrast to the message of *Misery*, an experience radically different to the repetition by an anonymous indiscriminate reader of the word 'Misery' and all it implies, one that instead exploits to the full the potentials of horror by both enacting and evading the reductive simplicity of repetition.

King's works constantly develop and expand in the senses of being added to and, like *The Stand*, republished in 1990, and *'Salem's Lot*, in 2005, being revised and reissued in new expanded editions. They exist in a complex and reiterative set of relations to

Gothic conventions. While Gothic motifs, themes and concerns resonate throughout his immense oeuvre, the relations between this oeuvre and conventional understandings of the Gothic are best understood as mobile, flexible, sometimes contradictory and always productive. Gothic exists, throughout King's writing, as a spectral, trace effect of that writing, a product both of the failure and the persistence of words. Linguistic uncertainty and indeterminacy, effects of repetition, periphrasis, verbal encryption, anagrammatisation and other verbal tricks and insistences (like, for example, the description of Carrie's telekinetic powers as a 'latent talent' (*C*, 15) or the subtle, divisive counterpointing of Annie's '*for-EN-sics*' and her 'frenzies' in *Misery* (*M*, 233)), revealed through close reading to be embedded throughout King's prose, indicate aspects of formal and generic ambivalence and mobility. King's works display what Michael R. Collings has called 'generic indecisiveness', an unwillingness or inability to be confined to singular generic categories.[7] They tend instead to fray at their generic edges, sprawl over boundaries, allowing different genres to seep into each other and constructing, in the process, different and astonishingly marketable generic combinations. Such 'indecisiveness', evident also in the formal complexity of novels like *Carrie* (discussed in chapter 2 below), is characteristic of the Gothic in its remarkably persistent series of historical survivals through relentless transformations and redeployments of other genres, from crime fiction to romance to Westerns. Many of these processes are exemplified in King's works, where mobility is again key: individual works frequently mutate genre, or juxtapose different generic features, within their own textual borders, contravening (as we will see in chapter 4 below) the classificatory 'law of genre' Jacques Derrida defines, but fulfilling, in Gothic terms, the contract implicit in and demanded by that contravention.[8]

Genre, Intertextuality

As Heidi Strengell notes in one of the few full-length critical studies of King, 'Most of King's novels and stories are generic hybrids'.[9] The same point might also be made about his critical writings, which tend, in delineating King's versions of the genres and traditions of horror, to combine encyclopaedic accumulation of detail, extensive paraphrase and plot summaries, and autobiographical interludes, with occasional critical or theoretical asides. The uses to which King's works put their 'generic indecisiveness' and 'generic hybridity' correspond to the themes and concerns of those works. Genres rely for their effects on shared meanings that are recognisable to readers, so that generic recognition invokes familiarity (just as genres rely on 'family resemblances' between texts) and initiates particular reader responses familiar to the experience of reading King. In that experience, genre is 'performed' – it 'takes place', Frow argues, 'in the interplay of readings and of the social force they carry'.[10] These readings and their social force also incorporate within this 'interplay' the effects of readings depicted within or put into effect by the texts themselves, like Annie Wilkes's 'reading' scrutinised in *Misery*, Rose's endless readings of signs in *Rose Madder* (1995) or the various re-readings and rewritings of canonical Gothic and other texts performed throughout King's oeuvre. They also mobilise the available critical and other readings and rereadings of those texts, enabling King's generic mixing to generate complex and critically significant meanings as they delineate his different engagements with Gothic. Genre is effectively produced by the recognition through repetition generated in the act of rereading. It depends for its effects on readerly familiarities that are established in prior acts of reading. As 'generic hybrids', King's works express a complex relationship to this process of generic recognition. They demand a kind of reading which is also, already, a 'rereading' for the first time, an inauguration of readerly recognition that is also (in typically Gothic terms) a resurrection of previous readings. They draw on a wide range of experiences that pre-exist the texts themselves and make possible a conception of the importance of rereading to the act of reading Gothic that enables us to argue, against David Punter's question, that no one ever 'reads' King, in any simple sense, for the *first* time.

The complex generic relations that delineate and define King's works imply both the generation of generic positions and identities and its ideologically loaded Gothic inverse, the *de*generation of discrete and clearly definable forms and structures into hybridical or mixed forms. This process, as we will see later, concerns much of

King's writing. In *Misery* this is made explicit, as Paul Sheldon thinks of 'popular fiction' as 'a degenerate sort' of art (*M*, 272). Generic relations furthermore depend upon and are produced by a proliferating series of intertextual referents that establish different traditions and different textual precursors as markers and delimiters of the ways King's works produce meanings. These intertexts, comprised of both specific texts and generic features and motifs, 'productively question ideas of origin, stability, and repetition'.[11] Such ideas are crucial to a comprehension of King's Gothic and are manifest in the concern of his works with key Gothic configurations of otherness in terms of beginning, authenticity, identity and difference, repetition and variation, the familiar and the unfamiliar, and the production and effects of monstrosity. Intertextual references abound in King's works (to say nothing of the *intra*textual network that binds many of King's novels and short stories, like those of his major precursor H. P. Lovecraft, into epic sequences and cross-referenced inter-allusive structures). Citations from fictional and poetic texts or from popular music and film are used to frame individual works. They are placed as markers at section and chapter breaks and work constantly to regulate and direct readerly attention in relation to the text being read. Allusions authenticate character, work to historicise and legitimise plot and context and offer a constant series of insights into how King's writing negotiates its own literary and cultural inheritances. Rarely attended to by critics, these different citations signify textual echoes, parallels and extensions. They mark the specific text in relation to a range of written, filmic and other traditions that informs and draws upon readerly competences in complex ways, establishing the oeuvre again in a complex set of relations to other texts and works, and inviting the encyclopaedic response from the reader that King's critical works often demand in demonstrating his own, authorial, readerly competence. Importantly, they also interrogate their own relations to traditions and origins, degrees of textual and ontological stability, and issues of repetition and citation, relations that are addressed in different ways within the individual works. These questions again relate back to the functions of Gothic and its willingness to raid its own textual corp(u)ses in search of narrative sustenance. King's uses of intertextuality, like his generic flexibility, define key aspects of his Gothic writing.

Genre and intertextuality thus provide initial ways of thinking about the possibilities opened up by 'rereading' King. To conceive King's works in relation to their uses of and deformations of genre and intertextuality is to establish ways of responding to David Punter's question. Rereading is, in effect, what Stephen King's Gothic is, initially, all about. In reading King we read his rereadings, and reread our own readerly relations to the traditions he appropriates, revises and redeploys in the act of rereading them. The intertextual interrogation of textual identity in terms of 'origin, stability, and repetition' impinges also on rereading as an activity that doubles and therefore puts into question the notional originality of any given reading, challenging its ostensible primacy and therefore its control over meanings. Generic and intertextual frames mark each reading as a rereading, insisting on familiar patterns, processes of citation and allusion and the readerly act of recognition as key elements in the construction, in King's case, of fictional worlds charged with recognisable significances. In this sense, King's works conform to the requirements of popular fiction and of specifically Gothic texts in fulfilling reader expectations that are generically and intertextually marked.

Popular fiction

King's works repeatedly deploy key features of the popular field: repetition and formulaic structure, sometimes excessive length and tendencies to over- or under-writing, legitimising uses of pre-cursor texts, clichéd or banal denouements, two-dimensional characterisation, sentimental bathos and nostalgia. These features relate King's works clearly to the well-known formal and stylistic limits of Gothic fictions and their traditions. Even his most sympathetic critics comment on these features. 'In all honesty', notes Tony Magistrale, King's best and most frequent critic, 'much of King's oeuvre would benefit from the tough advice of a good editor: there are, for example, a number of instances where King's work could be substantially improved as a result of some judicious editing'.[12] Overt references in the texts to historical and political contexts include frequent nods to Vietnam, Nixon and Watergate, Cold War cultural anxieties and other historical and political meta-narratives. These allusions enable us to locate the works historically, if not politically, alongside their relentless documenting of the jingles, catchphrases and brand names of late twentieth-century Western consumerism. But they mask a deeper, more persuasive set of concerns with the ideological tensions expressed in most popular fiction: imitation versus innovation, conventionality versus transformation, political acquiescence against resistance, subversion against reinforcement, and, of course, marketability against less marketable aesthetic values. These themes resolve themselves at surface levels into King's much-noted thematic concern with 'the struggle of Good and Evil', manifest in his fiction's ideological insistence on and privileging of conventional moral structures. Magistrale defines this 'struggle' within the tradition of American Gothic literature, linking it specifically to the writings of Nathaniel Hawthorne and summarising the moral position established in King's writing: 'while we all share in the capacity for acts of evil, each of us is likewise endowed with the potential for performing good'.[13] This Manichaean reading of King, revealed in his relentless analysis of adult suppressions of childhood freedoms, informs much criticism of his work and helps initially to locate it in relation to those American and other Gothic traditions on which King's writing heavily depends.

In a different vein, Harold Bloom comments on King's reliance on such traditions when he pejoratively notes King's 'remarkable absence of invention'.[14] This feature is a symptom of an absolute reliance on Gothic's cyclical, repetitive generic modality, a popular-fictional modality well described by Ken Gelder: 'Genres must be continually processed, re-animated, added to'.[15] One of King's many definitions of writing calls it 'a process of accretion' (*SW*, 392), where 'accretion' signifies this 'adding-to'. 'You put the two things together and somehow they connect', he states (*SW*, 392). Gelder's 'Processing' and 're-animating', combined with King's 'accretion', describe the popular Gothic writer's macabre activities structured by a foundational myth, that of *Frankenstein*, which in turn provides King with another metaphor for the moment of writerly 'creativity': 'You feel as Victor Frankenstein must have when the dead conglomeration of sewn-together spare parts opened its watery yellow eyes' (*OW*, 153). Elsewhere he argues, in an apparently unwitting but suggestive pun, during a discussion of the relations between literature and reality, that 'writing is not life' (*SW*, 398). This precisely expresses the Gothic text's relation to its themes: not death, but 'not life', lies at the centre of King's Gothic narratives. Their fictionality offers an assertion of the 'not life' that fiction, particularly Gothic fiction, creates. 'Not life' inverts the opposition of life–death; it expresses the 'un-' that undermines and unhinges the world of the Gothic in its concern with the unconscious, the undead, the uncanny, the unthinkable and unbelievable, and the unrepresentable.

King's mobile comprehension of writing's 'not life', its complex and problematic enactment of Gothic concerns with mortality, and other key motifs and modalities of the macabre ('My obsession is with the macabre', King states in the 'Foreword' to *Night Shift* (*NS*, 7)), will be a recurrent concern of this book. King's 'obsession' may be with the macabre, but it is also, this book contends, with the Gothic world of the 'un-', the 'not life' that is created by Gothic writing and the Gothic writer and by reading and the reader. This 'obsession' develops throughout his career in a variety of forms, grounding his versions of Gothic in a complex textuality that plays across the surfaces of his narratives and which is eminently susceptible to critical rereading. For King the experience of writing is inevitably Gothically charged. Words and paragraphs, King writes, 'quicken and begin to breathe' like monstrous creations; 'building entire mansions of words' becomes the writer's business, the staging of versions of the genre in which 'stories are relics, part of an undiscovered pre-existing world' (*OW*, 153–4, 188). The power of words to animate (and re-animate) and to construct 'mansions', the story as 'relic' from an 'undiscovered' past world: these are the parameters of a conception of Gothic as a ghostly script, as inscription, as instruction for performance and as inscribed tradition in which versions of the encounter between self and other find themselves allegorised, throughout King's oeuvre, in the staged relation between the writer and the reader, a relation that can be detected from his earliest work onwards.

Others

King's multiple versions of Gothic engage, then, in processing, re-animating and adding to the genre's various written histories in order to stage a series of encounters between writers and readers.

These, in turn, suggest deeper levels of significance, in which Gothic's obsession with writing expresses its concern with different construct- ions of otherness. For King, otherness is principally contemporary, motivated sometimes directly by current political and social anxieties, and expressed as a recurrent, ineradicable feature of an otherwise familiar, endlessly reread social reality. King's contemporary figures of otherness are multiple: they may be gendered (*Carrie, Misery*), racialised (*The Green Mile, Thinner, Bag of Bones, Duma Key*) or sexualised (*Gerald's Game*), or they may reside within and express American fantasies of colonial and neo-colonial history (*Pet Sematary*). They may be monstrous or becoming-monstrous (*It, The Tommy- knockers*), spectral (*The Shining*), uncanny (*The Dark Half; Secret Window, Secret Garden*), possessed by demonic forces or human desires (*Christine, From a Buick 8*). They may constitute themselves as readers (*Misery*) or as other kinds of consumers (*Needful Things*). Their manifestations can distort and redefine conventional comprehensions of time (*The Langoliers*) and space, history and place (*The Shining* and *'Salem's Lot*), private and public, familiar and unfamiliar (*Cujo, The Girl who Loved Tom Gordon*). In any of these configurations they may reveal themselves as belonging to and inhabiting 'us' in ways that threaten and destabilise even more disturbingly our own con- ceptions of our selves. They are often mechanical objects, haunted cars or laundry machines, or (more commonly) writing machines that encode a rhetoric of the machine that spills over into other dimensions of King's fictional world. Such metaphors provide, for example, ways of comprehending repetitive human activities and their relations to desire. They also express a conservative anxiety about technology and its effects and suggest a coupling of King's Gothic to a theoretical framework of machinic relations and inter- connections (discussed in chapter 4 below) that mobilises a critique of Gothic's assimilative, combinatory generic and intertextual tenden- cies. They are, above all, profoundly intertextual, dependent upon their elective affinities with specific and recurrent Gothic and other tropes, motifs and traditions, extensively drawn upon and often re- petitively alluded to throughout the oeuvre.

In their most powerful and extreme forms, these varieties of others become 'Other', versions of the big Other of psychoanalytic theory, excessively significant and threatening in their symbolic weight. In doing so, they tend to become externalised projections, figures of the othernesses King's writing locates within the self. In *It* (1987), for example, the big Other is a polymorphously perverse thing, an 'It' that manifests itself as the deepest childhood fears of those who encounter 'It', and therefore as a multitude of things, uncontrollably diverse in appearance, as various in its meanings and grammatical functions as the word 'it', which plays powerfully across the textual surface of the novel. *It* (discussed in chapter 8 below) symbolises through this linguistic repetition the monstrosity implicit in a notion of the unconscious, the hidden but determining element of the Freudian conception of the divided self, and therefore latent in each of us, a script which each follows unwittingly and which inscribes itself covertly into the novel's texture. Through such configurations of otherness as an emanation or expression of the self's fears and anxieties, King's work offers interrogations of selfhood and of the effective agencies of the self as 'a creature of phantasms'.[16] The self is constituted as an imagined and unstable agency, deluded in its sense of autonomy and consistency, continually under threat from without and within, and (most threateningly) potentially other, or monstrous, to itself. King's works repeatedly examine the stability and viability of conventional constructions of selfhood in post-modernity, not least in its own inevitable relation to death, which may be considered *the* defining Gothic motif. King's Gothic, in turn, is ideologically constrained by a failure to transcend a gendering of that 'Otherness', a reduction of the monstrous 'Other' to a feminine-coded figure of specifically masculine anxiety that connects the feminine to death, constructed in opposition to a masculine selfhood and creative force figured by the male writer. This is the basic paradigm of King's writing, noted by critics like Hanson[17] and Schroeder:[18] a feminine-coded monstrosity threatening and countered by a masculine creative agent. This structure both repeats and fails to redefine a set of relations wholly intrinsic to the reactionary gender politics associated with Gothic from its earliest inceptions. It indicates an ideological restriction of King's writing to which we will repeatedly return.

The staging of different encounters with otherness is frequently examined through King's preoccupations with the figure of the writer and the 'secret act' of writing, with all the questions of relations to others that 'secret' implies (*FPM*, 306). King's Gothic insistently explores the connections between writing, constructions of 'Otherness' and the position of the writer in relation to these connections and constructions. His consistently male writers, from Ben Mears in *'Salem's Lot* to Scott Landon in *Lisey's Story* (2006), are inscribed into symbolically complex relations with the social worlds they inhabit. Their writing-acts become allegories of the processes of fictional construction and critical analysis that King's texts relentlessly perform. These processes can be read as large-scale myths of the reader–writer–text relation (as is offered in *Misery*) or, again, as small-scale patterns, local and insistent anomalies of language, like the play of initials between *'Salem's Lot*, *Lisey's Story* and Scott Landon. Such lexical games suggest an embedded or covert elective affinity, a cryptically inscribed connection between texts and characters across the oeuvre. Part of the project of rereading King's works as expressions of contemporary Gothic concerns will involve tracing such connections, repetitions and patterning recurrences in order to explore the complexities of King's language in its attempts to map writing's social potentials, its provision of ways for the reader to encounter and come to understand forms of otherness.

Beginning Writing

The question of traditions and their representation and deployment in contemporary Gothic writing is a recurrent concern of King's work, and will be explored more fully in chapter 3 below. A key element of King's particular strain of the Gothic is manifest in the deliberate ambivalence expressed in his texts over the question of which tradition to identify with, or where within available traditions to locate their sources and what the consequences of such choices might be. This might explain his recurrent references to high-cultural literary texts, in particular, as motifs offering some guarantee of value or legitimacy to the ostensibly popular text. Allusions and citations insert into King's texts traces, fragments and elements of other texts and other writings, redefining the works as structurally plural and profoundly dialogic in their constant writing back to traditions. Furthermore, the precursor texts which King's works incorporate are themselves multiple in their origins, members of pre-existing genres and traditions that predispose their potential meanings to instability and unreliability. If the contemporary text is susceptible to rereading and to all the transformations of interpretation implied by that susceptibility, then so too are its intertexts and precursors unreliable as origins, susceptible in turn to other rereadings (including those performed by the contemporary text). This version of the structural ambivalence of Gothic writing is evident too (in the form, perhaps, of an anxiety) in King's critical writing, with its alertness to how critics of his work fail (in a quote he attributes, in his late manifesto text *On Writing*, to Amy Tan) to 'ask about the language' (*OW*, x). This failure is also, for King, a critical failure to situate his work in relation to those traditions of literature of which critics *do* ask questions of the language – a failure this book hopes partially to redress.

This failure extends deeper into King's oeuvre in its concern with an insistent trope: '*why* did I want to write about writing?' (*OW*, x; italics in original). This question insists in different ways from his earliest novels onwards, as we will see in chapter 2 below. It helps us initially to locate his version of Gothic in relation to a conception of the genre as provisionally and unreliably located in the unstable textual world of the book. Anne Williams notes of the putative 'first' Gothic novel, Horace Walpole's *The Castle of Otranto* (1764), that 'Information about the origin, provenance, and physical condition of the text figures prominently in Walpole's "translator's introduction" to the first edition'.[19] Furthermore, this 'first' Gothic novel, as Jerrold Hogle has argued, is itself 'counterfeit' in origin and as 'source' of the Gothic, combining in its allegedly originary form 'several long-standing literary forms'.[20] Gothic, it seems, is not and never has been what it seems. Dispossessed of its putative source, it 'possesses no original' and from its false non-outset it proceeds to construct a proliferating, unstoppable generic hybrid of illusory or unreliable origin, a composite mode accommodating different and sometimes conflicting pre-existing literary forms, styles and genres, themselves always already predicated on previous forms.[21] Hogle argues elsewhere that Gothic has its 'basis' in 'the signs of already partly falsified signs' and in 'representations of representations'.[22] Such a 'basis' can only ever be unstable, illusory, spectral, a basis in a confusion of origins with repetitions that erases any putative primacy of 'origin'. This anoriginality partially repudiates Bloom's attack on King's 'absence of invention', making such an assertion redundant as a critique of Gothic writing. We can situate a provisional enquiry into King's versions of Gothic in the ways his texts respond to this endless anoriginality and how they repeatedly perform and deform the unstable, repetitive, generic non-basis of Gothic traditions.

On Writing, subtitled *A Memoir of the Craft*, tries to respond to the question of '*why*' the author wants 'to write about writing'. The book offers no less than three 'Forewords' before launching into a long autobiographical narrative entitled 'CV'. This narrative is insistently repeated in King's interviews and critical writing – it is related again, for example, in 'On Becoming a Brand Name' (1980: *SW*, 39–70). The author's 'CV' in *On Writing* begins with an untitled introductory page before offering a memory of self and desire: 'My earliest memory is of imagining I was someone else' (*OW*, 4). Clare Hanson argues that 'King's fiction is concerned above all with origins, with the grounds of being'. Hanson's reading of King locates this concern in relation to psychoanalytic questions of origin, of 'primary / primal movements and experiences'.[23] But the problems presented by origins or beginnings (problems signalled critically by words like 'primal' and 'primary') are clearly evident in the uncertain, staccato opening of *On Writing* and are addressed in other ways in King's writing. The difficulty of beginning, and the attempted resolution of that difficulty in the recourse to autobiography and thus to the ostensible authority-from-life of the authorial self, delineates all King's writing as a form of resurrection, an exploration and demonstration of the power of the writer to bring back (the past, former selves) to life. Paul Sheldon, the writer-hero of *Misery*, confronted by Annie's readerly demand for a new 'Misery' novel, despite the death, in the supposed final 'Misery' novel, of the eponymous character, nevertheless thinks '*I could bring her back*' (*M*, 69; italics in original).

This is a repeated trope of King's Gothic: the writer's desire expressed in the power of writing to resurrect, its spectral authority over death, which is also the thorny problem of beginning, because that which is resurrected is, in the Gothic mode, always already returning, beginning again and thus not really a 'beginning' at all. One of King's best-known short stories (collected in *Night Shift* (1978)) is entitled 'Sometimes They Come Back'. *Pet Sematary* (1983)

---

is expressly concerned with what Jodey Castricano has called 'the economics of revenance'.[24] *It* explores at great length the mixed desire for and horror of returning to and re-enacting childhood events. King's writing performs Derrida's insistence, in *Specters of Marx*, on the difficult logic of haunting as a coming-back, 'a malaise of perception, hallucination and time', the logical impossibility of the ghost's 'return' as ghost: each haunting is a singular return, the coming back of that which did not exist before, an inaugurating returning-to, an impossibility – 'Repetition *and* first time . . .' (italics in original).[25] For Derrida, each apparent first haunting is, like the false origins of the Gothic genre itself, a return of that which was always already there. Belated, historically anachronistic and persisting uncannily beyond its time, this logic is embodied in the unholy trinity of resurrections in *Pet Sematary*, or in the final cry of the thing that haunts and possesses Jack Torrance in the Overlook Hotel in *The Shining*: 'NOT TOO LATE!' (*S*, 403; emphasis in original). Resurrection, repetition and rereading thus constitute the Gothic trinity that provisionally defines the generic spaces King's writings occupy. Each opens the possibility of the anoriginal origin, the failure of the first (appearance, occurrence, reading) to be primary and initial, the non-beginning that haunts Gothic writing and, in its deliberate distortion of the basis of Christian myth, drives its horror. As Castricano puts it, 'Whatever returns had better be Christ, or there is going to be trouble'.[26] In Gothic, and particularly in King's Gothic, whatever returns is *never* Christ; the genre resides, precisely, within the spaces marked out by that 'trouble'.

Like Walpole's text at the anoriginal historical moment of the Gothic, King's writing writes into itself the inscription of authorial power as a power of returning and of making return, simultaneously locating at its putative origin something that is also elusively central – a spectral, scripted version of the King, the symbolic Law of the Father. If, as David Punter has argued, King's work insistently re-iterates 'the "presence" of King-the-writer himself, the King who announces himself on every title page, the writer in Maine who is in constant touch with his legions of fans and who is dedicated to supplying them with the product they want', then this 'King-the-writer' is also inscribed, repetitively, in other ways into the oeuvre, as, for example, an insistent lexical tic.[27] From the 'Crimson King' of the *Dark Tower* sequence and related narratives to Eddie King, murdered by an axe-wielding madman in *It*, from Cora Rusk's 'Date with the King' in *Needful Things* (*NT*, 576) to King's own Martin Amis-like guest appearances as 'that fellow who lived up Bangor way' in books like *The Tommyknockers* (*T*, 352) or, more coded, as writer Steve Kemp in *Cujo* who (evoking King's instructions to aspiring writers) 'wrote a lot' (*C*, 59), King relentlessly cites himself as a constant reminder of his fictions' authorial 'origin'. This insistent self-reflexivity is most ludicrously evident on the first page of *The Eyes of the Dragon* (1987), a book written for children by a father who has inscribed on this single page his own surname, in different forms, no fewer than twelve times. Such reminders are offered also in the contents of the narratives that constitute King's versions of Gothic: narratives of childhood, fictionalised versions of King's own life and of the places he has lived in and in the recurrent figure of the writer, the expression, again and again, of the author's own vocational identity.

Such self-reference betokens Gothic's ambivalent generic concern with paternal authority and patriarchal law as well as with their undermining by the inherent instability of origins, repetitions and destinations. It conforms to the popular fictional branding of King's name as signifier of particular qualities (if not, for many critics, of 'quality' in the abstract sense). In 'On Becoming a Brand Name' King addresses his market value directly, seeking via another long autobiographical narrative to repudiate his commercial status by asserting his writerly identity as his priority: 'Being a brand name is all right. Trying to be a writer, trying to fill the blank sheet in an honourable and truthful way, is better' (*SW*, 69). Questions of honour and truth bear at best a tenuous relation to Gothic concerns with falsity, surrogacy, anoriginality. Offering figures of authorial identity in so many surrogates implies the endless masquerade of identity as repetition, as non-beginning, as differentiation and closure, rather than a 'truthful' representation of the self. In 'trying to be a writer' King essays the act of writing itself: performing this act momentarily fulfils the desire to write. King's versions of Gothic extend this double movement in manners both transformative and repetitively reiterative of the genre's history. The hesitant, deferred opening of *On Writing* and its reliance on autobiographical narrative and on a 'Toolbox' of advice to aspiring authors reveal writing to be a recurrent trope symptomatic of a concern with authority, displaced onto a series of Gothic anxieties about origin and the inheritance of generic legitimacies.

Beginnings (Again)

We can initially trace these anxieties, in their textual expressions, through the opening pages of *'Salem's Lot*. This early novel (King's second) reveals the complexity and subtle effects of King's 'generic indecision' and of his intensive, self-conscious use of intertextual references, and how they destabilise and ceaselessly renegotiate the text's formal insistence on its own origins. *'Salem's Lot* revisits the vampire myth, transplanting it into contemporary small-town America and gathering together a band of men – a writer, a teacher, a doctor, a priest and a schoolboy – to combat the vampire invasion. Botting notes of the vampire that, 'consuming bodies, it transforms beings, contaminating them with its own appetites and desires'.[28] King's version of the vampire in this novel expresses the negative, pessimistic fulfilment of this myth. *'Salem's Lot* is a novel of failure and despair: of the failure of belief and faith, the failure of consumerism as a social ideology, and the failure of Fathers to rule and of heterosexual love to redeem and, in its representation of the undead and their uncanny, persistent afterlives, a novel of the failure of endings. It is also a Gothic novel concerned with the failure of beginnings.

'Salem's Lot 'opens', or perhaps fails properly to begin, with a complex and confusing sequence of formal manoeuvres, tropes, textual frames and citations, a proliferation of 'beginnings' that have drawn the attention of at least one critic:

> At the beginning of *'Salem's Lot*, after the Prologue (which sets up the very important sense of unease that marks all good horror literature), King immediately introduces the Marsten House, the source of evil that will figure centrally in everything that will happen later in the story. It is essential that the Marsten House, from the first moment we lay eyes on it, be scary. King predisposes the reader to see it that way by quoting, just before the actual story begins, the first paragraph of Shirley Jackson's *The Haunting of Hill House*. This is, especially with

that memorable phrase, 'not sane', and its eerie last line, an outstanding bit of evocative writing. But King is doing more here than paying tribute to a distinguished predecessor. Always the pragmatist, he gets full value from the epigraph by the inevitable carryover of those associations to his own Marsten House.[29]

The overriding impression of Alan Ryan's critical description is of a proliferating confusion of origins (a confusion and 'carryover' we will encounter in different form later in King's 'first' novel, *Carrie* (1974), and which is symptomatic of his work in general) that confuses, more deeply, the very possibility of origin itself. It emphasises, from its own destabilised outset, King's writing as an exploration of its own problematic origins and of the illusory grounding of those origins in already inscribed repetitions. Rereading the opening pages of the novel reveals the extent of this complexity and the difficulty Ryan demonstrates of describing it critically. The establishment, at the beginning of his analysis, of 'At the beginning', is immediately displaced, as Ryan notes, by 'after the Prologue'. The 'Prologue' is itself already a second 'beginning' that formally precedes but chronologically follows the 'beginning' of the novel, questioning immediately where the novel actually 'begins'. The 'Prologue', textual precursor to the novel itself, incorporates within itself a long citation, an extended quotation from a newspaper, the Portland Press-Herald. This article, we might note, is read twice within this 'Prologue' before we read it, read first by the so far unnamed 'tall man' and then reread by the unnamed 'boy' (SL, 5–6). The press article narrates the 'revelation' or 'discovery' of the unexplained decline of the Maine town of 'salem's Lot; it relates, in effect, a draining away of the population, a kind of suspended, originary 'ending' that the novel will proceed to represent and account for.

The novel's 'beginning', its second 'beginning', the 'beginning' after the 'beginning' of the 'Prologue', is then preceded again, as Ryan describes, by another anoriginary moment, 'just before the actual story begins', displacing the reader into yet another text and its 'beginning', 'the first paragraph' of Shirley Jackson's novel. The introduction into King's novel, 'immediately', Ryan asserts, of the Marsten House, is thus not really 'immediate' at all, but is heavily mediated by false beginnings and mistaken origins, inserted passages from another novel, from a fictional newspaper report and from the narrative's future, the 'Prologue' narrating events after the ensuing action of the novel. These false starts gesture repeatedly, for Ryan, towards essences – the Marsten House as 'the source of evil', its figuring 'centrally' and its 'essential' scariness – which are subtly undermined by generic knowledge of the forms and functions of houses in Gothic writing – that their 'essential' uncanniness is, for example, actually dependent on a cause which, we assume, the narrative will reveal. The proliferation of false origins establishes 'the actual story' on a basis of textual non-actuality, a receding and preceding sequence of displacements. This sequence is extended further in another direction by King's short stories 'One for the Road', a sequel to the novel, and 'Jerusalem's Lot', a 'pre-text' for the novel (and itself an exercise in the pitfalls of textuality, false leads and misreadings), both published later in *Night Shift* (1981). Both these supplementary stories return, furthermore, as appendices or additions to the republication of *'Salem's Lot* in 2005 in a thirtieth-anniversary 'Illustrated Edition', along with several hundred pages of what the publisher's blurb calls 'Previously unpublished material and a new introduction by the author' (and also an 'Afterword'). These additions supplement the 'original' text, giving the novel a strangely textualised 'afterlife' or 'undeath' of its own and further implying its 'original' incompleteness.

Ryan's critical description of the opening of *'Salem's Lot* alerts us to these complexities, but glosses over further complexities of the novel's opening structure, other paratextual passages that secrete themselves in spaces within the novel's covers, but before the multiple beginnings of *'Salem's Lot*. These include an initial epigraph, comprising an English translation of the opening verse-paragraph of Giorgio Seferis's Greek poem 'The Return of the Exile' (1938) (not named or dated in King's novel), and, before that, an 'Author's Note' comprising a conventional paratextual set of acknowledgments and authorial disclaimers. There is also, before that, a dedication which includes another citation: 'For Naomi Rachel King – "... promises to keep"', the quote from Robert Frost's 'Stopping by Woods on a Snowy Evening' invoking another level of returns (the poem narrates a pause in a journey of returning; it was also famously quoted by J. F. Kennedy, suggesting a political resonance to King's dedication).

Seferis's poem (used again by King in 1987 as an epigraph for *It* and ignored by most critics of both novels) invites particular interpretations, as does King's later quotation from Shirley Jackson. It is a poem of return, ostensibly a dialogue between a returning exile and someone who has remained in their shared homeland. There are several possible reasons why King has included it. The returning exile states later in the poem, 'I'm looking for my old house, / the tall windows / darkened by ivy', and eventually recognises the conflict between the nostalgia of return and the reality of death:

> Now I can't hear a sound.
> My last friend has sunk.
> Strange how from time to time
> they level everything down.
> Here a thousand scythe-bearing chariots go past
> and mow everything down.[30]

Seferis's poem describes the themes of return and its impossibility and of return as repetition that structure King's novel, themes which insist as contradictory configurations of desire throughout his oeuvre. Ben Mears, at the displaced, anoriginal beginning of the narrative, is returning, looking for a house to 'return' to which is, however, not his 'old house'. The poem King cites as his novel's epigraph also invites into that space the pervading awareness of mortality that imbues King's Gothic. Seferis's returning exile is also experiencing a kind of dying, entering an 'alien' country that is, symbolically, the land of the dead (a space that will become, in the poem's history, the dead land of Nazi-occupied Greece). The novel's version of the land of the dead is the vampire-ridden town of 'salem's Lot. It offers a provisional figure for King's vision of contemporary America, elaborated in different ways in later novels like *The Stand*, *Pet Sematary* and *Cell* (2005).

'Salem's Lot draws, furthermore, not only on Jackson's *The Haunting of Hill House*, a novel offering a complex analysis of notions of home and returning, but also on the social matrices constructed in popular novels like Grace Metalious's *Peyton Place* (1956) (in the 2005 'Afterword' King includes *Peyton Place* in a list of books described by his mother as 'bad trash' (*SL*, 589)). The novel alludes in the naming of

the Marsten House to the writer Richard Marsten, a pen-name of Evan Hunter (b. 1926), who also publishes under the name Ed McBain. The Marsten House derives also from Richard Matheson's *Hell House* (1971), a novel set in 'that pesthole up in Maine'.[31] The citations and allusions King deploys in opening his novel construct a resonant and profoundly dialogic series of echoes of popular fiction and literary texts, poems and novels, that serve not so much to locate *'Salem's Lot* as to *dis*locate any simple generic positioning of the novel. Far from being merely 'susceptible' (in Punter's word) to re-reading, the novel's opening demands a series of rereadings which help to emphasise the extent to which rereading is structured within the experience of consuming genres like Gothic. In its problematically structured opening pages, King's novel addresses covertly a series of questions about the complex, anoriginal origins of his 'brand' of contemporary Gothic in a variety of traditions, fictional and poetic, Gothic and ostensibly peripheral to Gothic modes. In this complex figuring, King's Gothic is, in generic terms, both 'alien' (to use Seferis's word for the 'non-existent country' his returning exile has imagined into existence) and 'familiar'. It is, in Freud's sense, 'un-canny', disconcerting in its simultaneous inhabiting of and displace-ment from familiar Gothic traditions.

What is clear by now is that *'Salem's Lot* is, in formal terms, deeply concerned with questions of origin and its impossibility and thus with questions of repetition, citation and return. The novel offers a Gothically labyrinthine sequence of false clues and then, reissued in 2006, appends to its textual body further texts and passages, called 'Deleted Scenes', that extend and deepen its complexity. It launches a series of false starts, a formal stuttering that is reflected, furthermore, in its content, which, in the opening pages, is all about returning. The narrative begins with a double return: the decision, towards the end of the 'Prologue', to return from Mexico to the town after the narrative has ended – '"I'm going back", he said' (*SL*, 11); and Ben's action, at the 'beginning' of 'Part One – The Marsten House', chapter 1, of returning to the town before the arrival of the vampire, with accompanying 'memories' and a 'burst of recognition' (*SL*, 17–18). Ben is returning here to the town he last saw when he was 'nine', 'coming back to a town where he had lived for four years as a boy' and experiencing the cognitive processes of recollection and recognition, an 'original sense of excitement' based on how 'more and more things began to seem familiar', 'familiarity' both undermining and reinforcing the 'originality' of the experience (*SL*, 17–18). The trope of returning and the excitement of the newly recognised are balanced in these opening pages by the significance of persistence: on seeing the Marsten House, Ben murmurs, 'Still here' (*SL*, 19), signifying its transcendent role, surviving amid the familiarity inculcated by his return and yet aloof from that world, unfamiliar, uncannily persistent.

Before Beginnings

'Salem's Lot, then, opens with an extended revision and doubling of the trope of returning. This trope problematises the very notion of beginning, invoking other Gothic openings-as-returnings (like the opening lines, say, of *Wuthering Heights* (1848)) and establishing returning itself as an insistent feature throughout King's subsequent works. The novel establishes itself on a series of returns and repetitions of that which existed before its beginning, signifying temporal difference and change, but drawing also on odd persistences, symbolic intensities (like the Marsten House) that signify sameness across time ('Still here') rather than difference. The trope of returning is given a further Gothic twist early in the novel by another kind of recognition, in which Ben himself becomes the thing recognised. As Susan Norton recognises him from the photograph on the jacket of the book she is reading, she performs a series of repetitive acts: 'She looked up and saw him. [. . .] She looked down at her book; looked up at him again and started to rise; almost thought better of it; did rise; sat down again' (*SL*, 22). 'I thought I was seeing a ghost', she says to Ben, using an odd tense, the past continuous, to describe her experience. 'I thought I was seeing' (*SL*, 22) implies persistence, the survival of the same, within the difference of the experience; uncanniness ('seeing a ghost') is rendered momentarily familiar by the tense's suggestion of continuous, rather than anomalous, experience, a continuity evocative of repetition.

'Salem's Lot, as is well known, returns to a central Gothic text, Bram Stoker's *Dracula* (1897) (King may have chosen the name 'Straker'

as a coded homage to Stoker), just as the short story 'Jerusalem's Lot' revisits Lovecraft and Poe. King has often alluded to the intertextual dependence of his novel on this major precursor: 'Without *Dracula*, I think, there is no *'Salem's Lot'* (*OW*, 245), he notes in an aside in *On Writing* and, in an earlier interview with Eric Norden, published in *Playboy*, he notes the relationship, adding: 'I've never made any secret of that'[32] (the issue of 'secrecy' in relation to King's Gothic is something we will return to in chapter 2).The mechanics of this rewriting have been extensively explored by Strengell, who calls the novel 'King's *Dracula* Look-Alike' and maps its correspondences to the precursor novel via an analysis based on the formalist model of narrative devised by Vladimir Propp.[33] The status of *Dracula* as precursor invites other kinds of enquiry, though; King calls his use of earlier texts 'literary homage' and describes *'Salem's Lot* as 'my own vampire novel', suggesting issues of ownership and authority as recurrent concerns (*OW*, 245; *DM*, 85). His comments on reading *Dracula*, in the 2005 'Afterword' to *'Salem's Lot*, link these concerns to questions of origin and primacy and return us to rereading, repetition and resurrection, those key elements of King's Gothic. The 'Afterword' is all about reading *Dracula*: 'I first read *Dracula* when I was nine or ten', King writes (the age, we recall, at which Ben Mears last saw the town of 'salem's Lot), noting his mother's construction of the book as 'trash' and exaggerating for himself its absolute and unique trashiness: 'That one was in a class by itself' (*SL*, 589). '*Dracula* was my first encounter with the epistolary novel', he elaborates; he comments on the novel's form and on 'the original strangeness of reading such a patchwork', notes his perception that *The Lord of the Rings* was 'just a slightly sunnier version' of *Dracula* and describes the novel (in an echo of Jim Burden's description of reading a *Life of Jesse James*, at the beginning of Willa Cather's *My Ántonia* (1918)) as 'the first fully satisfying adult novel I ever read' (*SL*, 590).

'Original strangeness' and 'first' experiences thus abound in King's recollected memories of reading *Dracula* as a child. Stoker's novel becomes a particular kind of myth within King's own extended mythologisations of (his own) childhood, an ur-text laden with original significance, on which his own work is grounded and which exerts a powerful influence on his literary imagination. It introduces him to a form ('the epistolary novel', deployed in King's first published novel, *Carrie*) and to a tradition, and enables him later to redefine other texts (like *The Lord of the Rings*) in relation to its authority. The primacy of Stoker's novel is established as central to King's own development, and is elaborated in his subsequent discussion of later encounters with American revisions of the vampire myth in various E.C. comics (*SL*, 591). *Dracula*, however, returns, to be reread and to exert a different kind of influence: 'I reencountered *Dracula* in 1971, when I was teaching a high school English class called Fantasy and Science Fiction' (*SL*, 591). 'I came back to it', King writes, using the rhetoric of uncanny Gothic returns, 'with some trepidation, knowing that a book read – not just read but studied and taught, even at the high school level – at twenty-four looks a lot different than one read at the age of nine or ten' (*SL*, 591). Reading, rereading and the 'difference' between them are the telling features of King's discussion. Reading differs in relation to age and to purpose (books read as a child are not 'studied'; books read in 'high school' are different for teachers and for students). *Dracula* becomes, in this double process of critical evaluation, a text not simply original and primary in its functions, but multiple, repeatedly encountered, varied according to use and to pleasure: 'My students enjoyed it, and I'd say I enjoyed it even more than they did' (*SL*, 592). The novel's original primacy and uniqueness ('It was in a class by itself') is modified now into membership of a group, an elite: '*Dracula* [. . .] is one of the great ones' (*SL*, 591–2). Rereading *Dracula* opens up its uniqueness, subjecting it to different kinds of reading and different readings, exposing it to a democratising process of critical scrutiny and analysis, making its rereading a shared experience that contributes, in turn, to its rewriting as plural, rather than singular, a text that generates rewritings of itself, such as King's own *'Salem's Lot*. This shared experience in turn revises the symbolic significance of the key motif in *Dracula* identified by the child King, 'the intrepid band of adventurers' who gather to pursue the vampire to its death, the motif of (male) group agency in response to (feminised) threats that will dynamise so many of King's own narratives (*SL*, 590).

Rereading affords, for King, new pleasures which are shared and social, and which culminate in the pleasure of creative resurrection and adaptation, the combining of Stoker's novel with the 'what-if?'

hypothesis of a vampire appearing in 'America of the 1970s' and, with 'the fleshy leeches of the E. C. comics, creating a pop-cult hybrid that was part nobility and part blood-thirsty dope, like the zombies in George Romero's *Night of the Living Dead*' (*SL*, 592). The generic familiarity of the Gothic novel opens up the space for its recombination and redefinition in terms of the genres and traditions it provokes, and within which it covertly persists. Rereading and rewriting, as acts of returning to texts that involve the transformation of ostensibly unique, originary experiences into plural, repeatable events, are integral to this opening up. King's writing, in this sense, is characteristic of a prevailing postmodernist sense of the simulacrum as the dominant order of contemporary representation. Lacking a beginning or an ending, the simulacrum disembodies signification, suspending the sign's animating power within the fields of repetition and pastiche that constitute postmodern cultures. As Botting argues, even Gothic's focus on the visceral, the abject, the disordered regime of the body and its horrors (what King calls 'the gag level of revulsion' (*DM*, 39), a description that alludes also to the comedy of Gothic, its pantomime resurrections and absurd recurrences), cannot separate it from the 'absolute coding of simulation'.[34]

Part of the argument of this book will concern the significance of the many ways in which connections between the repetition of returning and the repeated acts of reading and writing that structure King's works suggest an initial approach to a critical consideration of his use of the Gothic mode. King's Gothic can initially be understood as repetitive and tradition-dependent; generically fluid and 'indecisive'; heavily intertextually and intratextually ordered; enacted reiteratively and insistently in the representation of processes of writing and reading and the tropes and figures they afford for a description of an analysis of the writer's 'craft'; and coded by contemporary political and ethical concerns with otherness and its intermittent mutation into a predominantly feminised 'Otherness'. The relationship between *Dracula* and *'Salem's Lot* offers an initial expression of some of these features and the potentials they offer for a critical reading (a rereading) of King. This rereading will begin with a discussion of *Carrie*, King's first published novel and an initial expression of his Gothic, focusing on that novel's establishment of the central theme of the Gothic tradition of writing and its relation to another of King's major tropes, that of telepathy. It will then extend this exploration of King's relations to Gothic and other traditions through a discussion of the trope of doubling, as explored doubly in *The Dark Half* and 'Secret Window, Secret Garden' (chapter 3); through an analysis of genre, via Gothic's relations to science fiction, in *The Tommyknockers* (chapter 4); and through the Gothic revision of the reader–writer relation offered in *Misery* (chapter 5); before developing analyses of some of the key tropes of King's Gothic – temporality and chronological disjunction (chapter 6); place and the location of horror (chapter 7); and the monstrosity of otherness and its tendency to become a feminine 'Other' (chapter 8). The concluding chapter will explore King's narrative endings and outline possible future routes of critical enquiry and engagement with his works. This book will offer through these thematic concerns a series of exemplary, but partial and necessarily selective, readings and re-readings of King's Gothic writings. King's monstrous oeuvre will be gestured towards but, in practice, critically partitioned, reduced, destructured into manageable chunks (corresponding to current critical orthodoxy in its reading of a 'canon' of major King works), in order to practise the kind of textual analysis he often, in his own critical writing, demands of his critics. To do critical justice to King's 'care' for 'the art and craft of telling stories on paper' (*OW*, x) is a consistent concern of this book; the readings offered will trace some of his writing's Gothic concerns.

2

Carrie's *Gothic Script*

'The horror of it should have been monotonous, but it was not.'
(*C*, 167)

Beginning with Carrie

King's first published novel, *Carrie* (1974), emerged amid a wave of popular Gothic and horror texts in the USA and England, including William Blatty's *The Exorcist* (1971), Anne Rice's *Interview with the Vampire* (1976), Jay Anson's *The Amityville Horror – A True Story* (1977), Peter Benchley's *Jaws* (1975), Peter Straub's *Julia* (1975) and, in England, Colin Wilson's *The Space Vampires* (1976) and James Herbert's *The Rats* (1974) and *The Fog* (1975). Within this contemporary Gothic resurgence *Carrie* establishes a series of Gothic themes, tropes and motifs that will recur throughout King's works. Centring on a narrative of teenage trauma and consequent social destruction, it explores the world of American youth, analysing religious extremism, bullying and suffering, humiliation and revenge and conflicts between the individual, the social group and the family. It establishes a basic narrative structure of gradual accumulation and eventual explosion of violence that will organise many of King's subsequent novels. Its style, form and language gesture towards surface elements familiar from American postmodernist fiction. It nods to its historical context, suggesting a reading in relation to Vietnam, Cold War and Watergate paranoia which the novel implies but also largely evades, offering only surface references to these contexts, although its overt political meanings include clear and more coded, politically conservative, commentaries on the agendas promoted by the women's rights movements of the 1960s and 1970s.

Carrie also displays, in the interstices of these multiple potential concerns, a self-reflexive and profoundly Gothic engagement with the acts and products of reading and writing. It presents these as traces of historical affect, evidence offered within a pastiche legal-discursive framework that simultaneously reinforces and problematises the novel's verisimilitude. Carrie's concern with texts is King's initial expression of his relation to Gothic traditions of writing, and its overriding metaphor for this concern is offered in the figure of the supernatural mental powers of telekinesis and telepathy. This chapter will explore some of the ways Carrie affords such an entry for King's writings into Gothic traditions of writing, and how the novel relates this to its social concerns in powerful and problematic ways. It will read the 'Gothic script' into which Carrie inserts its readers, evident in its prevailing concern with writing and writers, textuality and the traditions of Gothic fiction, relating these to the motif of telepathy, a metaphor connected to the activities of reading and writing, and also to King's critical commentaries on writing and writers.

Carrie concerns a teenage schoolgirl, Carrie White, butt of her class's bullying contempt and victim of her mother's religious funda-mentalism, who unaccountably develops telekinetic and telepathic powers. These enable her, after disastrously being elected Queen of the school Prom and being, at her crowning, humiliated, to exact a violently destructive revenge on her schoolmates and on the people of the town they live in. The narrative opens with a news report of a rain of stones, a supernatural event borrowed from Shirley Jackson's *The Haunting of Hill House*, the novel later cited (as we have seen) in the epigraph to *'Salem's Lot*. Jackson's central character, Eleanor Vance, experiences at the age of twelve, soon after her father's death, 'showers of stones' falling on her house.[1] King draws on this episode and its symbolic significance in Jackson's novel in order to establish, via that novel's place in the American Gothic tradition, his own

text's specific relation to that tradition and to other traditions sub-
sumed into Gothic. Jackson draws heavily on Shakespeare's *Twelfth
Night* (*c*.1601) and her novel directly alludes to canonical works like
Samuel Richardson's *Pamela* (1740) and, importantly, *Dracula*. *Carrie's*
'rain of stones' links King's novel to another text by Jackson: he
notes, in *Danse Macabre*, 'the rain of stones which ends Jackson's
story "The Lottery"', a story about, among other things, the horror
of ritualised tradition and its impact on social conformity (*DM*, 47).
Stoning, in these two episodes, is a signifier of contradictory powers:
of apparently motivated supernatural agency and of the potentially
devastating arbitrary and yet predictable, traditionally sanctioned
power of the mob. It indicates, in Jackson's works, an ambivalent
destructive power, magical and/or political, offering a potential
symbol for the ways in which democratic agency can be perverted
by forces both external to and yet structured within it. *Carrie* opens
with an analogous event, a supernatural raining of stones which is
then symbolically repeated as a socially enacted ritual in the girls'
'bombarding' of Carrie 'with tampons and sanitary napkins' as they
'chant' an 'incantation', '*PER*-iod' and 'Plug it *up*' (*C*, 12–13, italics
in the original). Repetition and citation thus establish King's connections to a tradition of American popular Gothic and its concerns
with notions of power and agency, the forces of social conformity
and their effects upon individual freedoms. The girls' chants furthermore establish early in the oeuvre the metaphorical potential of
symbolic flows and blockages – in this case of blood and social power
– that will dynamise many aspects of King's Gothic.

Carrie *and Gothic Tradition*

However, *Carrie's* debt to and extension of this popular Gothic tradition goes much deeper than simple plot repetition and overt allusion
through reiterating specific events. Most critics of the novel are alert
to the obvious colour symbolism of Carrie's surname and its counterpointing by the redness signified in various ways in the novel, including Tommy Ross's surname. Through such structures the novel
establishes its own use of what Neil Cornwell identifies as 'the colours
of the fantastic' and their symbolic force, deploying colour symbolism

as an iconography of Gothic emotions, and connecting *Carrie* to the symbolic structures of Gothic.[2] Focusing on the surname 'White', Heidi Strengell points out that 'Clearly, the girl's name has a significance', and notes 'the tradition in American letters in which whiteness and inscrutability are two points of a triangle whose third point refers to the futility of interpretation'.[3] This tradition, analysed in different ways by Toni Morrison (1992) and other contemporary critics, establishes whiteness at the core of an American identity that represses racial and other differences but retains a destabilising uneasiness with the 'blankness' of the white: 'It was the whiteness of the whale that above all appalled me', Ishmael tautologically comments in Melville's *Moby-Dick*.[4] Carrie White's surname implicitly locates her character within and in relation to this tradition, which is symbolically embedded at the ambivalent heart of American democracy in the presidential White House (in *Carrie* the White family's home is 'the White house', 'a political joke' (*C*, 28)). Strengell's 'futility of interpretation' sits oddly in this symbolic tradition. As we will see, *Carrie*'s whiteness is not that of Melville's whale, but instead the blankness of the page awaiting inscription with the (bloody) ink of Gothic.

Critics of *Carrie* tend to focus via the surname 'White' on the novel's overt concerns with conventional Gothic oppositions such as purity and (feminine) blood, and femininity and monstrosity (for example, Hanson)[5] and the ways colour symbolism mobilises these concerns through a framework conventionally read in terms of fairytales. Such connotations are conventionally connected in turn to theories of abjection and its cultural-symbolic connections to bleeding and menstruation, as in Hanson's analysis of how the novel 'pivots on the reader's horror of the abject as it resurfaces in adult life'. Hanson's sophisticated Kristevan reading, to which we will return later, calls the novel a 'purifying rite of passage' which exorcises 'the power of the abject', symbolised for Hanson by menstrual blood.[6] For Hanson and other feminist critics, *Carrie* establishes at the outset of King's oeuvre an unsettling and problematic construction of femininity to which he repeatedly returns but which he fails adequately to resolve, a theme to which the final chapters of this study will return. Other critics expand on the connection between abjection and the novel's use of fairy-tale iconography and motifs, as in Chelsea Quinn Yarbro's early analysis of *Carrie's* use of 'the Cinderella myth' and Linda Badley's later reading of the novel as 'a dark modernization of "Cinderella"'.[7] This echoes Douglas E. Winter's description of it as 'a dark modernization of the Cinderella story'.[8] Later still, Strengell shifts attention to *Carrie's* first name, noting that '"Carietta" [Carrie's full name] echoes the four-syllable "Cinderella"'.[9] Most criticism of the novel focuses in these ways on its analysis of religion or its use of fairy-tales, locating the Gothic of *Carrie* in relation to specific, popular-cultural and oral, traditions. James Egan, for example, in a reading that largely ignores *Carrie's* evident suffering, invokes religious parallels when he describes the climactic destructions as 'the mutation of evangelism into parodic form' by 'a demon who rejoices in the chaos she creates', while Alex E. Alexander calls the novel, problematically, 'A Universal Fairytale' which 'catalyzes fantasies about social and sexual anxieties'.[10]

These readings of the novel gesture towards its relations to and its working out of questions of tradition and inheritance, either of the psychoanalytic past of the subject or of the novel's relations to other popular generic traditions. Each reading suggests, but doesn't fully explore, the possibility that *Carrie* may offer a complex engagement with specifically *Gothic* traditions that opens them up to accommodate King's versions of Gothic. This possibility is indicated initially in the name 'Carrie', which, like the opening 'rain of stones', King has borrowed from Shirley Jackson's novel, where it is given to Eleanor Vance's patronising, oppressive older sister.[11] Carrie's name thus embeds within King's first novel an onomastic notation of tradition and of the text's insertion of itself into tradition. The name 'Carrie' carries within it a performative function, the enactment of a repetition which is also a textual resurrection, a borrowing which also rediscovers the potential for extension, or the carrying on, of the (oppressive, burdensome) Gothic past. What, then, might be carried over, or carried on, into *Carrie*? What burdens does *Carrie* carry, what functions does the novel carry out, and how does it tell us of these functions?

The word 'Carrie' is inscribed repeatedly, presented and re-presented, in a variety of forms in addition to that of the name, throughout the novel. It is present in the recorded testimony of one of the cited witnesses to Carrie's childhood, Estelle Horan, whose connection to American traditions is indicated by the comment that she 'still carries the thin, difficult soil of New England somewhere inside her' (*C*, 30). It is symbolically implicated in the death of Carrie's father, Ralph White, 'when a steel girder fell out of a carrying sling' (*C*, 18); the 'steel girder' prefigures another 'steel girder', the one on which Billy Nolan later balances the two pails of pig's blood (*C*, 130) that will fall on to Carrie and Tommy at the Prom, suggesting that the death of Carrie's father symbolically prefigures her own humiliation, and the 'carrying sling' is later echoed by Billy 'Carrying the pails back to the trunk' of his car (*C*, 107). Carrying and what is carried – buckets of blood – assume particular resonances here. 'Carrie' becomes, eventually, in the novel's documentation of its events, a dictionary entry describing a verb that has entered American English as a consequence of the novel's events: '*to rip off a Carrie*: To cause either violence or destruction' (*C*, 220; italics in original). 'Carrie' is present as proper noun and verb throughout the novel, embedded in synonymous actions like transporting, moving or conveying, and in the acts of vengeance carried out by Chris Hargensen and, eventually, by Carrie herself.

The repetitive reinscription in different forms of her name intensifies as Carrie approaches death. The word is repeated as a name twenty-three times, becoming a punctuating, accelerating incantation, in the short scene where Chris and Billy try to drive their car into her to kill her (*C*, 200–1). But Carrie's name echoes, too, and perhaps symbolically implicates her, in the ways *Carrie* enacts, in its eponymous heroine's name, the carrying over of its events in the scientific speculation initiated by the White Commission over the likelihood of there being 'carriers' of the telekinesis (or 'TK') gene (*C*, 95–6). Carrie and *Carrie* are in effect genetic and generic 'carriers'. They are, in the novel's pseudo-scientific speculation on her origins, transmitters and receivers of a rogue gene, a metaphor for the version of Gothic King inherits and extends. Carrie's name and that of her author (and even the initials of her author's wife, Tabitha King, to whom *Carrie* is dedicated) are entwined in this passage's discussion of 'TK' in relation to other genetic disorders, such as haemophilia or 'King's Evil', first of the many self-inscriptions in King's works. The author's description, in a conversation in 'An Evening at the Billerica Library' in 1983, of horror as 'an outlaw genre',[12] echoes the description in *Carrie* of 'the outlaw gene' (*C*, 96) connected to Carrie's 'TK' abilities. Amid this lexical interplay of names, initials and self-inscriptions, genes and genres seem connected. One form of inheritance, the genetic, echoes and doubles the other, the generic. 'TK', in turn, becomes an abbreviation signifying the strange, uncanny locus of Gothic horror in *Carrie*, establishing the paranormal at the unstable centre of King's ostensibly 'normal' American world and connecting it to a fantasy of catastrophically disruptive femininity.

Carrie, then, is, in its eponymous repetition of its protagonist's name, covertly concerned with the lexical potentials of that name to signify as a verb and, through this, with a genetic inheritance which can also be read as a symbolisation, a version of a generic inheritance carried on into the novel. 'Outlaw genes' and 'outlaw genres' play against each other, via traces and repetitions of the name 'Carrie', across the novel's textual surface, inscribing into the text a Gothically coded script of generic / genetic significance that emphasises *Carrie*'s concern with traditions of textuality and writing. *Carrie* establishes at the beginning of King's writing career, through this play on its heroine's name, a 'hidden script', a coded set of acknowledgements to and dependencies upon a Gothic tradition always already in the process of returning within that writing, necessarily coded into it. Read in this way, *Carrie* indicates clearly that Stephen King's writing immerses us from the outset in a Gothically inscribed world of generic returns and resurrections. This immersion is, initially, into the world of Gothic textuality.

Carrie *and writing*

While alerting us in its opening pages, through its emphasis on textuality, to its overt written-ness, *Carrie* deploys a series of Gothic motifs and features in rapid and effective succession, constituting the 'hidden script' lurking behind and within the screens offered by different narrative modes and forms. The opening pages of *Carrie* mobilise, through a series of differentiated discourses and generic allusions, a generically diverse range of surface devices that initially and disconcertingly motivate it towards realism and modernism in constructing its Gothic world. The novel's first words (after a short page of dedications and acknowledgements) are 'News item' (C, 9): they foreground its initial effort to construct and sustain, through a neutral, ostensibly disembodied narrative voice, the generic appearance of documentary realism and 'factual' exposure and presentation. These are immediately undercut by the narrative's non-realist, Gothic, substance, evident in a variety of types of content. These include what the news item actually reports, the apparently supernatural 'rain of stones', and the centrality of the house to these opening events. We have also the incomplete, fatherless family structure introduced here ('Mrs White, a widow, lives with her three-year-old daughter' (C, 9)) and the narrator's deliberately premature and suspense-breaking 'revelation', again on this first page, that 'Carrie White was telekinetic' (C, 9). This revelation of a significant non- or anti-realist dimension – a supernatural dimension, like the reported 'rain of stones' with which the novel's action begins – as central to the novel's action, is also, paradoxically, motivated by a documentary-realist narrative drive to expose or reveal, or at least to unconceal, a destabilising resistance to the suspense associated with Gothic artifice, a tendency to lay bare their suspense to which King's writings are frequently prone.

In terms of style and structure, *Carrie* is overtly modernist and documentary in composition, even 'eccentric',[13] although such formal 'eccentricity' has clear Gothic, if not fairy-tale, precedents. Four discernible and distinct types of documentary discourse are evident on the first page alone, effecting (again paradoxically, in generic terms) 'a portrait of Carrie as if she were the object of a Cubist painting or sculpture'.[14] Critics rarely note the novel's formal modernism: its fragmented, incomplete narrative, its reliance on counterpoint and juxtaposition, its deliberate subversion of any single stable point of view (even that of its putative omniscient narrator and its author, himself inserted into the narrative as Carrie's English teacher 'Mr Edwin King' (C, 69)) in constructing incomplete portraits and narratives. Strengell's extensive discussions of the novel, for example, make no mention of its formal distinctiveness, while Anne Williams notes but does not analyse the 'other modes of discourse' that 'supplement and interrupt the main plot'.[15] Tom Newhouse notes, in contrast, that *Carrie* 'employs a third-person narrator as well as the multiple points-of-view common to epistolary documentation', and comments on how 'King's new objectivism' leads to 'a meticulous realism'.[16]

Written during the Watergate investigations and published in April 1974, four months before Richard Nixon's resignation, this overtly modernist textuality resonates in relation to specific American and mid-1970s senses of the difficulties of ascertaining a singular 'truth' or 'main plot' in comprehending political and historical complexities. *Carrie* constructs a textual space in which modernist devices can be seen (in Brian McHale's words) to 'tip over into postmodernist uncertainties', suggesting not realism and revelation, but, instead, secrecy and concealment as counterpoints to any potential insight into reality through textual accumulation and detail of description.[17] Fredric Jameson, commenting on postmodern narrative in American films of the 1970s, notes that 'one of the peculiarities of Watergate [. . .] was that it turned from the outset on information and representation rather than anything substantive'.[18] Similarly, *Carrie* is comprised of (largely sceptical) legal and journalistic conjecture and questionable witness statements, documents of uncertain factual value and other ultimately insubstantial forms of knowledge unaccountable in rational terms. The legitimacy of its discursive elements is, at best, superficial, predicated on a seeming *lack* of information, as Sue Snell implies: 'On the subject of Carrie White, we're all relatively uninformed' (*C*, 208). The American historical context is, as noted above, only tangentially alluded to in the novel. Carrie's father, Ralph White, dies in the historically resonant year of 1963, echoing the symbolic death of the American 'father' in the Kennedy assassination (*C*, 18). The Gothic death of the paternal and its traumatic or liberatory consequences for the postmodern symbolic, analysed recently by Botting in a chapter entitled 'Daddy's Dead',[19] is a recurrent motif in King's works and prominent in later novels like *'Salem's Lot* and *Pet Sematary*.

Carrie's suspicious discursive composition also firmly locates it in relation to a Gothic, anti-realist literary tradition of composite texts, including *Frankenstein* and *Dracula*, texts that gesture to 'documentary' veracity in order further to emphasise the uncanniness and monstrous incongruities of what they describe. *Carrie* incorporates into its textual body news items, graffiti, extracts from books and memoirs, magazine articles, transcripts of interviews and court hearings, and fictional narrative interrupted by stream-of-consciousness passages, to construct a text of fragments, a composite text that ultimately seems to cohere only in its telling. Even then the narrative is finally incomplete, subtly subverted by questions of reliability, motivation and other internal inconsistencies that interrogate the basis and reliability of the extensive but speculative body of knowledge constructed in the novel. The opening 'News item', concerning the apparently supernatural event of a 'rain of stones' on a house, alludes, we have already seen, to *The Haunting of Hill House*, structuring textual repetition and generic reiteration into the opening of the novel. The emphasis on repetition is evident at the level of lexis: King's 'rain of stones' is 'reliably reported by several persons' (*C*, 9), so that 'reported' is repeated from the preceding headline, 'RAIN OF STONES REPORTED' (*C*, 9; emphasis in original). Storytelling and narrative reliability are emphasised, despite their implicit conflict with *what* is reported, as the 'rational' or authoritative grounds of the narrative's Gothic uncanniness. Nicholas Royle notes of an early use of the word 'uncanny' that it 'is explicitly concerned with language and storytelling', and King's writing, in *Carrie* and elsewhere, makes much capital from this connotation.[20]

Carrie establishes its relations to the Gothic uncanny by initially raising issues of narrative reliability and formal flexibility, but it also locates them, characteristically for King, in a variety of contemporary, realistic and recognisable locations, from the girls' locker-room of the American high school to the suburban family home onto which the opening stones rain. This familiar domestic space contains an unfamiliar, uncanny space, the secret 'closet' to which Carrie is banished by her abusive mother, 'the home of terror, the cave [. . .] where all hope was extinguished' (*C*, 53–4). This internalised, domestic uncanniness contrasts dramatically with the novel's version of the external, public and recognisably contemporary world of America, with its popular-cultural references, its frequent citation of familiar brand-names, its promiscuous high-school kids, the world, indeed, that King's writing makes its own. *Carrie* locates its Gothic vision initially within this tension. Its uncanniness secretes itself within familiar spaces, defamiliarising them, shading them with Gothic taint, challenging their cultural and ideological hegemony and offering, in that challenge, a nascent critique of American social values.

The novel quickly deploys the language of psychology to establish different levels of significance as its Gothic parameters and to spatialise its construction of the human psyche, differentiating the realism of 'surface' meanings and reportage from the implicitly non-realist 'subconscious level where savage things grow' (*C*, 9). This level, in turn, is connected to a sense of narrative predestination ('this had been building''since the first grade' (*C*, 9), we are told by the narrator) that *Carrie* will inexorably fulfil. The novel's beginning is thus backwardly displaced, making it susceptible to kinds of uncertainty similar, again, to those noted earlier in relation to *'Salem's Lot*. Narrative opening extends back throughout *Carrie* into a dim, partially excavated childhood history later briefly fleshed out by narrative flashbacks. Through the discourse of psychology, Gothic tropes of the hidden, the forgotten, the known–but–denied, the always–already and the fatalistic, the rational and the 'savage', are firmly established on the novel's opening page. Entry into *Carrie* is thus effected in a different way to the complex intertextual opening of *'Salem's Lot*, through a complex series of generic and formal devices which establishes the conflicting symbolic and representational codes that structure the novel.

But the novel also expresses (as this generically complex, overtly *written* opening implies) a coded but constant concern with the act and products of writing, locating this key Gothic trait as the basis of King's version of Gothic. Writers, writing, texts and inscriptions (like the 'Graffiti scratched on a desk' on the opening page) punctuate the fragmented narrative, which repeatedly draws attention to its written–ness and to the demand to read it. Susan Snell's memoir expresses this self-reflexivity: she laments Carrie's death, pointing out that 'Nothing can change her back now from something made out of newsprint into a person' (*C*, 124). Carrie is thus, in the 'present' of the novel's post-Carrie's-revenge narrational frame, constructed as a version of, and a textual product like, the 'News item' that begins the novel. The novel's different narrative frames and discursive forms reconstitute her retrospectively as a text, like the novel named after her, and as textual spectre within that novel, haunting the nightmares of the survivors in the text's present.

Carrie White is emphatically a *written* figure of the Gothicised feminine, suggesting a deeper gender-political significance to the functions of writing that King's works will subsequently elaborate. The novel's emphasis on the complex retrospective construction of the eponymous character suggests that narrative temporality in *Carrie* is itself problematic, a complex mixture of repetition and retrospect, prediction and forgetting, foretold, planned and random events, past and present tense narration, memory and desire. Acts of writing, and their products, are prominent throughout the novel and are embedded within these complex temporal frames as expressions of recording and prediction. Susan Snell's written memoirs comprise a substantial portion of the narrative and she refers frequently to *The Shadow Exploded*, an academic text cited throughout the novel, as 'the only half-decent book written on the subject' (*C*, 76). That book in turn quotes Bob Dylan in offering 'lines that might serve as Carrie's epitaph: *I wish I could write you a melody so plain* . . .' (*C*, 220–1; italics in original). Headmaster Mr Morton (a name which onomastically inscribes death into the novel's authority structures) introduces writing homonymically into Carrie's very identity by mistaking her name as 'Cassie Wright' (*C*, 20). In doing so he dramatically emphasises the significance accruing to that name.

Writers, furthermore, populate the classroom world of *Carrie*. Tommy Ross is a published poet (*C*, 84–5), and when Carrie dreams of trying to hide with her mother, the narrative invokes poetry by alluding to T. S. Eliot's *The Waste Land*: 'But the rock would not hide them; the dead tree gave no shelter' (*C*, 76) (as we will see, King's writings are extensively haunted by echoes and citations of Eliot). Carrie herself is a repetitive writer; the novel quotes her poem written on paper 'decorated with a great many cruciform figures which almost seem to dance' (*C*, 69) and offers lines from another Bob Dylan song 'found written repeatedly on one page' (*C*, 38) of one of her school books. Blood and writing momentarily mingle in one of the unwittingly fatal actions that condemn Carrie's Prom Night; as she and Tommy vote for themselves at the School Prom, she accidentally breaks the pencil, drawing 'a small bead of blood' which Carrie 'blotted [. . .] away with her napkin' (*C*, 144–5). Carrie's writing is an expression of her solitude: '*Alone*', which will become a key word in King's oeuvre, recurs as a one-word refrain early in the narrative (*C*, 39–40; italics in original) and one of her poems concludes 'Why do I feel so all alone?' (*C*, 69). She is, paradoxically, the undeveloped, nascent prototype of King's writer-solitaries, figures recurring throughout his works, usually as male novelists, like Paul Sheldon in *Misery* or Mort Rainey in 'Secret Window, Secret Garden'. The 'work' she eventually produces is the novel's apocalyptic action, textualised into the novel itself, a 'work' that 'unworks' in its immense destructive force, a force of which the fiction struggles to make sense.

Writing's symbolic ordering of experience is deeply encrypted in the narrative logic of the novel, the contemporary action of which begins with a 'period'. Carrie's first menstruation (occurring with emphatic symbolic force in 'Period One' (*C*, 10) of the school day) marks a series of ends, continuities and beginnings that establishes writing itself as another version of the hidden script of *Carrie*, its narrative 'sentence'. The 'period' links Carrie to her mother's symbolic connection with death through her own 'period of bereavement' after her husband's death in 1963 (*C*, 18). A 'period' is also, of course, a full stop, the punctuation at the end of a sentence. Carrie's period punctuates her progression (the 'sentence' of her life) from child to adult. It is symbolically repeated in her being drenched in pig blood at the Prom. This symbolic 'period' ends one potential narrative 'sentence', that of the fairy-tale, a harmonising and redemptive narrative potentially enacted in the Prom Night sequence, and leads inexorably to a different kind of sentence, the death sentence for all involved in this prank.[21] It is an event repeated a third time in the 'slow course of dark menstrual blood' Sue Snell experiences as Carrie dies, near the novel's end (*C*, 212). The opening period, inaugurating the novel's contemporary action, is thus an end and a beginning, both the unrepeatable singularity of the first time – Carrie's first menstruation – and an inauguration of an event to be repeated, enacting Carrie's entry into an adult female symbolic world. It is an event coded in terms of a female cycle of bodily repetition whose agency moves from Carrie herself, to those around her who seek to harm her and eventually to Sue, initiating the symbolic repetition that structures the novel's movement between self and other, individual and social.

The 'period' returns again, in another form, in Carrie's final act of revenge, the crucifixion of her mother. Carrie uses her powers to slow down her mother's heart towards death while Margaret

White recites in her death throes the Lord's Prayer. Carrie completes her mother's recitation, and the stopping of her heart, with the words 'Full stop' (C, 193). The period – the 'full stop' – thus returns in the *arresting* of the pumping of the maternal heart and the flow of maternal blood, the fluid that symbolically circulates most obviously through *Carrie* and which is mentioned on virtually every page of the novel. This 'Full stop' severs the mother–daughter bond to which Carrie has always been sentenced, a bond paradoxically established by Margaret White's severing of her daughter's filial connection (at Carrie's birth, she 'apparently cut the umbilical cord herself' (C, 18)), which she replaces with a symbolic bond based on a fundamentalist interpretation of Scripture. The period is another figure of the 'blocked' (C, 41) objects of the repression of female reproduction – of menstruation, of pregnancy – that punctuate the novel, and of the flows implied and resisted by these objects. It contradictorily expresses both flow and blockage, connection and severance, the movement and the stillness of language, as writing (like blood) circulates through and across the novel. Writing, blood and menstruation interlink throughout the novel: Sue, working on the Prom Night mural, experiences 'monstrous writer's cramp', a phrase that links *Carrie*'s Gothic concern with the potential monstrosity of the feminine to writing via an echo of the menstrual cramps Carrie herself experiences after her first 'period': 'Cramps came and went, in great, gripping waves' (C, 25).

In keeping with the flows of blood and the circulation of the novel's internal symbolic structure in the narrative's relentlessness ('*They all hate and they never stop*' (C, 25; italics in original)) there is no full stop at the end of *Carrie*. What begins problematically, uncertainly, with a period ends in incompleteness, or rather with a capitalised name, like a grammatical sentence inverted or reversed. The novel closes (but does not finish) with another repetition, another emphatically *written* text of narrative continuity, a letter from one Amelia Jenks that documents in semi-literate writing another supernatural phenomenon, opening a new fictional space of continuation that is also a repetition, a recurrence, a rebirth or resurrection of Carrie and of *Carrie*. The final word of this letter (and of the novel) is the abbreviated and period-less name of its signatory, 'Melia' (C, 222), a name lacking its initial 'A' and therefore deformed, unbegun, a name furthermore implying an 'amelioration' or a 'making better' that the novel's closing repetition resists. 'Melia' connotes in Greek myth the nymphs who sprang (like the Erinye) from the blood spilt when Uranus was castrated by Cronos. The name thus extends the novel's concerns with blood and (re-)generation, introducing to it a mythic (rather than fairy-tale) emasculation that further abbreviates a patriarchal line. 'Melia', like Carrie, writes, and in her writing resides the final, unfinished example of the Gothic force of *Carrie*, the force of repetition-as-return and insistence. Carrie's death, in *Carrie*, ends with her displaced resurrection, an implicit reincarnation in the similarly named child 'Annie'.

We might initially argue, then, that the hidden script of *Carrie* and its relations to the novel's representations of writers and writing concerns not only the Gothic symbolism of white and red signified by her surname, but also the coded meanings embedded in the name she shares with the text, and how that name signifies through the novel. It is connected to the Gothic colour symbolism – 'you sign your name you sign it in blood' (*C*, 137), Margaret White thinks – but it carries other resonances too, not least the resonance of 'carrying' itself. *Carrie* is, in this sense, about different kinds of 'carriage' and 'miscarriage', the latter including Margaret White's earlier miscarriage ('I lost the baby and that was God's judgment', she tells us (*C*, 190–1)) and the implicit miscarriage signified by Sue Snell's climactic menstrual flows ('Her period was late. Almost a week late. And she had always been as regular as an almanac' (*C*, 142), we are told earlier). The wider effect of Carrie's name signifies the novel's 'carrying on' of traditions and textual motifs that resonate in genetic, generative and generic terms. Borrowed from a major precursor novel, the name 'Carrie' marks a Gothic inheritance, a trace that signifies all that King's novel assimilates and passes on into its own revised version of the Gothic tradition. Carrie's name, signifier of difference in the text, traces its own signification across the novel, a difference always eluding simple or accurate definition. It remains, instead, a detached signifier, as each discursive element in the novel tries and fails to pin it down to a different meaning: psychological, legal, familial, political, religious. The name carries its own evasion of definition. Carrie White remains, at the end, only a figure: unknown, uncomprehended, unassimilated, an excess of the symbolic world the novel constructs and therefore also potential, an impending return, a carry-over of her own destructive power. *Carrie*, in effect, marks how the Gothic genre carries on generically and genetically, via the novel's final, period-less letter, into another present, the present of the next or the to-come, the potential (generic / genetic) repetition of the novel's events. In another kind of carry-over, it suggests how Carrie's look of '*misery*' (*C*, 34; italics in original) will return (connected with, again, the name 'Annie') as a complex noun later in King's work, just as the name 'Mears', central to *'Salem's Lot*, can be found hidden in *Carrie* in the name 'Thomas B. Mears', the first body to be identified in Chamberlain (*C*, 160). Open-ended, *Carrie* opens also the spaces of writing-as-return and repetition that will be occupied by King's subsequent works, and expresses in complex ways Gothic's concern with writing's materiality, figured in indelible, bloodlike signs. Like the 'red plague circle [...] you could scrub and scrub and scrub and still it would be there, not erased' (*C*, 26), these are markers of Carrie's difference, and of the differences signified by the sign 'Carrie'.

Carrie *and telepathy*

Carrie's differences locate the novel in a complex textual situation that demands and rewards the kind of careful reading not usually granted popular fiction. Central to these differences, constitutive of Carrie's 'difference' from others in the novel and acting throughout as figures of reading, are her telekinetic and telepathic powers. The relations between these powers as markers of difference and the novel's concern with the processes of writing and their reading open the space for a consideration of King's theorisations of writing in his own critical work. Like writers and writing, telepathy, literal and metaphorical, is everywhere in King's writing, a recurrent trope with a variety of functions. In an interview with Martha Tomases and John Robert Tebbel in 1981 King, asked about the contemporary reputation of parapsychological investigation, responds to the question seriously and talks of telepathy as 'a capricious phenomenon'.[22] The prevalence of this 'phenomenon' in his works suggests that it carries an insistent force or potential and works as a convenient recurrent signifier. His writing affords spaces in which this phenomenon takes on specific symbolic functions in relation to prevailing metaphors of writing and reading.

Carrie's telepathic powers connect her to King's many other child-telepaths, including Danny Torrance in *The Shining* (1977) and Charlie McGee in *Firestarter* (1981) (effectively a rewriting of *Carrie*, and dedicated 'In memory of Shirley Jackson'), who asks her father, in a bracketed monologue, '(*is it telepathy Andy? Is it?*)' (*F*, 49; italics in original). Other examples include Ellie Creed in *Pet Sematary* (1983) and Leo in *The Stand* (1979), 'a little boy who seems to be a telepath' (*St*, 754). John Smith, in *The Dead Zone* (1979), an adult version of this trope rendered childlike and 'innocent' by his accident and coma, develops precognitive telepathic powers. New telepathic abilities characterise those who have undergone the 'becoming' in *The Tommyknockers* (1988), facilitating the communication – '*touching a different mind*' (*T*, 513; italics in original) – necessary to their new communal existences. *Rose Madder* (1995) offers a version of telepathy to explain the insights of its psychotic policeman Norman Daniels: '*In his years as a cop, Norman had come to believe that telepathy was perfectly possible . . .*' (*RM*, 118; italics in original); 'It's almost like telepathy' (*RM*, 210), Rose notes of his hunches and intuitions. The monster in *It* (1987) displays telepathic abilities in its communication with the group who intend to kill it – '*Telepathic*,' thinks Ben Hanscombe, '*I'm reading It's mind*' (*It*, 840; italics in original). And in *From a Buick 8* (2002), the haunted car's effects on people are linked to this thread of meanings: 'We've all heard it whispering. No idea what it's saying. [. . .] Only inside my head, going from the inside out. Like telepathy' (*FB8*, 154). In many of these texts telepathy is clearly connected to writing; a key example is the 'telepathic typewriter' (*T*, 189) built by Bobbie Anderson in *The Tommyknockers*, discussed in chapter 4 below.

Telepathy is thus in King's works not so much a 'capricious' parapsychological phenomenon as a recurrent, almost normalised metaphor, a way of imagining social communication beyond the sensory channels, and ultimately a figure for how writing performs this communicative effect. Connected to writing, it also invokes the act of reading (the reading of minds). As Nicholas Royle has argued (in relation to Salman Rushdie's *Midnight's Children* (1981)), "'telepathy" remains a cryptic and uncanny term, always already other and "more than itself", figuring a crisis in intelligibility and sensibility, an irreducibly interruptive moment in *reading*' (italics in original).[23] Royle's earlier study *Telepathy and Literature* argues that such a connection facilitates a rereading of the representation of communication and telecommunication in modern writing. Telepathy, he argues, is 'a concept and effect intimately bound up with writing and death, the spectral and unprogrammable'.[24] It figures, as it surely does in *Carrie*, 'an uncanny reading-machine', one that may be 'interdependent with literature'.[25] Telepathy, Royle suggests, is a potent metaphor of communication, one structured by the advent in modernity of telecommunications technologies that facilitate different versions of communication at distance. It offers, furthermore, a metaphor for the interface between shared unconscious meanings and shared social meanings, the point at which individual urges seem to coincide with the desires that drive the social mass. Royle's extended discussions of the metaphor of telepathy do not address King's writing; telepathy offers Royle, instead, a figure of the ways that (mainly) nineteenth- and twentieth-century narrative fiction mobilises, through devices like point of view and omniscient narration, the readerly illusion of being able to read the thoughts of other people, paradoxically a fundamental device of realism. Royle also develops an analysis of the 'telepathy effect' theorised by Jacques Derrida, which he elaborates in relation to a critique of 'omniscience' in literary narration. Telepathy, Royle argues, 'opens up a humbler, more precise, less religiously freighted conceptuality than does "omniscience", for thinking about the uncanniness of what is going on in narrative fiction'.[26]

Alongside its concern with writers and writing, *Carrie* displays an extended preoccupation with the acts of reading and rereading as challenges to narrational omniscience. The novel insistently scrutinises testimonies, records, recollections and documentations of the events it describes and tries to comprehend while, at the same time, refusing a single omniscient point of view. King's third-person narrator, fragmentarily present, assumes a position of authority more stable than those offered by the different analytical discourses the novel presents; but this position is also questionable, reliant on local focalisations and adumbrated itself at certain points by the narratives it elsewhere compromises. In one generic sense the novel constitutes through this concern a Gothic crime narrative in which the criminal is both obvious and concealed, and, in realist or documentary terms, impossible. Characters like Sue Snell are presented as readers as well as writers (for example, *C*, 70), their consuming of texts mirroring the novel's production of them. Reading closes the circuit opened by the novel's emphasis on its own textuality and opens the novel's critique of teenage loneliness to scrutiny in terms of King's concern with figuring otherness. Reading is both a solitary act and a social obligation. Individual characters read, reread and comment upon each other's testimony, just as the 'White Commission' sets in motion an extended, politicised rereading of the novel's events. *Carrie* establishes in the figure of the telepath, and specifically of the telepathic child, a motif of otherness constructed by and in the act of reading that will recur throughout King's writing and that figures the individual and social activities, processes, effects and potential liberations of reading.

The word 'telepathy' is used only once in *Carrie*, where it is explicitly connected to books and reading, as Sue Snell struggles to account for her 'peculiar knowledge' of Carrie: 'She didn't know how she knew. It bore no relation to anything she had ever read about telepathy' (*C*, 202). Telepathy is comprehended in King's works as a kind of reading (just as knowledge is likewise connected to reading), a privileged access to private mental processes figurable through conventional metaphors of 'mind-reading' and thus constituting minds as kinds of text. In *The Dark Half* (1989), popular novelist and King-surrogate Thad Beaumont is asked, 'Do you read minds as well as write books?' (*DH*, 101). King repeatedly refers to telepathy in his discussions of writing, usually in relation to the reader's connection to the writer via the text. In *Danse Macabre* he asserts that 'those who love books and love the language know that the printed word really is a kind of telepathy' (*DM*, 405). And in *On Writing* he answers the question of 'What Writing Is' with a simple statement: 'Telepathy, of course' (*OW*, 77). King's elaboration of this definition is by example: he describes at length the process of writing and the demands of readerly imagination in effecting the 'telepathy' of writing. He implicitly notes, in a reference to a 'far-seeing place' (*OW*, 78), the notion of distance (*tele-*) embedded in

the word and connects this to the temporal displacement of communication facilitated by writing, its ability to record information
for future consumption:'If that's how things work out, then you are
somewhere downstream on the timeline from me' (*OW*, 77). King
elaborates here and elsewhere in his repeated use of telepathy as a
metaphor in his fiction a concept of writer and reader in a telepathic
relation structured by the temporisation and spacing associated with
writing as *différance*. This enables him to construct a metaphor of
writing as the transmission of information, without apparent speech
or any other direct contact between addresser and addressee, across
time and space. Leaving aside the apparent erasure of the medium
of the word in his model of writerly communication, King's theory
does draw attention to the reader–writer relation: 'We're not even
in the same *year* together, let alone the same room . . . except we *are*
together. We're close. We're having a meeting of the minds' (*OW*,
79; italics in original).

King's version of telepathy here gestures towards writing's communicative effect in offering a figure for a kind of reading. Valentine
Cunningham, for one, has noted the potential of King's telepathic
'closeness' to imply, among other things, 'close reading',[27] a critical
description that successfully elides King's definition of writing as
telepathy with a theory of *reading* as telepathy. This 'meeting of the
minds' is King's most theorised version of the encounter between
self and other that structures his entire oeuvre. Telepathy enacts the
encounter with otherness that defines the Gothic dimensions of his
writing in its exploration of otherness as that against which selfhood
must be defined and as that which simultaneously threatens and
provides the possibility of stability for the constructed self. But his
concern with telepathy might also hint at a deeper anxiety (explored
elsewhere in the oeuvre, for example in the short story 'Word
Processor of the Gods' (in the 1985 collection *Skeleton Crew*)) about
the apparent power of the written word to influence or transform
reality. This power is manifest in *Carrie's* connection of telepathy
with telekinesis. King's insistence, in his discussion of writing as
telepathy in *On Writing*, that writing (not telepathy) be taken
'seriously' (*OW*, 80), signifies the investment inherent in his conception of the telepathic potential of the written, and of the potential
of the telepathic as a metaphor.

If telepathy figures, for King, writing's ability to communicate across time and space, reading and writing are also clearly valued acts of conjoining, of social connectivity, acts that signify the potential achievement of a social 'closeness'. At the same time, as the 'telepathy' metaphor implies, they involve some notional secrecy. They are covert performances, irrational, unthinkable or at best repressed in scientific or realist terms. In *Carrie*, as we've seen, telepathic powers are from the outset both laid bare *and* secret: 'What none of them knew, of course, was that Carrie White was telekinetic' (*C*, 9). The novel's opening page both asserts and refutes the non-knowledge of her secret ability. Its scientific status within the novel's fiction remains suspended, both evident for all (including the reader) to see and experience, and suppressed, discredited in the final statement of the White Commission, which alludes to 'some cellular changes which *may* indicate the presence of *some* paranormal power' of which 'we find no reason to believe that a recurrence is possible or even likely' (*C*, 221; italics in original). Telepathy, it seems, is condemned to remain simultaneously revealed and concealed in *Carrie*, something nobody knows and something every reader is made immediately aware of on the first page. Tellingly, King makes use of a key American text in describing his critical comprehension of writing as 'telepathy'. 'For years', he writes, 'people have argued about whether or not such a thing [as telepathy] exists [. . .] and all the time it's been right there, lying out in the open like Mr Poe's Purloined Letter' (*OW*, 77).

Poe's 'The Purloined Letter' (1845), a well-known allegory of the trope of secrecy and revelation that structures detective fiction (and an inaugural text in that genre), narrates the theft and recovery of a potentially compromising letter, 'an affair demanding the greatest secrecy'.[28] Circulating (somewhat like the Prom night scenes of *Carrie*) around a King and a Queen, a letter and a deceit, it deals with the detective Dupin's seemingly miraculous ability to interpret and solve the mystery of the letter's theft and concealment, and to recover it. Subject to a famous series of readings by Jacques Lacan, Jacques Derrida, Barbara Johnson and other eminent critics and theorists, Poe's story is a complex allegory of reading as an act of secreting (a process we will explore in the next chapter), of the reading of texts secreted in full view, inscribed with meanings displayed and concealed in their displaying.[29] Lacan's reading of the story, for example, hints at meanings significant for King's Gothic, not least in its reading of the story's concern with 'the communion established between two persons in their hatred of a common object', a version of telepathy, and in its addressing of 'intersubjectivity' and 'the very subjectivity which constitutes an Other as absolute'.[30] Lacan reads the narrative for its events and content, linking these to an allegory of how desire displaces along the chain of signification. Derrida, alert rather to the frames of telling and the structures of encoding of Poe's text, offers a closer textual analysis and describes the story as 'this affair of writing' and 'a scene of writing'.[31] 'The Purloined Letter', constructed by theorists as an allegory of how critics have failed to answer the question King seeks to address of 'what writing is', affords a multiple set of links with popular, literary and critical writing. Poe's story emphasises the importance of reading within these structures, and its invocation by King in discussing writing suggests ways of theorising the functions of telepathy in his work.

Carrie clearly establishes some of the ways King's Gothic writing exploits and depends upon the potential social connectivity enacted in reading and writing and figured, in this instance, by telepathy. The novel's use of the notion of 'secrecy' is a key element of this concern. Telepathy and telekinesis, as 'internal' mental processes that manifest themselves in the novel in 'external' effects, demonstrate the complexity of writing's representations of the self in literature. The secrecy of telepathic ability involves, also, the exposure of that secrecy (any telepathic communication necessarily involves two people, presumably revealing at least one as a telepath). In *Carrie*, the 'secret' is constructed as something internal that is exposed: as Clare Hanson has argued in a bracketed aside to her feminist analysis of King's writing, *Carrie* constructs blood as something 'that should remain *within*'. In the scene where Carrie is drenched in pig's blood, Hanson argues, 'The surface of life is peeled back [. . .] to show the abject which lies "behind" it, that which is "secret"' (italics in original).[32] The paragraph Hanson quotes (*C*, 167; Hanson's essay misquotes 'coloured' as 'covered' and 'patter' as 'pattern') demonstrates the rhetorical confusion in *Carrie* of interior (mind) and exterior (sight), contained (blood) and container (body), and secret and exposed (the telepathic act and the mind of the character, revealed to the reader by the novel's stream of consciousness). Carrie's telepathy both demonstrates and undermines the Gothic text's reliance on the secret. Revealed by the narrating voice on the first page of the novel and demonstrated as developing in force and effect throughout the narrative, but also rejected (or at least underplayed) by the sceptical rationalist tone of the White Commission, it constitutes a secret simultaneously hidden and exposed, withheld and shared. Like the functions of writing in *Carrie*, it is both overt and coded, secreted within the text; the two are intimately connected throughout King's work.

The recurrent trope of telepathy in King's writing figures, then, a deeper concern with communication as social connection. Carrie's telekinesis and eventual telepathy may thus be read as another form of textual encounter within this novel so replete with representations of writing, a communicative act of inscription that simultaneously opens a space of reading. When, at the end of the novel, Sue Snell experiences Carrie's telepathic power, she understands, in hitherto unimaginable ways, through a form of 'sharing', the other that is Carrie: 'They shared the awful totality of perfect knowledge' (*C*, 210). This 'awful totality' is knowledge of Carrie's otherness, her self's knowledge of itself – her history of suffering, her alienation and isolation, the bullying to which she has been subject – transmitted absolutely to another person, a knowledge that momentarily transcends the scope of the novel's language: 'The mixture of image and emotion was staggering, indescribable' (*C*, 209). Sue's encounter with this 'other' is sublime, beyond the power of the text's language to articulate. The novel's metaphor for the telepathic encounter between Carrie and Sue is a reader in a library:

> The sensation was terrifying. Her mind and nervous system had become a library. Someone in desperate need ran through her, fingers trailing lightly over shelves of books, lifting some out, scanning them, putting them back, letting some fall, leaving the pages to flutter wildly
>
> (glimpses that's me as a kid hate him daddy o mommy wide lips o teeth bobby pushed me o my knee car want to ride in the car we're going to see aunt Cecily mommy come quick i made pee)

in the wind of memory; and still on and on, finally reaching a shelf marked TOMMY, subheaded PROM. Books thrown open, flashes of experience, marginal notations in all the hieroglyphs of emotion, more complex than the Rosetta Stone. (*C*, 210; emphases in original)

This remarkable passage, largely ignored by most critics of the novel (Hanson notes only that, in this moment, Sue 'finds herself drawn unwillingly into Carrie's mind at the point of death'),[33] locates within the human psyche the library, repository of textual information and inscription, a place familiar to Gothic texts from *The Castle of Otranto* onwards. It redefines Carrie, with her telepathic abilities, as the ideal reader. It offers through this image an allegory of the novel itself, constructed of texts and allusions and generic debts, internalised in the image of a human consciousness as a 'library' of emotions and repressed childhood memories of desire and hate and abjection, in which the novel itself becomes figured in Sue's mind. What becomes 'read' in such a process is the textuality of consciousness itself, 'the infinite nature of the work' that 'is just the mind's infiniteness', as Maurice Blanchot puts it.[34]

Derrida notes of 'The Purloined Letter' that 'Everything begins "in" a library: in books, writings, references. Therefore nothing begins. Only a drifting or disorientation from which one does not emerge'.[35] The 'library' in the passage from *Carrie* is an image of Sue's mind, a resource (full of recorded, inscribed memories re-enacted in stream of consciousness) on which Carrie draws in her search to understand exactly how she has been constructed as other by Sue and her peers. Telepathy offers here an image of a disturbing, violent, disorientating intimacy (Sue experiences 'the feverish feeling of being raped in her most secret corridors' (*C*, 210–11), a confused image of woman-as-library-as-victim that unfortunately reinforces the novel's some-times bizarre sexual politics). It emphasises the written-ness of human subjectivity that King's writings will henceforth relentlessly elaborate as central to his Gothic vision. Telepathy, Derrida argues (in relation to psychoanalysis), 'is indeed a question [. . .] of admitting a foreign body into one's head'.[36] This passage from *Carrie* enacts, in Sue's willingness to be exposed to this kind of telepathic reading, precisely such an admission of and to the 'foreign', a belated response to the ethical demand that circulates through King's novel in Carrie's refrain of '*Alone*'. Her socially enforced solitude offers a kind of exclusion of the other which King's writing constantly explores. Aloneness, *Carrie* implies, generates a monstrosity which, in this novel, is specifically and insistently feminine. Only an ethical response to 'aloneness' can ameliorate it, reducing the risk posed by the monstrous but simultaneously threatening (as Melia's closing, non-ameliorative letter implies) its return. In the case of *Carrie* this response comes too late but is nevertheless there, present as a possibility in Sue's behaviour, her attempts to redress the injustices of Carrie's bullying. These attempts are undermined by the novel's events, consequences of another kind of monstrosity, that produced in the refusal of ethical behaviour in the social world of Chris Hargensen and her friends.

Carrie's contact with Sue enacts the ethical encounter with the 'stranger within', an experience of uncanny doubling that is simultaneously a welcoming-in of the other within the self, and the encounter of the self with (and within) its own 'secret' otherness. It reinforces the sense that Carrie is Sue's uncanny other, an aspect of her self externalised, a possibility implicit in the use of the word 'Flex' to describe both Sue's physical pain when writing ('She flexed her hand' (*C*, 97)) and the enacting ('*Flex*' (*C*, 86)) of Carrie's psychic power. Chris Hargensen's stream of consciousness struggles to separate the two girls – 'i'd like to crown that fucking snell bitch carrie too' (*C*, 100) – suggesting they are closely connected in the perceptions of others. Carrie's 'terrifying' intrusion into Sue's mind demonstrates the potentials of the figure of telepathy to stand for writer–reader relations. Derrida describes the experience of such an encounter with the other as being 'more intimate than one is oneself, the absolute proximity of a stranger whose power is singular *and* anonymous' (italics in original).[37] Such intimacy is hinted at in the implication at the end of the novel of Carrie's 'return' or possible reincarnation in the infant Annie, suggesting metempsychosis or the transmigration of souls as a closing figure of the intimacy of telepathy, its transference of one mind into another. Such a figure might also stand for how one text appears, cited and recited/re-sited, within another in *Carrie*'s intertextual play, offering Gothic figures of the persistence in writing and its echoes of the textualised genes of tradition across generations and genres. Carrie's 'singular *and* anonymous' telepathic power, a figure ultimately of *Carrie*'s relations to Gothic traditions of writing and reading, mobilises through such figurative potentials King's analysis of the uncanny Gothic dimensions of writing and their mapping of the other's relations to the self. The novel establishes at the beginning of King's career the importance to an understanding of his work of Gothic conceptions of tradition and genre, writing and reading, and the other's threat to and demand on the self. The next chapter will elaborate some of these themes in relation to the Gothic trope of doubling, already implicit in *Carrie* but central to two key later texts.

3

Disinterring, Doubling: King and Traditions

ℒ

'*Don't make me tell you twice.*' (*DH*, 11; italics in original)

'For it goes without saying that the god of writing must also be the god of death.'[1]

'Oh yes, there's naturally a higher charge for two figures than for one.'[2]

Traditions

If *Carrie* establishes King's continuation of Gothic traditions, the texts examined in this chapter reveal their strange doubling. This doubling can be traced across the oeuvre and marks the relation of King's Gothic to traditions. It signals also the establishment, intra-textually within King's works, of different versions – repetitive, vestigial, fragmented or Gothically monstrous – of tradition. King's works self-consciously and conspicuously shadow the major European and American Gothic writers and works, echoing and repeating their themes, motifs and rhetoric, drawing (for example) on the American sense of Gothic place and on onomastic and other textual resources. They also demonstrate through citation, allusion and imitation an extensive, complex and densely allusive set of relations to non- and para-Gothic popular and literary traditions. Particularly in his critical writing, King regularly expresses a strong sense of the authority of tradition for the contemporary writer. This authority is repeatedly invoked through the key trope of homage through repetition. Literary traditions are alluded to or imitated in his writings in doubled forms, as traces of the persistent past and as motifs resonant with contemporary significance. Traditions are reiterated and re-inscribed into King's specific version of contemporary American Gothic, the genre in which he self-consciously and belatedly works, summarised by one critic as a tradition 'in which domestic intimacy is menaced by its dialectical other, an unearthly, cosmic and always malignant force'.[3]

Tradition itself might provisionally be understood as one figure (along with monstrosity, which we will turn to later) of this 'dialectical other' against which King's works pitch themselves and through which they structure their concerns. His writing struggles with overbearing Gothic and non-Gothic traditions of textual achievement, traditions he repeatedly 'buries' with (and within) his own excessive texts, only to witness again their relentless, uncanny disinterring within those texts. Such Gothic rhetoric is not inappropriate; King's repeated revisions of this construction of tradition-as-otherness into different forms of Gothic threat (monsters, 'Bad Places' and other tropes we will consider later) constitute an intervention into the Gothic tradition as other to contemporary writing, an other that both doubles it and extends it. It invites a particular kind of reading that is already, in *Carrie*, implicit in the image (discussed in the previous chapter) of Sue Snell's mind as a library, presenting itself to be read by Carrie White's telepathic mind, a potent image of the encounter of the self with a terrifying, intrusive and unaccountable 'other' that lies at the heart of all Gothic. Telepathy figures, here and in Other comparable meetings, a kind of empathy. The library, a repository of texts, offers King another complex figure of traditions as an immense, textualised resource, available to the contemporary writer and reader, comprised wholly of the otherness of writing, an otherness that *Carrie* reifies as a metaphor of selfhood, of the individual mind. If the burden carried by *Carrie* can be conceived as a version of the inherited weight of tradition, then that tradition is both other to and uncannily within the work of the contemporary writer, as it is other to and within the self.

'The melodies of the horror tale', King writes in his critical survey of Gothic traditions, *Danse Macabre*, 'are simple and repetitive' (*DM*, 27). Tradition, the repository and the reiteration of these 'melodies', exists in a double relation to the individual text, both desired and resisted. It offers in its repetition an uncertain and uncanny guarantee of the problematic, displaced and unstable textual 'originality' we have seen already in *Carrie* and *'Salem's Lot*, and embeds itself in other kinds of repetition within the structure of King's own critical arguments. Magistrale, for example, notes 'the repetitive raising of issues' as a theoretical limitation in King's *Danse Macabre*.[4] Furthermore, tradition recurs as a version of itself in the theme of doubling that preoccupies Gothic texts and to which King's writings are no exception. As Marshall Brown notes, 'There can be few traditions so beset with second selves and *doppelgängers* as the gothic novel'.[5] The double relation of tradition to the text and the different kinds of doubling, including the doubling of tradition itself within King's texts, are the subjects of this chapter, which will read *The Dark Half* (1989) and its later companion or revision text, the novella 'Secret Window, Secret Garden' (1990), in a double critical engagement, viewing these texts as different but connected analyses of the Gothic dimensions of the written text and its relations to tradition. Each text concerns a writer who is, in some way, blocked; each centres on specific kinds of debt and repayment incumbent on its central protagonist; and each offers a strange doubling both of tradition and of itself. This indicates the doubled relations between these two texts which, together, offer an extended meditation on the burden and responsibilities of inheriting a tradition.

Doubling, in these texts, performs functions associated with the figure of apotropoeia or the warding-off of death, a balancing of repetition's function in relation to tradition of effecting a kind of raising of the dead. In each text the fictional writer creates (consciously or not) an uncanny other self, his double, his 'brother', through which he enacts a kind of 'warding-off'. The double, as is well known, is an uncanny harbinger of death. Louis Creed, in *Pet Sematary*, performs an instinctive apotropaic movement when he first encounters his resurrected cat: 'He shot both hands out in a primitive warding-off gesture' (*PS*, 160). In *The Dark Half* in particular, the arrival of the double enacts a form of the return of the dead which, Slavoj

Žižek argues (in relation to *Pet Sematary*), is 'the fundamental fantasy of contemporary mass culture', a fantasy with which King's books frequently engage.[6] But the functions of doubling in *The Dark Half* and 'Secret Window, Secret Garden' are rendered more interesting by the curious doubling relationship that pertains between the two texts, in that the latter is a rewriting, and thus a doubling, of the former, as if the burial, resurrection and reburial narrated in *The Dark Half* were still incomplete, unable to pay off the symbolic debt that the novel seeks to address. This debt is, of course, a form of the specific debt to tradition experienced by the popular novelist. In these discussions questions about key Gothic themes of secrecy, doubling, death, resurrection and the law will be related to the readings of tradition in King's writing and its doubling – repetition, invocation, imitation or otherwise – in individual texts.

King and Eliot

Harold Bloom (no fan of King, as we have seen) argues that he 'emerges from an American tradition one could regard as sub-literary: Poe and H. P. Lovecraft'.[7] In his note to 'The Sun Dog', King defines his complex generic productivity as a 'site' on which other writers, Gothic and otherwise, have also worked: 'Franz Kafka had an office here, and George Orwell, and Shirley Jackson, and Jorge-Luis Borges, and Jonathan Swift, and Lewis Carroll.' He goes on to list contemporaries including Thomas Pynchon, Kurt Vonnegut and Peter Straub (*FPM*, 735–6). This list, unlike Bloom's, blends literary and popular authors. King's argument, that the two levels of production are linked by shared aspects of theme, suggests a way of thinking his own relation to tradition. The 'site' of Gothic on which King writes is analogous to the 'field' of popular fiction theorised by Ken Gelder, with its generic limits, gendered reading politics, specific modes of production and consumption, and specific non-aesthetic claims to value.[8] King refers to horror fiction as a 'field' in the 'Foreword' to *Night Shift*: 'The field has never been highly regarded', he notes (*NS*, 12). 'I think of myself as an American writer', King writes elsewhere (*SW*, 332). Peter Straub paraphrases the word 'American' here to connote 'the best, truest tradition of American fiction' (*SW*, xiv).

Leaving aside the question of what 'best' and 'truest' might mean in this context, King's relations to tradition clearly extend beyond the traditions of the fictional and Gothic and draw on traditions far wider than those 'sub-literary' sources noted by Bloom. His writings are haunted, for example, by a major non-Gothic American writer, T. S. Eliot, whose poetry is a recurrent point of reference as early as *Carrie*, where paraphrases of Eliot have already been noted. *The Waste Lands* (1991) is the title of the third volume of King's massive fantasy work *The Dark Tower* (1982–2004), a novel sequence replete with references to Eliot, of which other volumes feature chapter titles taken from Eliot's poem. *The Shining* quotes 'The Love Song of J. Alfred Prufrock' ('*In the room the women come and go*' (*S*, 152; italics in original)). *'Salem's Lot* alludes to Eliot's 'Sweeney Among the Nightingales' in its description of Dud Rogers's 'arms, which dangled apelike almost to his knees' (*SL*, 67). *Hearts in Atlantis* (1999) repeats this citation alongside another from *The Waste Land*: 'Apeneck Sweeney spreads his knees; the typist puts a record on the gramophone with automatic hand' (*HA*, 50). *Pet Sematary* alludes to 'Eliot's poem about the hollow men', quoting that poem and 'Prufrock': '*I should have been a pair of ragged claws* [. . .]. "Headpiece full of straw, Church"' (*PS*, 332; italics in original). Such insistent, repetitive allusions and citations bind King to a generation of mid to late twentieth-century writers profoundly influenced by the authoritative cultural weight accrued by Eliot's poetry, affected by that weight into what is sometimes a talismanic performance of repetition, a verbal invocation of lines that resonate with indeterminate meaning. But they also suggest the kinds of generic crossings and hybridical productivities that King's writerly versatility generates (and which will be explored in more detail in the next chapter). They contribute furthermore to a potential rereading of Eliot's poetry in modernist Gothic terms, linking King's work to other (late-)modernist revisions of Gothic. Andrew Smith and Jeff Wallace, for example, open their discussion of 'the mutual obsession of the Gothic and the modernist' by noting the 'recontextualisation of the Gothic within Eliot's myth of modern decay and dislocation'.[9]

Eliot's persistent prominence in King's writing indicates a reliance on traditions extending beyond the fictional and the strictly popular or 'sub-literary'. Eliot's own critical work on tradition, and its recent

theorisation by Jane Goldman and others, offers a suggestive framework for thinking about King's relations to traditions.[10] Goldman,
in particular, offers a Gothicised reading of modernism and of Eliot's
pivotal essay 'Tradition and the Individual Talent' (1919) that resonates
in relation to King's work. She describes Eliot's famous definition
of tradition as 'an ideal order' of 'existing monuments' as 'a graveyard
metaphor', in which each new work of art becomes 'a monument
to the poet's identity', offering a comprehension of 'tradition' as 'the
interment of the nation's literary greats'.[11] Goldman makes little of
Eliot's own borrowing from immediate tradition, specifically his use
of T. E. Hulme's writings on tradition, which clearly prefigure Eliot's
in language and tone. Hulme's *Lecture on Modern Poetry*, probably
delivered in 1908 and unpublished in his lifetime, talks of the poet's
particular sensitivity to 'the competition of the dead'. Hulme's lecture
makes extensive use of a Gothicised rhetoric of death and renewal,
transience and strange immortality. Art forms 'decay', like an old
religion where 'The carcass is dead and the flies are upon it'; images,
for Hulme, are 'dead' and then 'born in poetry'.[12] Such terminology
of death, decay and implicit resurrection haunts Eliot's essay in its
radically different context a decade later, establishing repetition within
modernist theorisations of tradition as a cycle of mythic decline and
renewal that provides the mythic structure of much modernist literature. Eliot's concern with metaphorical monuments in attempting
to represent his conception of tradition's persistence is related by
Goldman to the historical context of his essay, read as a response to
the horror of the First World War. Such connections have not been
missed by King's readers: Robin Furth's *Concordance* to *The Dark
Tower* comments on that series' use of Eliot's poetry, and reiterates
the well-known fact that Eliot's poem 'was written in the aftermath
of World War I, when Europe was still in shock over the death and
destruction caused by modern weaponry'.[13] Eliot's conceptions of
the work as 'monument' and of tradition as 'interment' resonate, as
we will see, with *The Dark Half.*

King's own critical versions of tradition are largely untheoretical
in style. His critical writing, while meticulously open about his
borrowings and reference points, rarely uses the word 'tradition',
and he develops no overt theoretical conception of the writer's
relations to or responsibilities towards traditions. Michael Kilgore,

interviewing King in 1980, asked him 'Do you feel as if you're part of a tradition, and if so, who are other members of that tradition?' King replied:

> I feel that way very much. I mean, I discovered Poe when I was in grammar school, I guess, and from Poe I went on and discovered people like Ambrose Bierce and some of the other classic short-story writers, and H. P. Lovecraft. And then some of the modernist people [. . .] like Richard Matheson and Robert Bloch. And all of those people played a part in teaching me how to write [. . .][14]

Here, in short, is the 'sub-literary tradition' disparaged by Bloom, a tradition nevertheless generating its own popular-cultural field of meanings, styles and forms, and a vibrant and immensely productive current in the subcultures of modern and postmodern American writerly and cinematic production. Locating himself in relation to such a tradition, King asserts a particular American, male, white sense of his own position as inheritor of the American Gothic line. King has reworked each of these writers: Matheson's *The Shrinking Man* (1956) in *Thinner*, Poe's 'William Wilson' (1839) in *The Dark Half*, Lovecraft in the short story 'Crouch End' (in 1993's *Nightmares and Dreamscapes*), Bloch in *Misery*. These reworkings further assert an appropriative relation to this tradition that affirms the Gothic nature of the contemporary text's dependence on tradition. As we have seen, King is also heavily indebted formally, thematically and narratively to *Dracula* and other canonical Gothic texts. Tradition for King is largely a matter of homage, acknowledgement and sometimes more or less transparent imitation.

King does, however, concentrate extensively in his critical writings on what Eliot calls the 'individual talent', suggesting another version of the underlying tension between social and individual demands that structures his version of American Gothic. In *On Writing*, for example, he writes of 'deposits of talent' that make easy for some the King commandment for writerly success to 'read a lot [and] write a lot' (*OW*, 116–17); and in *Danse Macabre* he comments on 'the talented individual', but notes here, in contrast, that 'talent is a dreadfully cheap commodity, as cheap as table salt' (*DM*, 104). *Danse Macabre* and *On Writing* are extensively concerned with defining and describing different traditions of popular fiction and film and their necessary relevance to King's own literary output, in relation to this emphasis on individual creativity understood as 'talent'. Both books offer exemplary lists of texts and films, demonstrating King's own extensive consumption of work from different traditions. *The Dark Half* and 'Secret Window, Secret Garden' are concerned, rather, with exploring how tradition, manifest in the productive 'individual talent' fictionalised in characters who are clearly authorial surrogates, replicates itself in the contemporary text.

Burying Tradition in The Dark Half

The Dark Half (1989) is perhaps the most autobiographical of King's texts.[15] Echoing his own invention and killing off of the Richard Bachman pseudonym it concerns a novelist, Thad Beaumont, whose oeuvre is divided into works written under his own name and those produced under the pseudonym George Stark. The latter, more numerous than and far outselling the former, trouble Thad so much that in order to suppress this alter ego and its threatening productivity he enacts a fake 'burial' of his pseudonymous self, complete with '*papier-mâché*' tombstone' (*DH*, 27; italics in original) and media attention. This stunt backfires when someone starts murdering everyone involved in it; this someone is revealed to be George Stark himself, Beaumont's fictional alter ego returning from a fictional burial to exact horrific revenge and to force Thad to resume writing under his now manifest pseudonym. *The Dark Half* is a fable of writerly creativity gone monstrously wrong, a version of the allegory of the author enslaved by a popular readership that King constructs more effectively and more economically in *Misery*.

    The Dark Half invents a writer and his relations to different traditions, shadows of the real (that is, authorial) writer and traditions the novel analyses, in order to destroy them in a ritual burial that literalises Eliot's metaphor of the writer entering tradition via a monumental gravestone. The stone is a marker of his death and consequent absence, but also of his persistent significance, his posthumous relevance and influence. The dependence of Gothic on deception and fakery theorised by Jerrold Hogle[16] is made transparent in the process of symbolic interment that mobilises *The Dark Half*. The narrative relates a mock funeral, 'a posed job' with 'bogus sextons', photographed by a woman trying to publish a book satirising 'the American way of death' (*DH*, 26–7). The deceased is a fictional character, a fake alter ego or nom de plume, symbolically killed off so that the real writer may live (again): 'He was dead, dead and publicly buried, he had never really existed in the first place' (*DH*, 95). The question of what, in the writer's world, is real and what is imagined, haunts *The Dark Half* as it also haunts its doubling sequel, 'Secret Window, Secret Garden'. It establishes the uncanny basis of King's enquiry into 'the strange no-man's-land which exists between what's real and what's make-believe' (*FPM*, 303). The novel thus locates itself firmly within a series of Gothically inflected tropes: the cyclical movement of death and resurrection, the linking of death and the fake (embedding the Gothic hope/fear that death itself might be 'fake'), the confusion between symbolic and 'real' actions, and, at their centre, the writer's desire to live and to live on in writing.

The Dark Half explores the writer's position in relation to a conception of tradition as embodying the (controllable) order of the dead, an order disordered by the uncanniness of resurrection. The specific literary and cinematic traditions principally addressed in this novel include the Gothic line of descent from James Hogg to Robert Louis Stevenson that addresses the uncanniness of doubling; the modern American Gothic tradition of *noir* ('All very *film noir*', one character remarks (*DH*, 111)); the police procedural, elaborated with extended detail that deflects, and distracts from, much of the novel's allegorical force (but which, as we will see, establishes key tropes of doubling in the text); and the tradition of 'gross-out' (*DM*, 40) horror King claims as his own, that concerned with 'the gag reflex of revulsion' (*DM*, 39). The novel alludes extensively in terms of plot devices and motifs to Poe's 'William Wilson' and Stevenson's *The Strange Case of Dr Jekyll and Mr Hyde* (1886), and to *Frankenstein* as both novel ('It wouldn't matter if they ran to the end of the earth; they would get there, look around, and see George Stark mushing after them behind a team of huskies' (*DH*, 224)) and film ('You make it sound like the part of *Frankenstein* where the lightning finally strikes the rod on the highest castle battlement and juices up the monster!' (*DH*, 33)). Alluding to wider literary circles, it cites Hemingway, Kafka and Orwell (*DH*, 80), Conan Doyle (*DH*, 210), *Brideshead Revisited* (*DH*, 111) and *Treasure Island* (*DH*, 183). These various references suggest, if not diverse lines of high and low cultural generic descent, at least an awareness of literary traditions as potential resources. They combine in *The Dark Half* with an extended and self-reflexive analysis of the writer and the writing process, suggesting another layer of tradition, that of allegory and postmodern self-consciousness.

Through its pastiche of Gothic, police procedural and *noir* languages and conventions, *The Dark Half* enacts a series of writerly fantasies constitutive of King's Gothic. These include the horror implicit in the ambivalent power of the writer to create and destroy, the writer's uncanny ability of self-redefinition and self-naming, and of imagining into existence non-existent beings, events and places, the power of words to evoke the unimaginable, and the symbolic authority of the written text that overrides, in the moment of reading and writing, that of the real world. It grounds these fantasies in its enquiry into the apparent epistemological power of the writer:

> How could he know so much? People asked him that all the time. They used different words to express it – how did you make that up? how did you put that into words? how did you remember that? how did you see that? – but it always came back to the same thing: how did you *know* that? (*DH*, 158; italics in original)

This passage questions the uncanniness of the writer's knowledge, which is comparable to that uncannily gained by Carrie's telepathic intrusion into Sue Snell's mind. The implicit answers presented in *The Dark Half* are that writers know not what they know, that whatever is creative in writing is largely a product of unconscious and apparently uncontrollable and monstrous forces, and that the creative power of the writer exceeds authorial control in alarming, potentially destructive ways, threatening the very basis of society (symbolised in King's novel in a banally conventional heterosexual family and their policeman friend). The potential horror of the unknowability of the writer's knowledge is thus the symbolic concern of *The Dark Half*. The novel subjects the writer to scrutiny that reveals some kind of secret, unknown knowledge at the centre of fictional creativity.

The crux of this haunting question turns on doubling and its uncanny effects, the 'layer upon layer of falsity' which the novel piles on in its representation of King's autobiographical renunciation of his fictional alter ego, Richard Bachman.[17] We learn early in the novel that Thad Beaumont, father of identical but mixed sex twins (thus establishing identity and difference as key motifs), had in his childhood an operation to remove from within his own cranium an undeveloped twin which he believes was a tumour. Thad's writerly alternative self, his 'secret identity' (*DH*, 109), George Stark, writes novels about a character called Alexis Machine, 'a fiction by a fiction' (*DH*, 114) (a name that the 'Afterword' acknowledges derives from Shane Stevens's novel *Dead City*; George Stark's name is borrowed from one of the pseudonyms of Donald E. Westlake, Richard Stark (*DH*, 32)). Stark, symbolically 'killed off' by Thad in a publicity stunt, returns from the 'dead' as a resurrected ghost of a representation, a spectre of a counterfeit.[18] This ghost is inextricably and inexplicably bound to its 'real' author, the murders it commits having Thad's fingerprints 'all over the scene of the crime' (*DH*, 97).

Stark is, furthermore, explicitly connected in the novel's rhetoric to Thad's tumour. Thad thinks of him as 'some weird cancer in human form' (*DH*, 150), and the graphic descriptions of the process of decay to which he is subject by the novel's economy of writing as life-force reinforce this perception. At the same time he 'is' Thad, possessing those aspects of Thad's identity – voice-prints and finger-prints – on which modern police technology relies to determine identity. Within this detailed police procedural discourse, Thad and Stark are one: legally, and in terms of the epistemology of evidence on which the novel draws, there is no difference between them. Names and identities thus circulate in *The Dark Half* through a restricted, generically second-hand economy expanding on and constrained by different traditions, binding characters to each other and the novel to those traditions. Pseudonyms add further dimensions to this relation to tradition. The novel notes that,

George Stark was not real, and neither was Alexis Machine [. . .]. Neither of them had ever existed, any more than George Eliot had ever existed, or Mark Twain, or Lewis Carroll, or Tucker Coe, or Edgar Box. Pseudonyms were only a higher form of literary character. (*DH*, 150

Thad also refers to the structure of doubling within which he is enmeshed as 'my William Wilson complex' (*DH*, 125; italics in original), cementing the connection with Poe and the American Gothic tradition that has so far remained implicit. In a crucial scene that reconciles Thad to the initially suspicious Law and exonerates him from apparent culpability for murder, the novel addresses the fakery and counterfeit actions and identities involved in doubling and, in this novel's terms, its impossibility. Thad is suspected of 'not just one murder but two', ('Two!', Liz Beaumont repeats, emphasising by repetition the increasingly ludicrous doublings of this novel (*DH*, 96)). The Sheriff notes that 'Not even identical twins have identical prints' (*DH*, 97). The identity-marker that apparently 'connects' Thad and Stark is thus precisely that which distinguishes them, forcing the Law to recognise not their weirdly shared identity, but their apparently impossible difference. The novel's proliferation of twins and doubles gives rise to an anxiety about difference initially located in identity, which eventually extends to an analysis of the writer's difference from tradition.

But the fakery of doubling extends deeper into this novel. Thad believes the Sheriff's 'casual' questioning to be 'counterfeit' (*DH*, 98), while later discussion centres on 'counterfeit fingerprints' (*DH*, 102) and Liz's distrust of the 'counterfeit [. . .] monstrous teasing' (*DH*, 308) of Stark's voice. Liz's previous miscarriage (echoing the carriages and miscarriages of tradition in *Carrie*) is revealed to be of 'twins' (*DH*, 98), so that birth and failed birth doubly double each other, situating female reproductivity problematically within the novel's analysis of male creativity. Thad has published two books under his own name: the new novel will 'be my third' (*DH*, 98)), threatening to destabilise his hitherto doubled output. We're told that 'Stark messed with some of the conventions of the mystery story' (*DH*, 99), in ways analogous to King's adaptation of the Gothic tradition. Nothing in this novel is not doubled. There is, as Hogle argues of Gothic fiction more generally, 'no place at which points of reference are not already spectres of counterfeits'.[19] Resurrected,

Stark daubs the phrase 'The sparrows are flying again' over the corpse of one of his victims. The same phrase ('It's the same . . . *It's the very same*' says Liz (*DH*, 122; italics in original), again embedding verbal repetition within individual utterances) is insistently scrawled by Thad in his fugue moments.

In *The Dark Half* doubling is repeatedly connected to falsity, implying in turn an anxiety about the contemporary text's repetitions and reiterations of the traditions it inherits. Hogle's reading of Gothic relates the process of Gothic counterfeiting to the process of abjection. In this process, 'the most multifarious, inconsistent and conflicted aspects of our beings in the West are "thrown off" onto seemingly repulsive monsters or ghosts that both conceal and reveal this "otherness" from our preferred selves as existing very much *within* ourselves' (italics in original).[20] This reading sheds light on the symbolic function in King's novel of George Stark and his impossible resurrection in relation to the writer's relation to tradition, a concern that extends throughout King's work. Hogle's historical displacement of Gothic counterfeits from the period of Gothic emergence, backwards on to Renaissance counterfeits of medieval signs, can be adapted to apply to King's reworking here and elsewhere of modernist literary traditions. *The Dark Half* alludes, among others, to a wide range of modernist literary figures, from Hemingway to Agatha Christie. Modernist writing is, for King, what Hogle calls an 'evacuated signifier',[21] a motif of textual authority to be both imitated and debunked. The generic loyalty of *The Dark Half* is ultimately, but problematically, to the popular traditions it inherits, even if it eventually adds little to them beyond the excess of its own counterfeit versions of repetition as insistence.

Tradition Doubled

In *The Dark Half* tradition dies, is buried and returns within the trajectories mapped out by the works of the contemporary novelist. The novel offers no philosophy of tradition or theorisation of its force. Instead, it seeks tropes and images through which to articulate a sense of debt that finds expression through repetition and the coded workings of the motifs of doubling outlined above. A more complex comprehension of tradition can be constructed through the work of Simon Critchley, who defines two senses of philosophical 'tradition': '(1) as something inherited or handed down without questioning or critical interrogation; (2) as something made or produced through a critical engagement with the first sense of tradition, as a de-traditionalisation of tradition or an appeal to tradition that is in no way traditional'. He goes on to qualify this distinction, suggesting that 'consciousness of tradition' may only emerge with 'a *modernity* [understood] as that which places in question the evidence of tradition' (italics in original).[22]

The first of these definitions, we might argue, approximates the dominant conception of tradition in King's works: something inherited which is also reiterated in acknowledgement of that inheritance. Critchley's stronger, second definition is less detectable in King's works, which are not on the whole innovative in their interventions into or transformations of inherited tradition, but tend instead to reflect it back upon itself. Tradition, as either the repetition of or the generation of something new in response to that which is handed down, becomes significant in the process of the (modern) perception of the productive tension (generative of new elements of tradition itself) between its problematic authority (the burden it presents to the modern writer) and its potential loss. As Leslie Moran has argued in relation to connections between the Gothic and the law, this sense of potential loss is a condition of the possibility of Gothic:

> As an imaginative mode and philosophical schema the Gothic is an effect of and response to modernity experienced as the loss of tradition, the loss of the divine and sacred as organising principles of moral truth and order. In the Gothic the sacred and the divine return in the secular form of nature. [...] While the return threatens to destroy, the terror it evokes offers the possibility of new sensations, new insights, new social orders.[23]

In this reading, the Gothic 'imaginative mode' is understood as an extended enactment of the dialectic of 'loss' and 'return' of tradition, historically dependent upon and responding to broad paradigm shifts and developments in intellectual culture. Gothic offers an interrogation of the differences between that which (uncannily) returns from the past and that which, it appears, has been lost of the past, as different and analogous sources of a paradoxically similar emotion, that of horror. It explores the conflicting potentials of destruction of and liberation from tradition afforded by the 'new'. Tradition dies, to be resurrected by and within the 'new' as an uncanny presence, an unwonted persistence. The novelty of Moran's 'new social orders' may also be their uncanniness, while Gothic itself embodies tradition and the 'new' in threatening, circular, interdependent relations. Gothic enacts (its own) tradition firstly as a kind of repetition. It offers a critical response that 'de-traditionalises' tradition, transposing it into a non-modern historical narrative, redefining its apparent absence from (or its repression within) the new and the modern as such an uncanny presence.

Gothic's appeal to tradition is, in Critchley's terms, 'in no way traditional', but is instead transformative of tradition, allowing its return in Moran's 'haunting and disturbing forms' and positing tradition as parasitic, vampiric upon the present and the future. The Gothic text performs and sustains its own vampiric textuality by feeding off its precursors in grossly public, excessively transparent ways. King's writing conspicuously inserts itself into these relationships, further redefining and extending them in ways disdained by much contemporary criticism, as in Harold Bloom's critique (in a book of essays on King, edited by Bloom himself) of King's 'general remarkable absence of invention',[24] an absence arguably structural to most Gothic writing. *Dracula* draws its lifeblood from Le Fanu's *Carmilla* (1872); *'Salem's Lot* draws its own from *Dracula*. Stevenson's *Dr Jekyll and Mr Hyde* (1886) redoubles Hogg's *The Confessions of a Justified Sinner* (1824), and is redoubled again by *The Dark Half*. Gothic figures, obsessed with death and endlessly dying, refuse to die, becoming posthumous versions of and re-enactments of their own traditions. Gothic's own traditions are replete with serial returns – *The Return of Dracula, The Mummy Returns, The Return of the Living Dead* – that indicate the genre's indebtedness to the logic of repetition and mark the oscillation between repetition and difference as a symbolic vacillation around and across the border of death.

Gothic's 'sublime [. . .] *awareness* of mutability' (italics in original)[25] is also its awareness of its own generic task, to explore the possibilities of symbolically overcoming mutability through the repetition or persistence of a dead life. Tradition becomes, in this sense, a parodic version of repetition as insistence, the insistent return of the dead and the outmoded, demanding, like George Stark, to be continued textually. Gothic compresses tradition to habitual tics and motifs that signify the uncanny and ultimately unwanted or threatening persistence of the past, its insistent presence in the present and the threat of its distorted, uncanny persistence into the future. Gothic's 'continuity', its outliving of its own historical moment and its recurrent re-adaptation to and resurrection within new contexts, in new disguises, suggests versatility, a mobile pervasiveness that insists against its own putative borders on the possibility that all traditions can be infected by Gothic traditions in a kind of double movement. As Gothic modifies by its uncanny presence the configurations of tradition, so tradition impacts upon and deforms, through incorporation or marginalisation, the force and effectiveness of Gothic modes of writing. This double movement is characteristic of the kind of reading that King's Gothic demands, and finds its expression in the novella 'Secret Window, Secret Garden', to which we can now turn.

Secreting: 'Secret Window, Secret Garden'

Speaking in 1979 of his writerly productivity, King commented: 'I'm not a fast writer, but I stick to it. I write 1,500 words a day, and the stuff just piles up. It's a constant secretion. I have the feeling that if I stop, I won't be able to do it again.'[26] King here connects the 'constant secretion' of writing to an anxiety about an interruption to the repetitive act of writing – 'doing it again' – were he to 'stop' writing. This is the fear of writer's block explored in *The Shining*, *Misery* and *Bag of Bones* (1998) and central to 'Secret Window, Secret Garden'. Writing as 'a constant secretion' suggests also writing as uncontrolled but 'secretive', secreting itself and its meanings within itself. It also implies writing as the construction of a place in which things (meanings) may be secreted, hidden or concealed.

We might note here some uses of the word 'secret' in texts we have already looked at, for example *'Salem's Lot*, where Matt Burke reminds us of the Gothic potential of the small-town community that King's fiction repeatedly mines: 'Not all the gossip in a small town is open gossip. There are secrets' (*SL*, 230); and Ben Mears, revealing to Susan the major recent business transaction in the town, the selling of the Marsten House, remarks that the buyer's identity 'Seems to be a deep, dark secret' (*SL*, 40). *Carrie*, too, has its secrets, like the 'top secret' (*C*, 101) ballot for King and Queen of the Prom, or Mrs White's injunction to Carrie: 'Go to your closet. Pray in secret' (*C*, 55). But, as we have seen, what is noticeable in *Carrie* is how such secrets are made public, exposed, revealed by the narrative's relentless laying bare of its action. Secrecy in *'Salem's Lot* seems, in contrast, to be connected to closed, concealed spaces within the novel's complex social world (such spaces become, in the epigraph to *Pet Sematary*, explicitly connected to death and burial: 'Death is a mystery, and burial a secret' (*PS*, 5)) – and within that world to business transactions, specifically the buying and selling of property (houses like the Marsten House, or the antiques in Straker's shop). Both are significant aspects of that novel's plot and both connections link 'secrecy' to the ease with which Barlow's vampiric reign is established and to the susceptibility of the town to being transformed, secretly, in the midst of contemporary America, into a land of the dead, through the plot-like manoeuvres of Straker, Barlow and their vampire acolytes. One secret of *'Salem's Lot*, we might adduce, is hidden in the covertly played rhyme between 'Lot' and 'Plot', signifiers of objects of sale and auction, land and property, on the one side, and on the other of narrative order, conspiracy and secrecy, markers of a 'plot' to take 'ownership' of the 'Lot', uncovered and contested by Ben and his colleagues. The 'secret' thus operates in two distinct, different ways: to conceal, in its non-sharing, and in being shared in its telling, to reveal. It invites a double reading around which *'Salem's Lot* revolves.

Etymologically, 'secret' derives from the Latin '*secernere*', meaning 'to separate, distinguish, secrete'. 'Secrecy' has to do with separation, disconnection, distinguishing as 'hiding (something) away' from others.[27] The secrecy productive of the social disconnection he diagnoses in small-town America is, of course, subject to repeated critiques in King's writings. In texts like *'Salem's Lot*, secrecy betokens a critique of social atomisation, a failure of the systems of social interaction and communication implied elsewhere in the oeuvre by telepathy, perhaps. We also find an analysis of the secrets contained within or belonging to (the properties of) other people, but simultaneously contained within the social sphere and available to exposure in writing, which, being published, reveals them. King's use of 'secrecy' to describe his writing opens the space for a consideration of that writing's social functions, its concerns with critiquing social disconnection. Jacques Derrida's assertion that 'Others are secret because they are other'[28] affords a theoretical perspective from which we can examine King's scrutiny of the otherness of others, their difference from ourselves, and the ways his writing constructs scenarios and plots in which that otherness becomes threatening, monstrous and alienating. King's fictions, in this reading, extend and elaborate Gothic literature's consideration of the 'secret otherness' of others and its relations to secret dimensions of the self.

The 'secret' also concerns the text itself, that which is 'secreted', King suggests, becoming itself a place of concealment and revelation, a double structure like that of the secret. 'Secret Window, Secret Garden' relocates these concerns with the secret into the apparently private world of the male writer and his pathological disconnection from the social world, the result of a drastic failure of writing's communicative powers. Secrecy in this novella has to do initially with the isolation, alienation and dislocation of the writer who borrows too heavily from and becomes unaccountably indebted to tradition. It gradually reveals itself to be a product and a cause of his internal psychological separations and divisions that cumulatively offer a severe critique of writing and its Gothic non-originality and which relate eventually to the connection between this novella and its precursor text. What is secret in 'Secret Window, Secret Garden' is also what is secreted by and within its central protagonist, the narratives he tells in constructing his fantasy world. These secrets require decoding in the relation of the novella to its own internalised tradition, marked by its reliance on its precursor text, *The Dark Half.*

'Secret Window, Secret Garden' is the second of four texts that comprise the collection *Four Past Midnight* (to which we will return later in chapter 6 in discussing 'The Langoliers'). It literalises a version of the writer's experience as a kind of doubling, an uncanny projection of the self into fictional forms and spaces that has disturbing and eventually fatal effects. As its title suggests, it is concerned with issues of secrecy and of what constitutes a secret, something both known and unknown; with how secrets relate to delusions, understood here as the fantasies characteristic of (even necessary for) the writer; and how secrets return in coded or encrypted ways to haunt those who possess or deny them. Its analysis of secrecy depends upon a comprehension of writing that informs King's oeuvre and which is outlined in the 'Note' appended to this novella, entitled '"Two Past Midnight": A Note on "Secret Window, Secret Garden"'. Though short, this is one of the most cogent and suggestive theoretical pieces on writing to be found in King's many critical or commentary texts. King writes here of writing not as telepathy, but as a 'secret act', 'this strange and dangerous craft' which is, he argues, 'as secret as dreaming' (*FPM*, 306). The 'secret act' of writing connects it to other Gothic secrecies and secretions (like the blood that oozes through *Carrie* or the vampirism that infects 'salem's Lot). Unlike the socially communicative act of telepathy, comprehending writing as a 'secret act' like 'dreaming' implies a certain privacy and isolation, an internalisation of unconscious and concealed processes of creativity secreted at the cost of their social dimensions. Writing, understood as being 'like dreaming', is an act of private intimacy, of secret expression and, like dreams, is potentially irrational or surreal, demanding specific kinds of readerly decoding.

This description offers an altogether darker conception of writing than that signified by, for example, the high-school poets and governmental inquiry documents of *Carrie*. In *Four Past Midnight*, writing is connected not to teenage expression or to the authority of governmental fact-finding, but to 'strangeness' and 'danger', to sleep, to the night of dreams and nightmares. In its suggestion of another 'secret act', that of masturbation ('The act of writing itself is done in secret, like masturbation', King writes elsewhere, in 'The Body' (*DS*, 399)), the phrase implicitly connects writing furthermore with a Freudian notion of repressed or concealed (and strangely non-reproductive, masculine) sexual activity. 'Secret Window, Secret Garden' is much concerned with what happens during or at the edges of sleep and with the confusions between sleep and wakefulness, the doublings and uncanny repetitions that arise from sudden interruptions – phone calls, knocks at the door – which betoken the intrusion of social and family worlds into the private world of the sleeper. These confusions lead to fundamental uncertainties about what is real and what is dreamt, and about whether dreams have, at certain points, been confused with memories. As the narrative repeatedly puts it, in a phrase repeated (not quite verbatim) from *The Dark Half*, '*Is it real* [or *live*], *or is it Memorex?*' (*FPM*, 382, 407; *DH*, 208; italics in original).

'Secret Window, Secret Garden', doubling the word in its title, analyses the 'secret act' of writing and in doing so offers another way of thinking about 'rereading King', where 'rereading' involves engagement with repetitions, reiterations, doublings and recurrences: precisely the subject-matter of the novella's plot. What, then, might be the 'secret(s)' and secretions of such a plot, and how might this 'secrecy' be read? The plot concerns Morton Rainey, a successful novelist (his initials imply a connection with M. R. James not pursued in the text; his first name repeats that of Carrie's headmaster in *Carrie*; and his abbreviated name, Mort, connects him to the death counterpointed by the love signified in the name of his ex-wife, Amy). Rainey is accused by John Shooter, an apparently unpublished writer, of plagiarism. The disputed text is a short story entitled (in Rainey's version) 'Sowing Season' and (in Shooter's) 'Secret Window, Secret Garden'. This second title repeats that of the novella, suggesting the *mise-en-abyme* structure of internal doubling and repetition integral to this text. Rainey, at the wrong end of a painful divorce, frantically tries to prove his innocence, seeking a copy of his own story in its first published form to confirm its precedence over Shooter's. As he repeatedly fails to do so, the dispute escalates. Rainey's cat is killed, the house ostensibly containing a copy of his story is burnt down in an apparent arson attack and he finds two crucial witnesses murdered with tools from his own garage. His world, as he seeks to evade the reality towards which the narrative drives him, becomes increasingly distorted and introverted until the plot resolves itself, slightly unsatisfactorily, through the conventional Gothic device of a case of split personality, a psychological doubling in which Rainey has 'invented' Shooter to murder his ex-wife and to express his own repressed guilt for an earlier literary theft which is eventually acknowledged. 'He *was* two men', his estranged wife Amy states: 'He was himself . . . and he became a character he created' (*FPM*, 478; italics in original). At the same time, the text seeks to sustain the further doubling possibility that Shooter seems to have been a 'real' rather than merely psychological presence in the narrative. He has left material traces of himself as evidence of his existence, not least a note written and signed in his handwriting.

Such a plot description indicates the extent to which this text relies upon repression, suppression and concealment as doubled processes which both establish and disestablish narrative events. The plot is driven by Rainey's apparently futile efforts to get a published copy of his story – 'an *original* copy', the text insists, not 'a Xerox' (*FPM*, 401; italics in original) – that would disprove Shooter's accusations of plagiarism. As the rhetoric here implies, the Gothic confusion over 'originals' and 'copies' familiar from *The Dark Half*, and consequent legal issues of ownership and provenance – issues of originality and creative precedence impinging upon questions of tradition and inheritance – reside at the heart of this narrative, figuring its allegory of the contemporary Gothic writer's anxieties over tradition and indebtedness. Told mainly from Rainey's point of view, the narrative must gloss over moments at which certain actions are performed. At one point 'a soft greyness came over his vision. When it drew back, he felt strange and frightened' (*FPM*, 453). In this blank space, the narrative later reveals, he excises from the magazine the pages featuring his own story, effecting a double repression, a kind of censorship of the text, a repression by the narrative of the repression he is enacting within the narrative, that of his own guilt at a much earlier act of plagiarism, his own excessive and dishonest reliance on the tradition from which he steals. In this repression the otherness contained within Rainey, that other self he represses, surfaces. It emerges in the interstices of the text as its own elision of its own narrative and of the (stolen, doubled) narrative it concerns, and as a 'real' persona, a doubled self, Rainey's own becoming-other to himself that is the repressed core of King's novella. The process of becoming-other experienced by Rainey is manifest in the projection of the alter ego John Shooter, a name comprised of the first name of the man from whom he earlier stole a story and the name of the town from which his wife's new partner originates. This projected alter ego, combining writerly and sexual jealousies, embodies a fantasy self, a figure of overtly phallic, Southern Gothic import (and much of the surface detail of this narrative seeks, not wholly successfully, to emulate Faulkner), a fantasised writer whose work doubles Rainey's own in impossible, uncanny ways.

Doubling is, of course, a key motif in Freud's description of the uncanny. Freud comments on how 'a person may identify himself with another, and thus become unsure of his true self; or he may substitute the other's self for his own'. He links the double, via Otto Rank's 1914 study *Der Doppelgänger*, to 'mirror-images, shadows, guardian spirits, the doctrine of the soul and the fear of death', and argues that as the motif of the double develops from its connection with 'primitive narcissism', it 'exercises a kind of psychical censorship, and so becomes what we know as 'the "conscience"'.[29] These Freudian versions of the double resonate with King's novella, lending it its particular uncanny form and effect. For Nicholas Royle, uncanniness itself is 'the experience of something duplicitous, diplopic, being double. It calls for diplomacy, the regulation of a strange economy, an art of negotiation which presupposes a kind of double talk, double reading, double writing'.[30] Everything in King's novella contributes to this 'strange economy' of the uncanny, an economy based here around a Poe-like series of thefts and gifts, refusals and acceptances, rewards and punishments (and, as we will see in 'The Langoliers', King draws extensively in the novellas of *Four Past Midnight* on Poe's 'The Purloined Letter'). The circulation of the disputed text is effected through this economy: a short story that shares its title with and so suggests itself as the one we are reading, but which also appears in the text with another title and is yet absent from it, apart from brief doubled quotations from the openings and conclusions of each version of it (*FPM*, 317–21). This circulation, in turn, is less a process of exchange and more a vacillation, a version of what Freud calls (in *Beyond the Pleasure Principle*) the *fort-da* game, the child's enacting of the symbolic absence (*fort*) and presence (*da*) of the mother through holding and discarding a toy.[31] This is the dialectic on which, Botting argues, 'All of Gothic fiction turns [. . .] its repetitions occluding some kind of excess to efforts of representation and theorisation'.[32] The contested text oscillates back and forth, 'occluded' by the narrative containing it, never revealed beyond its opening sentences but central to that narrative. Doubled, it is both secret and made public by its publication, and even this is double, as the story has been published twice, Rainey insists, in a magazine in 1980 and a short story collection in 1983.

Ending / Continuing

'Secret Window, Secret Garden' both brings to an end and continues or extends the themes of *The Dark Half*. Rhetorically and thematically an extension of the earlier novel, it also signifies a Gothic darkening of the precursor novel's tone, abandoning the mawkish family scenes of *The Dark Half* and its reliance on the rhetoric and logic of the police procedural and the *noir* thriller and forsaking the 'gross-out' physical horror of George Stark's decay, to scrutinise instead the internalised psychological decline of its protagonist. Like Alan Parker's *Angel Heart* (1987), a film to which it bears more than a superficial resemblance, 'Secret Window, Secret Garden' immerses us in what Botting calls 'a process that multiplies meanings and identities to the point where nothing is what it seems but an effect of narrative appearances', a 'process' expressed in a narrative that moves from the 'detective story' (of *The Dark Half*) to 'a Faustian tale of diabolical repossession'.[33] In King's narrative, what is repossessed is not a soul, but a text. The narrative expresses in its dispute over textual precedence and ownership a contradictory desire to continue writing, producing this novella, by stopping writing about writing. It also implies, covertly, the coded truth of this desire, which is that all King's writing has been, and is, and will be, about writing and the desire to continue writing, to extend the (secret, public) productivity of the writerly through its sustained drawing on a tradition that it may simultaneously seek to repress. In this sense, it embodies the absolute involution of King's concern with the figure of the writer, the folding of that concern into an analysis of the writer's descent into sociopathic delusion, his failure, among other things, to address appropriately the otherness of others. Anxiety over such an involution is addressed successfully elsewhere in the oeuvre, for example, in the involvement of writer Ben Mears in the group fighting the vampires in *'Salem's Lot*. Its failure here is evident in the novella's insistent concern with the writer's own internal concerns and self-divisions. 'Secret Window, Secret Garden' presents the male writer from the outset as anti-social, self-divided and self-destructive. Its negation of writing as productivity is figured in the novella's concern with constipatory metaphors of writer's block, to which we will return (*FPM*, 316). It indicates, amid these symbolic and thematic debts, repressions and unnatural retentions, a coded anxiety that King's work insistently returns to, expressed in 'Secret Window, Secret Garden' by the writer-hero: 'He felt guilty because writing stories had *always* felt a little bit like stealing, and probably always would' (*FPM*, 324; italics in original). The verb forms here indicate that what may be stolen by the writer is, it seems, tradition itself, the (secret) resource which (always) seemingly both facilitates and prohibits the Gothic author.

One 'secret' of 'Secret Window, Secret Garden' might then initially be understood as its plot revelation, that Shooter both *is* and *is not* Rainey (just as this novella both *is* and *is not The Dark Half*, and *is* and *is not* the novella with which its narrative is concerned). This suggests a contradictory double potential in the narrative. Shooter is, effectively, the 'secret' other within Rainey. He figures a secret, pre-emptive otherness revealed throughout the text (Shooter speaks first, his words opening the novella) and, at the end of the text, as Rainey's own guilt at an earlier 'accidental similarity' (*FPM*, 478), a potential plagiarism evident in one of his earlier texts but incompletely repressed, as Amy insists ambiguously that 'there was no question of plagiarism' (*FPM*, 478). The novella constructs Shooter throughout as an explicitly textual figure. Only ever represented from Rainey's viewpoint, he '*looks like a character out of a William Faulkner novel*' until, belatedly but crucially, he is apparently and uncannily perceived in a car wing-mirror by someone else: '*but you could see right through him, and the car, too*' (*FPM*, 308, 480; italics in original). The text, like its precursor, is replete with doubles, from the contested short stories (which are, like the fingerprints of Thad and Stark, '*exactly* the same' (*FPM*, 320; italics in original) and which both owe much to Poe's 'The Tell-Tale Heart'), to Rainey and Shooter as versions of each other. The phallic implications of Shooter's name, reinforced by the narrative's decryption of Mort's delusional self as deriving from the home town of the man with whom his wife has had an affair, Shooter's Knob, is further elaborated in a central scene in which Mort, thinking Shooter is in his bathroom, attacks him with a poker:

> He turned the knob of the bathroom door and slammed in, bouncing the door off the wall hard enough to chop through the wallpaper [. . .] and there he was, *there he was*, coming at him with a raised weapon, his teeth bared in a killer's grin [. . .] and he had just time enough to realise that Shooter was also swinging a poker [. . .] and to realise it wasn't Shooter at all, to realise it was *him*, the madman was *him*, and then the poker shattered the mirror over the washbasin [. . .] (*FPM*, 395; italics in original)

An extended Gothic mirror stage, this scene enacts the novella's central misrecognition of the self as the other. Its wordplay ('knob' repeating and embedding within the text's surface realism the name 'Shooter's Knob') and pronouns ('he' and 'him' working interchange-ably) effect, through repetition and doubling, a condensed version of the novella's Gothic economy. Its revelation – that 'the madman was *him*' – is, after all, one 'secret' of the narrative, revealed here as an open secret in an apparent moment of misrecognition which is actually a rare moment on Rainey's part of ironically accurate self-perception.

The mirror, here the location of the doubling of the writer, is also key to the novella's structure, as is implied in Shooter's eventual appearance in a mirror to someone other than Rainey. A 'rear-view mirror' allows the driver to see what is behind; seeing and failing to recognise or acknowledge that which is historically 'behind', located in tradition, is the secret concern of 'Secret Window, Secret Garden'. Mirrored himself by the bookshelves of his office (another figure of the Gothic library of the psyche familiar from *Carrie*), one wall of which displays 'various editions, domestic and foreign, of his works' (*FPM*, 319), Rainey meditates on the economies of narrative and ownership that define the themes of the novella:

> Well, a story was a thing, a *real* thing – you could think of it like that, anyway, especially if someone had paid you for it – but in another, more important, way, it wasn't a thing at all. It wasn't like a vase, or a chair, or an automobile. It was ink on paper, but it wasn't the ink and it wasn't the paper. People sometimes asked him where he got his ideas, and though he scoffed at the question, it always made him feel

vaguely ashamed, vaguely spurious. [. . .] But when you got a story idea, no one gave you a bill of sale. There was no provenance to be traced. Why would there be? Nobody gave you a bill of sale when you got something for free. (*FPM*, 323–4; italics in original)

The ideology of literary creativity and ownership propounded here works, like the text of 'Secret Window, Secret Garden', to efface its indebtedness to the 'provenance' it denies exists, that of tradition. Simplistic and reductive, it contradicts even Rainey's own version of the 'provenance' of his short story in the American Gothic trad- ition, expressed with characteristic denial of its own indebtedness to that tradition as 'no "Tell-Tale Heart"' (FPM, 320). But further indications of the force of tradition are evident. A story conceived as 'a real thing' echoes, perhaps, Henry James's short story of secrecy and representational doubling 'The Real Thing' (1892), a tale much concerned with 'the mystery of values'[34] that preoccupies King's writer. The doubles that deform and destructure Rainey's relationship to 'the real thing' – a relationship he seems to have overcome by creating, as Amy puts it, 'a character so vivid that he actually did become real' (FPM, 482; italics in original) – are also figures of the novella's relation to literary traditions, Gothic or otherwise, which it represses but which return insistently within the writing of its own repetition, its own self-doubling and its doubling of selves and of its precursor text. Such repetition exposes the secret, 'spurious' non-provenance of Gothic non-originality.

4

Genre's Gothic Machinery

༄

'Each "text" is a machine with multiple reading heads for other texts.'[1]

Carrie, The Dark Half and 'Secret Window, Secret Garden' enact in different and problematic ways the 'carrying-on' of the traditions of their predominant Gothic genre. King's writing carefully constructs this movement from a past of popular Gothic traditions into the Gothicised present: a familiar (but Gothically defamiliarised) present of media and consumer commercialism, brand-names and realistically rendered characters who speak the argots of modern America. But these texts also indicate in their formal complexities a version of the generic fluidity that King's writing frequently achieves. Such fluidity is evident in *The Dark Half*'s mixing of Gothic, crime fiction, police procedural and *noir* or in King's extensive fantasy output, which draws also on motifs borrowed from modernist and nineteenth-century English poetry alongside conventions deriving from the Western novel and the Spaghetti Westerns of Sergio Leone. Another key popular genre King relies on throughout his career is science fiction or SF, a genre proximally close to Gothic in terms of origins and development. King's particular use of the connections between the SF tradition and the Gothic will be explored in this chapter through a reading of *The Tommyknockers* (1988).

In what senses can *The Tommyknockers* be read as a Gothic novel? To any cursory reading the novel would clearly appear to be a science fiction text. Its narrative, plundered from dozens of SF films and novels from the nineteenth and twentieth centuries, is almost clichéd in its conventionality and generic predictability. This clichéd dimension is of course a recurrent feature of King's version of Gothic, an aspect of the tropes of repetition and reiteration that characterise his work. Generic novelty and innovation are rarely associated critically with King's writing. Ben P. Indick has noted, supportively, that King 'has constructed his work on a sure knowledge of the fiction of his predecessors',[2] while Herron argues, more critically, that 'King has not been even a *developmental* force in supernatural literature, as were Poe and H. P. Lovecraft'.[3] Indick, like most critics, relates King's writing to specific generic traditions, those of horror and the supernatural, which he discusses as elements of what he (problematically) describes as 'the original Gothic style'[4] of the eighteenth and nineteenth centuries. For such critics, King's relations to Gothic forms and motifs are at best conventional and at worst derivative. It is safe to say also that *The Tommyknockers*, read as a science fiction novel, adds little innovative to that genre, despite being published in the decade when its North American traditions were undergoing extensive revitalisation through major new works by William Gibson, Bruce Sterling and Octavia E. Butler. King has described his novel as 'a forties-style science fiction tale' (*OW*, 71), and its events clearly also relate to and to some degree represent sublimations of autobiographical experiences (of drug abuse and alcoholism) which he has narrated at length in *On Writing* and elsewhere. But these definitions reduce the novel's complexity and underplay its position in the oeuvre. They also ignore how the rhetoric and symbolic structure of the novel enact at different levels its formal conflation of genres, a kind of science fiction-becoming-Gothic. Its use of SF conventions, its thematisation at the level of narrative symbolism and rhetoric of those conventions and its combination of these conventions with certain Gothic images and tropes suggest that *The Tommyknockers* offers a microcosmic version of the functions of genre in King's Gothic. They suggest also ways of thinking about King's uses of generic models in developing his own versions of Gothic. The discussion below will explore how *The Tommyknockers* conflates writers and texts, machines and transformations, into a Gothicised form of pastiche science fiction and in doing so confirms ways in which King's oeuvre can be read as offering different allegories of writing. The novel invites an understanding of writing as an unconscious activity that works in terms of the operation of desire and its productivity – desiring-production – in relation to the machines and mechanisms that figure that desire and in relation to how desire affords insights into the operations of genre.

Genre's laws

Two theoretical injunctions help more clearly initially to define the generic territory of *The Tommyknockers*. Jacques Derrida famously defines, in critiquing what he calls the 'Law' of genre, that Law's insistence that 'Genres are not to be mixed';[5] and Ken Gelder, in his Pierre Bourdieu-influenced analysis of the 'field' of popular fiction, insists on another contrary 'Law', that 'Genres must be continually processed, reanimated, added to [. . .]'.[6] Two contradictory imperatives thus delineate the area of theorisations of genre: two contradictory versions of the 'Law' that regulates genre's productive desires to conform, to fit, to be recognisable. First, a definition of a prohibition (against generic promiscuity or miscegenation) imposed in order to sustain generic purity (explicitly, in Derrida's essay, in relation to a 'high-cultural', literary sense of genre); and second, an assertion (against purity or exclusivity) of genre's constant and essential movement and supplementation (explicitly, in Gelder's argument, in relation to a popular-fictional sense of genre). 'Genre', the French word for a kind, a literary type or class, signifies classification and is related, as Derek Attridge notes, to 'gender, genus and taxonomy more generally' but also to 'generation', 'generalisation' and 'genitive'.[7] Genre concerns generation and regeneration; within the field delimited by these conflicting injunctions genre offers an inherited and structuring classification system that is always mobile, unstable, shifting in response to readerly or historical demands. Within that mobility it can be understood as productive, a version of the productive powers of the unconscious. Genre, John Frow argues, 'has a systemic existence. It is a shared convention with social force', whose rules and effects are constituted, like the unconscious, at the shared level of social meaning, in contrast to the meaning embodied in a given individual text as an example of genre.[8] It thus enacts what Frow later calls (paraphrasing Georg Lukács) 'the discontinuity between person and social structure', a discontinuity central to the ideology of the Gothic in King's writing.[9] Genre, in effect, comprises sets of unconsciously inherited and socially imposed rules to which individual texts are subject and against which they react. *The Tommy-knockers* demonstrates how King's works explore the tensions arising within the individual text from these contradictory injunctions.

'Genre' defines precisely the 'processing' and 'reanimation', the generous 'giving' of textual life in the 'generation' of new fictional forms, that Gelder notes; and yet the concept of genre also insists that demarcation, classification, inclusion in and exclusion from clearly identified categories, remains, as Derrida's 'Law' implies, possible. Genres, Gelder and Derrida both imply, are, of course, always already mixed. The possibility of genre depends upon a notion of a formal and textual identity always already exceeding itself, each genre not fixed spatially or temporally but necessarily transforming, mutating, flowing into other spaces and becoming 'other' to itself in its efforts to respond to, assimilate, redefine or annul other generic positions which border it. Genre, like monstrosity, is 'interstitial', 'crossing the boundaries of the deep categories of a culture's conceptual scheme'.[10] In this sense, genre works like the psychoanalytic concept of desire, constantly in excess of itself, demanding and yet resisting containment, regulation, law. Generic classification involves, also, the inevitable impossibility of 'pure' classification, of simple identification of generic belonging or ascription of a singular generic identity to a given text. Derrida writes: 'Thus, as soon as genre announces itself, one must respect a norm, one must not cross a line of demarcation, one must not risk impurity, anomaly, or monstrosity'.[11] Genre's Law is connected, for Derrida, to normativity, to the imposition of norms and to the power (ideological, critical) that enables and supports classification as an imposition or enforcement of order. The 'monstrosity' of generic mixing, its double function as warning against and demonstration of the consequences of breaking the 'Law' of genre, is analogous to that monstrosity of desire and productivity which concerns the Gothic and its relentless and promiscuous crossovers into other generic modes. From *The Castle of Otranto* onwards, Gothic's proclivity for generic hybridity, for monstrous productions and transgressive desires, marks its identity as a manifest-ation of identity-as-desire, fluid, unstable, constantly degenerating or decaying, bordering other marginally Gothicised genres, inserting itself within them and transforming them into darker shadows of themselves.

In this reading Gothic is less a genre than a mode that assimilates different genres into differently inflected combinations – Gothic romance, Gothic crime, Gothic comedy and, in this chapter, Gothic science fiction – performing transgressive mixings and productions. The 'differences' deployed by these different combinations are where textual meanings are generated. As Thomas O. Beebee has argued, 'the truly vital meanings of a literary text are often contained not in any specific generic category into which the text may be placed, but rather in the play of differences between its genres'.[12] King's Gothic is no exception to this: fluid, ambivalent and indeterminate, able to assimilate or imitate, quote and mimic other generic forms both within and outside the conventionally literary or non-literary, it demonstrates the 'Law' of genre as the 'process' that Gelder defines even as it exploits (if only to resist them) the strict generic expectations implied by Derrida. King, like all writers, uses genre as a machine to generate meanings. He refers, in *Danse Macabre*, to the 'gothic novel' as 'a widget on the great machine of English-speaking fiction' (*DM*, 286), an image that both differentiates Gothic from and con-nects it to other genres. The differences between genres (like the tensions between realism, modernism and supernaturalism at the beginning of *Carrie*) generate conflicts, tensions, contradictions and ambivalences which in turn generate meanings. *The Tommyknockers*, as we will see, deploys a complex rhetoric in order to represent its own generation of meanings from differences, a rhetoric which finds echoes in the theoretical terms used by Gilles Deleuze and Félix Guattari. It mixes this rhetoric into other discourses, like science fiction, Gothic and other literary genres, in order to interrogate how generic meanings become significant. In a reverse kind of con-tamination, we can see, too, how Gothically inflected metaphors such as 'reanimation' permeate critical writing on genre. Fredric Jameson (a major critic of science fiction who is also generally dismissive of Gothic) writes, in *The Political Unconscious*, of 'The older generic categories' which

> do not [...] die out, but persist in the half-life of the subliterary genres of mass culture, transformed into the drugstore and airport paperback lines of gothics, mysteries, romances, bestsellers, and popular biographies, where they await the resurrection of their immemorial, archetypal resonance at the hands of a Frye or a Bloch.[13]

Or, indeed, in the critical attention of a Jameson. This passage (echoed in Bloom's criticism of King's 'subliterary' generic heritage, cited in the previous chapter) conveniently melds Gothic rhetoric with metaphors deriving from atomic science ('half-life') suggesting the merging of genres of discourse (science, science fiction, Gothic) within the discourse of literary theory. Jameson usefully distinguishes between two ways of thinking about genre, one which asks 'what it means' and another which asks, following Deleuze and Guattari, 'how it works'.[14] As we will see, this is a crucial distinction in reading genre in *The Tommyknockers*.

Science fiction and Gothic

The Tommyknockers is not King's first or only foray into science fiction. *The Stand*, as noted earlier, draws heavily on George R. Stewart's plague-apocalypse SF novel *Earth Abides*; *It* presents, eventually, an extraterrestrial monster; and several short stories (for example, 'Beachworld' and 'The Jaunt' in *Skeleton Crew* (1985)) are clearly generically science fiction. In *Danse Macabre*, ostensibly a critical discussion of 'The Anatomy of Horror', King doesn't distinguish clearly between horror films like *The Amityville Horror* (Stuart Rosenberg, 1979), and what he calls 'political horror films' (*DM*, 171), which to most readers would arguably be better classified as science fiction films. These include Christian Nyby's *The Thing* (1951) (*DM*, 171), which King discusses alongside George Pal's *The War of the Worlds* (1953), Michael Anderson's *1984* (1956) (*DM*, 177–9) and Boris Sagal's *The Omega Man* (1971). This last is based on Richard Matheson's *I am Legend* (1954), a key SF–Gothic crossover text; and *Thinner* (1984), published under the Richard Bachman pseudonym, is a thinly veiled version of Matheson's *The Shrinking Man* (1956). Indeed, a significant part of *Danse Macabre* is taken up with discussion of conventional science fiction texts rather than horror. This generic ambivalence or failure clearly to distinguish overlapping generic identities or texts suggests that King sees science fiction at least as a potential vehicle of Gothic and horror themes, if not as a sub-category of Gothic itself. Indeed, the whole chapter on 'The American Horror Movie – Text and Sub-text' drifts deeper into science fiction the further it progresses, returning via a brief discussion of Roger Corman's science fiction film *X:The Man with the X-Ray Eyes* (1963) to a series of concluding statements about horror movies (*DM*, 220–9).

King effectively maps out in his discussion a conventional conflation or confusion of genres of which other critics are often guilty. Barbara Creed's analysis of horror films in her *The Monstrous Feminine* (1993), for example, includes a chapter on Ridley Scott's *Alien* (1979), a film that is generically closer to science fiction than horror.[15] The plot of *The Tommyknockers* is, in science fiction terms, equally conventional. In a scenario deriving from Nyby's *The Thing* (which John Carpenter had remade in 1982), writer Bobbi Anderson (an author, unconvincingly, of numerous Westerns) discovers buried on her extensive inherited property a giant and apparently ancient crashed flying saucer. In excavating it she unleashes a strange, apparently radioactive force that transforms her and the people around her through a process the novel calls the 'becoming'. The saucer's radiation infects the air they breathe, turning them into aliens (the 'Tommyknockers' of the title) with remarkable but superficial inventive and adaptive technological powers, motivated towards the invasion of the planet (King has suggested that this aspect is autobiographical, 'the best metaphor for drugs and alcohol my tired, overstressed mind could come up with' (*OW*, 107)). Bobbi's sometime lover, the poet Jim Gardener ('Gard'), seemingly immune to the transformative effects of the spaceship because of a metal surgical plate in his head, offers the sole source of resistance to the changes, until the powers of the state are mobilised at the novel's end. The aliens, both transformed humans and apparently resurrected Tommyknockers (who turn out to be ancient, long-dead visitors incarcerated in their crashed spacecraft), establish a force-field around their town. They devise strange weapons and other innovations to protect themselves. The novel climaxes with the relaunching of the spaceship, the destruction of most of the transformed townspeople and the eventual restoration of order by a strange combination of state intervention and meteorology, in which the weather changes, clearing the poisoned air over the town, in a plot manoeuvre reminiscent of the viral demise of the Martians in Wells's *The War of the Worlds* (1898).

This plot, extended over King's characteristically excessive length, mobilises a series of devices which operate as markers of generic identity. These include a flying saucer, aliens, the horrific transformation of humans into something other than human with green blood and telepathic powers, fantastic technological innovation, a socially symbolic concern with atomic energy and a series of embedded allusions to key texts in the science fiction genre in fiction and film. These markers simultaneously identify the novel as a science fiction text and operate in counterpoint with a series of alternative generic markers which suggest a different, Gothic identity lurking beneath or within the more obvious textual identity. This Gothic alternative resides principally in the novel's exploration of body-horror and physical pain, its use of the trope of premature burial and resurrection, and its thematic examination of writing, inscription and reading. It deploys and combines SF and Gothic conventions self-reflexively, playfully: 'It's *both* Fu Manchu *and* green men from space. An alliance formed in hell' (*T*, 428; italics in original) announces one character, invoking the differential logic of 'both / and' with which the novel is deeply concerned. Its extended use of generic clichés and overworked conventions includes the most familiar of science-fiction devices, the flying saucer, as its central motif: 'No self-respecting science-fiction writer would put one in his story' (*T*, 172), we're told. But a *Gothic* writer might; the potential of the flying saucer as a vehicle of Gothic motifs, especially one long-buried and now exhumed, containing apparently resurrected aliens, a flying saucer as a symbolic crypt, is not missed by King. The flying saucer motif enables the novel's symbolisation of the uncanny persistence of the distant past through resurrection. Subsequently, the novel mobilises metaphors of contamination and degeneration, the notion of the other as an invasive, intrusive and transformational alien which is also a haunting, a telepathic ghost that figures a potential other-becoming-self and self-becoming-other. The flying saucer is doubly encrypted in the text: perceived by Bobbi early on in the novel as 'a coffin' resonating with 'the call of human bones' (*T*, 11), its flight, at the novel's end, is 'out of the earth's crypt [. . .] into thickening bands of smoke and hazy sunlight' (*T*, 681). A crypt encrypted in the 'crypt' of the earth, the ship is also a cipher of or encryption of the novel itself. Both are machines for the generation of the particular kind of transformation the novel calls 'becoming'. *The Tommyknockers* acts out the meeting of Gothic and SF as a drama of resurrection and transformation that reanimates each genre, a narrative of the process of becoming-other that allegorises the novel's inter-generic identity.

The science fiction credentials of *The Tommyknockers* are reinforced through extended allusions which generate the novel's identity in relation to tradition. The basic premise of *The Tommyknockers* arguably derives from H. P. Lovecraft's 'The Colour Out of Space'.[16] Lovecraft's tale, published in *Amazing Stories* in 1927, offers a pre-atomic age allegory of radioactive contamination of the American landscape by meteorite that might stand as a summary of King's novel: 'Strangeness had come into everything growing now'.[17] The opening pages of King's novel draw on Lovecraft's powerfully evocative prose in describing the woods of Maine. 'When I read Lovecraft, my prose became luxurious and Byzantine' (*OW*, 167), King tells us in *On Writing*. Lovecraft's 'blasted heath', with its Shakespearean overtones, becomes King's 'miles of wilderness' (*T*, 4), and Gard's surname clearly derives from the epicentre of the events in Lovecraft's tale, the Nahum Gardner family and their house (King may also have taken the name Thaddeus, used in *The Dark Half*, from this tale).[18] Angela Carter's description of Lovecraft's 'landscape of post-nuclear despoliation' connects it clearly to the themes of King's novel.[19] *The Tommyknockers* also reworks elements of Poul Anderson's science fiction novel *Brain Wave* (1954). Bobbi tells us that her name alludes to Anderson (*T*, 197), and *Brain Wave* features many generic SF motifs borrowed by King. These include accelerated technological innovation, telepathy as novel social communication and signifier of species advancement, and a giant spacecraft. Anderson's characters, their minds liberated as the Earth moves out of a restrictive interstellar force-field, build a ship that can travel faster than light.

In addition to these significant precursors, *The Tommyknockers* deploys a host of references and allusions to 1950s and older SF cinema, including frequent allusions to Roger Forbin's *Forbidden Planet* (1956) and its setting on the planet Altair-4 and to *The Day the Earth Stood Still* (Robert Wise, 1951). It notes Spielberg's *ET* and H. G. Wells's *The Invisible Man* (1897) and (as we have seen) *The War of the Worlds* in film and novel versions, citing 'The Martian heat-ray' (*T*, 46). It mentions the science fiction art of Frank Kelly Freas (*T*, 562) and the US Air Force files on flying saucers (*T*, 29). Science fiction traditions are repeatedly invoked as labelling motifs within the narrative and dialogue: '*Dear God*', thinks Gard, '*I've walked into a science fiction story from* Amazing Stories. *Right around 1947, I'd guess*' (*T*, 142; italics in original). The year 1947, that of the purported Roswell airbase incident, resonates in SF history. Science fiction, then, provides the initial overt generic parameters and reference points that mark out the novel's relations to a generic tradition. Its tropes of becoming-other, innovation and defamiliarisation reinforce this perception. But its relations to SF are clearly not singular: it draws on a range of SF texts from different media and different cultural, national and historical moments, questioning in the process the construction of any singular 'tradition' and demonstrating King's awareness of differences within the SF tradition. Such intra-generic differences ultimately problematise the reliability of 'genre' and 'tradition' as singular classificatory concepts.

Science fiction is, of course, itself a contested generic category identified, as Roger Luckhurst notes, by a 'mass of competing labels' and originating, Fredric Jameson suggests, in a historical moment of generic transformation, 'a mutation in our relationship to historical time itself'.[20] *The Tommyknockers*, exploiting this 'mutation' in its narrative, is more specifically a science fiction pastiche, an appropriation of conventional motifs transplanted with little, if any, recontextualisation from one historical context – the 1940s and 1950s – into another, the 1980s, in an act of generational repetition that is effectively, as Jameson elsewhere Gothically describes it, 'speech in a dead language'.[21] It draws heavily on allusions to and citations of an extended tradition of invasion and flying-saucer narratives from H. G. Wells onwards. Its publication in the late 1980s and its frequent references, in the wake of the Chernobyl (1986) and Three

Mile Island (1979) nuclear power plant disasters, to contemporary political and cultural anxieties about nuclear power generation and the nuclear industry more generally, motivate its critiques of US and international energy policy, critiques mainly articulated in a long, drunken rant early in the novel by Gard (*T*, 80–98).

Such concerns clearly mark the novel ideologically as dystopian and satirical, the reading supported by most critics who engage with it. Strengell, for example, argues that here and in *Dreamcatcher* (2001) 'King mocks scientific pretensions' to show 'how technology for its own sake may not be progress at all'.[22] King has commented on this ostensibly critical element in the novel: '[T]hat's what I'm talking about in this book –', he told Douglas E. Winter, implying a *Frankenstein* dimension, 'a guy who doesn't know what he's doing, yet who creates something capable of just blowing someone else away'.[23] This dimension of intended critique is, as is often the case with King, in practice largely overshadowed by other plot mechanisms that distract from it, but which also throw it into sharp relief, offering a different kind of analysis, an alternative mode of reading that reveals other agendas embedded within the novel. As Gard is warned: 'Poetry and politics rarely mix: poetry and propaganda, never' (*T*, 103). Mixing, its prohibition and its consequences are, as we will see, effectively what King is actually 'talking about' in *The Tommyknockers*: the mixing of narratives and allusions, the mixing of species and identities, and, above all, the mixing of genres. The other agendas addressed in *The Tommyknockers* refract and adumbrate this central concern. The novel explores power and its generation, the potentials of power and energy for generating new social mixes and combinations and, more fundamentally, the writer's task to find and mobilise metaphors that enable the political critique to emerge at levels other than the simply polemical. The novel's covert concern with the dynamics of genre, genre mixing and genre transformation constitutes one such level.

Generation and degeneration, contradictory processes and movements, pursue each other across the text. On the opening page, the landscape of Bobbi's estate features 'a rock wall [. . .] so old it had degenerated into isolated rock middens furred with moss' (*T*, 4). The superficially innovative Tommyknocker technology consists of adapted domestic artefacts that draw on a strange new source of energy like an 'electronic game [. . .] generating a strong glow' (*T*, 280) in one character's kitchen. Standing beside the excavated space-ship is, for Gard, 'like standing next to the biggest power generator in the world' (*T*, 432). The novel is intermittently concerned with technical issues, like 'generating capacity' (*T*, 447), as signifiers of the intellectual changes wrought on the people of Haven by the 'becoming'. Such changes might also make them 'degenerate into madness – the madness of schizophrenia as the target minds tried to fight the alien group mind slowly welding them together' (*T*, 289). The 'generation' of power and symbolically related themes like inter-generational conflict refract back into the novel's resurrection in the late 1980s of earlier, 1940s generic representations and ideo-logical concerns. Significantly, however, the Tommyknockers seem unable 'to create anything truly innovative'.[24] What they do instead is enable their victims to tinker with and adapt existing artefacts, producing new combinations of old objects. In this sense the actual products of the Tommyknockers are much like those of the genre of Gothic. The genre's adaptive belatedness, its constant appropriations and reworkings of the productions of older texts, older genres and older narratives, is likewise a form of generic tinkering, a mixing together of the already-existent to produce (in many cases) the less-than-new. *The Tommyknockers* typifies such a conception of genre as the manipulation for productive purposes of already existing narratives and motifs rather than the endless generation of the new. Genre does not innovate: rather, it recombines the pre-existent, processing, reanimating and adding to what is already there. What this novel adds to science fiction, specifically, is Gothic.

The Tommyknockers invites, then, through these structures, a double reading as SF-Gothic or Gothic-SF, each generic mode complementing and contrasting the other in a complex process of 'becoming-other' which is thematically central to the narrative. Each possible generic reading is furthermore encoded in features which are thematised within the narrative's concern with finding metaphors for the inventiveness of the writerly imagination. This thematisation suggests that *The Tommyknockers* covertly analyses the workings of genre within King's fictions. One way of reading the novel's significance within the oeuvre is to perceive it as an allegory of the productivity of writing and of the conflicting worlds it can produce. The novel relates events that befall two writers and which transform their writerly productivity in bizarre, destructive ways. To examine this process, we need briefly to explore the symbolic roles of machines in King's writing and introduce the Deleuzean theoretical framework which will enable us to connect machinic representations to desire and to generic representations in King's writing.

King's machines: desiring-production and becoming

The machine, like telepathy, is a recurrent, ambivalent structure in King's writing, an insistent trope that connects his texts, inviting connective readings and suggesting linkages and patterns that cross generic and textual borders. It defines a discursive space identifiable across the oeuvre of functionality, of machinic flows and exchanges (like the flows of blood in *Carrie*) expanding eventually to encompass the texts themselves, mobilising the possibility that King's texts, like machines, may be read better in terms of what they 'do' than what they 'mean'. King's machines are characteristically Gothic and un-canny: both familiar and unfamiliar, uncanny harbingers of other ways of writing and reading, expressing concerns with the writer, the body, the social, and with flows and blockages of desire across and through these structures. The 'shitty writing machine' of *Misery* (*M*, 173) establishes precisely the symbolic links between writing, the machine and the abject mechanical flows of the body that King's works address. Even telepathy as a metaphor of writerly inspiration is, as we will see in *The Tommyknockers*, machinic in its potential. In *The Shining* Danny Torrance, talking with Hallorann, suddenly per-ceives his 'shining' ability as 'some incomprehensible machine that might be safe or might be deadly dangerous' (*S*, 82). Danny's un-conscious, 'incomprehensible' machine, his 'shine' (echoing 'ma*chine*') is a kind of desiring machine, a mechanism of production rather than reproduction. Telepathy, discussed above (chapter 2), reconfigures itself at key moments in King's works into a social machine or a political machine with a dangerous tendency (seen in *Carrie* and *Firestarter*) to collapse together uncanny forms of production and destruction. Models of analysis developed by Deleuze and Guattari in books like *Anti-Oedipus* (1984) and *A Thousand Plateaus* (1988) suggest ways of reading King's works in terms of an understanding of the unconscious as a factory rather than a theatre, as a realm of production (desiring-production) rather than reproduction. The critiques articulated in King's works can be understood as products of function rather than meaning. They analyse the regulation of social life by flows and blockages deriving from the productive machine of the unconscious and from the abstract, ideological machine of social control (the machine of patriarchal Law). These are, not coincidentally, the twin sources of desiring-production in the Gothic novel as they are in culture more generally, the forces that drive the genre and orchestrate its effects.

King's works also involve the construction of generic identities and differences through machinic tropes of linkage, interconnection, contamination and flow. Lois Chasse, the machinically named elderly heroine of *Insomnia* (1994), asks a key question in King's oeuvre: on admitting her experience of the bewildering auras that figure that novel's version of imaginative productivity, she exclaims, 'What's it for, Ralph? Do you know what it's for?' (*I*, 358). This question reverberates throughout *Insomnia*: the novel meditates on ageing and rejuvenation (uncanny versions of the 'generation gap') as a winding-down and a winding-up, mechanical transformations of the body-machine understood in terms of interlocking characters and narratives. *Insomnia* constructs a space in which intersections between the real and the unreal, waking and sleeping, night and day, youth and age, afford flows and unblockings of desire that redefine character relations, and return us to the question: what is it for, or what can it do? A similar question is addressed in *Christine*:

> Engines. That's something else about being a teenager. There are all these engines, and somehow you end up with the ignition keys to some of them and you start them up but you don't know what the fuck they are or what they're supposed to do. [...] They give you the keys and some clues and they say, Start it up, see what it will do, and sometimes what it does is pull you along into a life that's really good and fulfilling, and sometimes what it does is pull you right down the highway to hell and leave you all mangled and bleeding by the roadside. (*Ch*, 60)

Christine, as befits a narrative about a seductive haunted car, comprehends desire machinically, as a complex machine formed of intermeshing parts (characters, bodies and body parts, organs, actions, events, places, things). 'Start it up, see what it will do' expresses the central desire articulated in the machinic metaphors, the cross-generic combinations and excessive textual productions that abound in King's narratives: they start up and we read what they will do.

In *Christine*, Arnie's 'fall[ing] in love' (*Ch*, 7) with a 1958 Plymouth Fury provides the desire that fuels the car's uncanny resurrection (it 'looked like a corpse that had been disinterred and left to decay in the sun' (*Ch*, 102)), introducing a perverse romance into the novel's postmodern, mechanised Gothic. But this masks the novel's deeper critique of the consumerist desires exploited by popular culture and reactionary nostalgia, alongside a barely articulated and destructive, reactionary desire to return to a time before parental pseudo-revolution. Arnie's parents, Michael and Regina, are old 1960s revolutionaries, 'University people to the core', as narrator Dennis puts it (*Ch*, 17), in that novel's version of inter-generational conflict. Christine, self-renovated and simultaneously haunted by her previous owner, becomes (in a recurrent science fiction trope in King's works to which we will return later) a kind of 'time machine' transporting Arnie back to the 1950s, simultaneously rendering the present 'like a thin overlay of film' (*Ch*, 401).

The writerly 'Toolbox' described in *On Writing* (*OW*, 81ff.) repeatedly constructs a fictional world of intertextual and machinic flows and blockages, becomings and transformations, interconnected desires and part-objects. These elements range from character as individual desiring machine or isolated engine of horror to the social assemblage – the network of relations that define society as a whole – as a machine for potential resistance, but also of reaction and oppression. King's works, understood in this way, constitute in totality a giant, endlessly proliferating writing-machine plugging into or disconnecting from traditions, genres, narratives, ideologies and abstract social machines and constantly reworking them into new forms. Within these forms it repeatedly redefines and represents itself in avatars of the creative drive of writerly desire. This desire is power ('Words are his Power' is the marketing tag-line on the covers of King's novels). Such power is figured throughout the oeuvre, in the energies generated in *The Tommyknockers*, or elsewhere in the murderous electrical current of *The Green Mile* (1996). Power operates in that novel at the level of the body, in 'endless flows' of water, tears and urine (*GM*, 340, 185–6, 205) and in the connection of these flows to writing, in names like 'Percy Wetmore' and 'Rolfe Wettermark' (*GM*, 209). Most forcefully, power constructs the social abjection of the prisoners who themselves flow down the 'Green Mile' and through the penal machine of Cold Mountain Penitentiary.

In *Anti-Oedipus* Deleuze and Guattari critique and reject the emphasis placed by psychoanalysis and semiotics on the interpretation of symbols and meanings. They redirect desire instead into a new functionality, asking the question we have seen in King's writings, the question reiterated by Fredric Jameson in relation to genre: 'The question posed by desire is not "What does it mean?" but rather "*How does it work?*"' 'What are the connections', they elaborate, 'what are the disjunctions, the conjunctions, what use is made of the syntheses? It represents nothing, but it produces. It means nothing, but it works' (italics in original). Desire, and more pertinently its orchestration of the movements of narrative, is, they assert, 'machinery', a set of mechanisms through which effects and consequences are produced.[25] Narrative, the storytelling so prominent in King's discussions of writing, is here understood as a machine for the production of desire: the logic of 'what-happens-next' juxtaposed with the suspensive desire for perpetuation ('I don't want this to end') alongside the teleological desire for resolution ('How does it end?'). Such a model affords important insights into the workings of King's narratives. It suggests that his exploration of generic mixing, an aspect of his overarching concern with writing and the writer, can be linked to the trope of machinic desire that recurs throughout his work.

In *Danse Macabre* King describes the work of the horror writer as 'a child's toy, something bright and shiny and strange. Let us pull a lever and see what it does' (*DM*, 456). Bruce Baugh notes that the Deleuzean question asks not of intentionality (not 'what is the work *supposed* to do?'), but of possibility: reading and writing are, in these terms, 'productive use[s] of the literary machine'.[26] Deleuze and Guattari assert that a book itself is 'a little machine'.[27] They theorise literature as 'an assemblage', an agglomeration of linguistic, generic and social codes that works to produce narratives, desires, articulations and lines of development or circumscription, flight and containment.[28] The literary assemblage works through flows and blockages, movements and transformations, like those traced on human bodies in *The Green Mile* as the repressive effects of state and legal power (King echoes in this novel Kafka's punitive writing-machine in 'In the Penal Colony').[29] In *The Tommyknockers*, characters suffer menstrual flows, nasal bleeding and tooth loss, and we read of the flows of desire and power in the 'becoming' that the town of Haven suffers. These flows are blocked by the barriers and obstacles (to telepathic communication or to leaving the town) that characters like Ruth and Gard encounter. King's books, obsessed with texts and writing, with their endless productivity and their relentless generic hybridity, can be read as assemblages of desiring machines. Machinic constructions are figured in characters, in the constructions of the social milieux of towns like Haven or Derry or Castle Rock and, above and around them, the abstract social machine of modern America and its components. The ambivalently constructed 'Status Quo Machine' (*T*, 192) of *The Tommyknockers* embodies this abstract machine, the system of political and economic forces that determine and are resisted by characters and their relations to its immediate effects, the economic and brand-name consumerism of contemporary capitalism, but also the military forces that arrive to save Haven at the novel's end. All are manifestations of the abstract machine of the Law, which is also of course a version of the Derridean 'Law of genre'.

The Tommyknockers deploys this machinic network of flows and blockages to offer an allegory of the consequences and potentials of generic mixing, centring on the potential linkages implied by genre itself. The novel's engagement with 1980s anxieties about 'nuclear-generated power' (*T*, 64) generates an allegory of the 'generating' powers of genre. Nuclear and other forms of power refract the novel's peripheral concern with what such power may in turn generate: social and political transformation, imagined in ideologically conventional American-dystopian style as a communisation which the novel calls 'becoming'. 'Becoming', as a process of transforming identity, echoes the Deleuze-Guattarian notion of 'becoming' as a resistance to 'being'. For Deleuze and Guattari, 'becoming-other' (or 'becoming-animal', or, more problematically, 'becoming-woman') are ways of comprehending identity in flux, continually changing into something other, liberated by this process from the confines of being and conventional politics of identity and self.[30] In King's novel, the destruction of individualism leads to the construction instead of another SF staple, the 'hive mind': those who 'become' in *The Tommyknockers* 'become' something 'hivelike and complete in itself' (*T*, 430), we're told. In Deleuzean terms, they 'become' a 'body without organs', a conglomeration of subjectivities that is, Deleuze and Guattari write, 'non-productive',[31] 'an un-mechanical machine with machinic attributes', as Anna Powell glosses it.[32]

Writing-machines

King's works, then, can be understood as machines that produce and endlessly recombine plots, characters, scenarios, events, actions. They are, in turn, productions of the various writing-machines that King deploys and starts up in many of his narratives. *Bag of Bones* (1998), for example, explores haunting legacies of American history through metaphors of automatic writing, writing-machines and answering-machines. The novel perceives writing itself as a machine that at the novel's end has ceased to work. It offers, in doing so, yet another metaphor for the writer's-block anxiety that haunts King's works: 'the machine which ran so sweet for so long has stopped' (*BB*, 515). The writing-machine works doubly in King; it is both literally mechanical (a typewriter, a word-processor) and a metaphor for a machinic form of writerly production, the desiring-production of the writer sometimes perverted or diverted by its connection with another desiring-flow (like that excessively embodied in *Misery's* Annie Wilkes, or disembodied in the phantoms that populate the Overlook Hotel in *The Shining*). King addresses its integration into the demonic rhythms of other machines, most powerfully expressed in the machine as *actant* in *The Dark Half*, George Stark's fictional alter ego Alexis Machine, literally '*a lexis machine*', a word-producing machine. In the short story 'In the Deathroom' King again reworks Kafka's infernal writing-machine in 'In the Penal Colony', offering as an instrument of torture a 'machine' connected to 'an object with a rubber grip' which resembles 'a stylus or some kind of fountain pen'. Describing the effects of this writing-torturing-machine, its operator dryly notes, 'Someday I hope to write a paper' (*SW*, 411). The flows and counter-flows of desire through writing and other machines orchestrate the production of meanings in King's narratives and indicate different encodings of desire as power. These include the writerly desire associated with the repeated self-representation of the author noted earlier.

The Tommyknockers, read in this framework, offers an extended allegory of writing imagined as desiring-production, a production of and by desire that illustrates the symbolic centrality of machinic structures of organisation to King's work. Two writers start up the novel's plot, which works, machine-like, to generate proliferating meanings that cross and re-cross generic boundaries. Poet Gard finds, in novelist Bobbi's cellar, a panoply of constructions: assemblages, interconnected machines, engines and power sources, a 'weird con-glomeration of components' that is, he observes, not 'differentiated' (*T*, 141, 138). The machinic assemblages produced by the characters, working and producing in baffling, excessive ways – science fiction machines geared towards producing uncanny Gothic effects, perhaps – embody aspects of the writer's unconscious, the unexcavated spaces and concealed, embedded mental processes of fictional productivity on which the writer relies. They figure also the generic frameworks that enable the generation of writing. Hidden in the cellar (con-ventionally a metaphor for the unconscious: D. H. Lawrence famously wrote of the Freudian unconscious as 'the cellar in which the mind keeps its own bastard spawn'),[33] Bobbi's machines gesture towards productivity as uncontrolled, untrammelled. This implies (as King's autobiographical account of this novel suggests) that the real horror in *The Tommyknockers* is not alien invasion or transformation, but writerly overproduction, the uncanny ability of the writer to write (and of the writing-machine to produce writing) in spite of blockages, impediments and other potentially disabling experiences.

The energy unleashed by the writing-machines and other meta-phorical devices is the energy of desire, the writer's desire to create, figured in the 'green light' (*T*, 15ff.) and unearthly glows (like the 'bright ball of light, no larger than a quarter but seemingly as bright as the sun' (*T*, 141) which heats Bobbi's water) that characterise the adjusted machines of the novel. The 'green light' first appears in Bobbi's dream early in the novel:

> And then, ahead of her, a terrible green light shone out in a single pencil-like ray. In her dream, she thought of Poe's 'The Tell-Tale Heart', the mad narrator's lantern, muffled up except for one tiny hole, which he used to direct a beam of light onto the evil eye he fancied his elderly benefactor possessed. (*T*, 15)

The 'green light' here signifies a variety of sources of becoming: the writerly desire (a 'pencil-like ray') to illuminate (figured also in the drive to excavate the buried saucer), the science fiction connotations of death rays later alluded to, via Wells's *The War of the Worlds*, 'raining green death on Hammersmith' (*T*, 46), and the Gothic connotations of Poe's tale (already noted as the source of Rainey's story in 'Secret Window, Secret Garden'). Later, the green light's effect is metaphorised as writing: 'A cricket hopped into the luminous pencil-mark one of these cracks printed onto the ground and fell dead' (*T*, 406). Writerly desire is thus simultaneously elucidatory, creative and destructive. It works in a variety of different directions, and combines Gothic and SF allusions to generate meanings.

As its exploration of the hazards of nuclear power suggests, *The Tommyknockers* is concerned with what 'makes things go'. Plugged into the creative forces unleashed from within her unconscious by her monumental efforts of excavation, Bobbi is driven into a symbolic overproduction that mirrors King's own overproduced, excessive narratives. Like his texts, her machinic assemblages (a supercharged water-heater, a multi-tone doorbell, a flying tractor) work overtime to achieve particular excessive effects. The most important machine she constructs is the 'telepathic typewriter' (*T*, 189) that enables her unconsciously to write a novel, which is 'just incidentally, the best thing she had ever written' (*T*, 148), a nice piece of wish-fulfilment on King's part. The typewriter, which Bobbi calls '*a dream machine*' (*T*, 162; italics in original), develops King's recurrent trope of the writing-machine, connecting the writer's unconscious with an assemblage of other machines that in this novel include its 'Status Quo Machine', a version of the Deleuzean abstract machine of ideology and governmental power against which King's characters are notionally, intermittently pitched. This is the overarching social machine that, as Brian Massumi puts it, 'makes things "*go* without saying"' (italics in original).[34] Bobbi's telepathic typewriter enables her to produce writing that, in being read, reproduces in the reader its own mechanical qualities, making characters 'go without saying'. Gard, reading her writing as it scrolls out, finds that 'he had read the material [. . .] in a mechanical, almost uncomprehending way' (*T*, 162). To demonstrate the telepathic typewriter working she quotes, mixing genres again, Shakespeare ('*Full fathom five thy father lies*') and a beer advertisement ('*My beer is Rhinegold the dry beer*') (*T*, 160; italics in original). But its productivity is clearly linked to the writer's unconscious. As she tells Gard, via the machine:

> *This poor old Underwood ran like a bastard for those two or three days, and all the time it was running I was in the woods, working around the place, or down cellar. But as I say, mostly I was sleeping. [. . .] [I]t's like a direct tap into the subconscious, more like dreaming than writing . . . but what comes out isn't like dreams, which are often surreal and disconnected. This really isn't a typewriter at all anymore.* (*T*, 161–2; italics in original)

This 'telepathic typewriter', tapping into Bobbi's sleeping and dreaming creative mind, epitomises all the writing-machines in King's oeuvre.

The 'undifferentiated' machinic mass suggests the condition of becoming which organises processes within the novel. Becoming describes both the novel's temporality (its constant movement towards new generic mixings and conditions) and its representation of identity as process, as incomplete, constantly transforming into something new and unfamiliar, uncanny. Gard notes 'the huge, the *profligate* amounts of energy that had been expended here' (*T*, 138; italics in original), a counterbalance to the potentially unlimited energy apparently released by the machines built by the possessed folk of Haven. The riot of machinic production that engulfs Haven expresses the unleashed writerly unconscious, the liberation of the forces of the id in untrammelled desiring-production imagined by Deleuze and Guattari at the outset of *Anti-Oedipus*: 'Hence we are all handymen: each with his little machines'.[35] Everyone in Haven becomes a 'handyman', the first stage in the conventional science fiction process of 'becoming-other' that the novel self-consciously maps. The Tommyknockers themselves are, we later learn, 'handymen' (*T*, 599), extreme embodiments of desiring-production in action: '*We . . . we make things. Fix things. We don't theorize. We build. We're handymen*' (*T*, 599; italics in original). Earlier, Bobbi, before her becoming, tells Gard: 'I'm not even a good handyman, let alone anyone's scientist' (*T*, 189). The machines produced or adapted by the people of Haven remove the labour of production and consumption, reducing their users to automatons. Significantly, money ceases to circulate in Haven during the 'becoming', indicating that an alternative economy of desiring-production has replaced the conventional system of symbolic exchange. But the machines' function is contradictorily liberating, too: in effacing the labour of production, the telepathic typewriter expresses a powerful writerly desire (as well as accounting symbolically for those blank autobiographical periods of literary production, products of alcohol and drug abuse, of which King writes in *On Writing*). Ultimately the machines of *The Tommyknockers* constitute and are products of desiring-machines, channelling and focusing the desire of the people of Haven. This is manifest for Bobbi in the irresistible desire to excavate the flying saucer: 'You've been *driven*' (*T*, 183; italics in original), Gard tells her, like the vehicle she adapts to dig with.

The notion of 'flow' offers one figure for this process of becoming. If becoming is produced in the liberation of desiring-production, in the excess energy expended in machinic innovation that King's characters have developed as a consequence of exposure to the ship's radiation (and have inherited from Poul Anderson's *Brain Wave*), then flows signify the ways in which this process is to be understood. The multiple functions and symbolic values of liquids in *The Tommyknockers* reinforce this implication. From spontaneous nosebleeds and menstrual flows (*T*, 17) and uncontrollable urination (*T*, 494) (connecting this novel again to *The Green Mile*) to a murderously adapted flying Coke machine, with its 'steady stream of quarters, nickels and dimes spew[ing] out of the coin return' (*T*, 587), liquids – particularly those associated with abjection – indicate and enact movement and change. Flows of blood or capital clearly allegorise sexual and political critiques that the novel leaves vestigial, suggested only as potential generators of significance within its chaotic and contradictory frames of reference. They indicate also a mobility that informs and deforms the novel's comprehension of generic identities. Flow indicates the fluidity of identity implicit in the notion of 'becoming', not least the novel's own 'becoming' as it melds together different generic features and elements into different combinations. In *The Tommyknockers*, flows delineate circuits containing 'becoming' and its contaminations. They offer alternative lines of flight (ways of escaping the ideological influence of the 'Status Quo Machine') to those embedded in the 1960s ideology of the writers Gard and Bobbi. *Their* flows are, initially, specifically textual; the 'telepathic typewriter' enables Bobbi to write an entire novel in a matter of days, an extreme form of writing in full flow. But her 'becoming' transcends the textual, leading to new combinations, new and ultimately disastrous lines of flight against which the novel eventually mobilises its conservative ideological retrenchment.

If genre's Law implies for Derrida 'an enforceable principle of non-contamination and non-contradiction',[36] *The Tommyknockers* subverts it to explore different constructions of boundaries and processes of generic 'distinction'. Genre and its transformative, processing potentials are implicit in the novel's opening sentence: 'In the end, you can boil *everything* down to something similar' (*T*, 3; italics in original). This statement asserts an underlying commonality between 'everything', achievable through reduction, through the process of 'boiling down'. This collapsing of distinctions and differences is figured throughout the novel in recurrent metaphors of contamination, transformation and becoming. It counters these processes with opposing desires for containment, specifically the 'containment' associated with nuclear power: the spaceship may be '*a great big containment housing that's already leaking*' (*T*, 464; italics in original). As we have seen, 'generation' and its ideologically loaded opposite, 'degeneration', are central to King's novel. Its (somewhat tokenistic, contextually conventional) concern with the side-effects of the generation of power by nuclear technology is balanced by the SF conceit of the discovery of a new source of power, generated from the mental and physical torture of living beings. 'Containment' and 'contaminant', as near-anagrams of each other, indicate the ways in which the novel plays with the rhetoric of 'becoming' which, in *The Tommyknockers*, is an extreme form of contamination, the consequence of an excess of contaminant and a failure of containment. These processes of contamination and containment, flow and blockage, are more than simply thematic in the novel. The novel opens with a series of contaminations and flowings-together: of youth and age in Bobbi's recognition of her own ageing (*T*, 3), of Bobbi's property and its blurred boundary with the 'wilderness owned by the New England Paper Company' (*T*, 4), and of its trees, mostly 'good hardwood relatively untouched by the gypsy moth infestation' (*T*, 4), an 'infestation' that clearly prefigures the discovery of the 'interstellar gypsies with' (significantly) 'no king' (*T*, 651), known as the Tommyknockers. Words, in these opening pages, contaminate each other: central protagonist Jim Gardener's name is echoed in Bobbi's 'garden' (*T*, 4); his abbreviated name 'Gard' compresses the 'good hardwood' of the 'garden' to signify his character (a faint intertextual echo not only of Lovecraft, but also, perhaps, of Henry James's Caspar Goodwood). Flow is indicated temporally in the complex mixing of memories and present experiences of these opening paragraphs, and geographically in the 'stream' which leads Anderson to safety when lost in the woods (*T*, 4).

The townspeople effectively 'become' machines geared towards the production, through transformation, of other machines. Their machinic characteristics are manifest in the spread of the 'becoming' to the domestic devices they construct, machines that make magic real. They include those in Bobbi's 'nutty workshop' (*T*, 138), with its 'batteries' connected to 'several different things' Gard can't identify: the modified water-heater, 'a weird Gyro-Gearloose combination' (*T*, 141), or a 'doorbell with a built in microchip that would allow the user to program a different song whenever she wanted to' (*T*, 137). Bobbi herself becomes machine-like as Gard imagines her 'growing more haggard as she screwed screws, bolted bolts, soldered wires' (*T*, 139). Bobbi and her machines embody the 'becoming-other' that the novel represents. She is effectively its prototype, figuring the transformation of human social reality into an alien, machinic otherness that unleashes within each transformed human vast potentials of destructive energy. That this energy *is* destructive rather than liberatory indicates the ideological limits of the world constructed in *The Tommyknockers*. This is not a transgressive or liberatory text, but one in which transgression is punished in order to facilitate the re-establishment at the narrative's end of the 'Status Quo Machine'. Anna Powell has argued of another conservative contemporary horror text, Clive Barker's film *Hellraiser* (1987), that it 'obsessively returns to the trope of wholeness, its consequent graphic disintegration and its possible renewal'.[37] 'The trope of wholeness', in a social sense, is what is restored constantly in King's Gothic texts. From *The Tommyknockers* to *Needful Things*, King offers allegories of social collapse redeemed by a return (often via the reassertion of ideological state apparatuses or 'status Quo Machines', like the army or the police) to social wholeness. Becoming-other, in these texts, is always under threat of being nullified by state power, confirming King's assertion in *Danse Macabre* that 'The writer of horror fiction is neither more nor less than an agent of the status quo' (*DM*, 56) and, of course, of the 'Status Quo Machine'.

Becoming-other, then, if it threatens that status quo, is nevertheless also the central metaphor for *The Tommyknockers*' exploration of generic transformation. The Tommyknockers themselves have no identity or name; neither do they appear alive in the novel. They occupy an empty space at the centre of the text, absent yet central, like Daphne du Maurier's Rebecca, their absence haunting the novel's action and its drama. Yet they are also present as the potential of desiring-production. In the becoming-other that the novel maps, becoming a Tommyknocker is the end-product of an accelerated evolution within the novel's exploration of what Derrida calls the 'parasitical economy' (surely a Tommyknocker economy!) which defines the Law of genre: 'a sort of participation without belonging', a 'division' and 'overflowing': 'the law of overflowing, of *excess*, the law of participation without membership' (italics in original).[38] Bobbi asserts such an interstitial non-identity when she insists that 'We're not a "people", Gard. Not a "race". Not a "species"' (*T*, 595).

Genre, King's novel suggests, consists of precisely this condition of potential, of participation without membership. Like the psycho-analytic conception of language, genre *speaks* us, offering, in the novel's terms, both 'an eerie sense of familiarity' (*T*, 495) and the strangeness of every new text in which we encounter it ('Every place has been a strange place to us', Bobbi tells Gard (*T*, 596)). King's version of Gothic science fiction demonstrates that genre, even when, like Gothic and like the Tommyknockers, it is 'perhaps dead, but somehow alive' (*T*, 567), is always mobile, flowing, 'becoming-other'. For Bobbi Anderson and the folk of Haven, 'becoming-other' ends in un-becoming, or the misery of death. Her writerly productivity and their machinic innovations lead in the novel's reactionary logic only to the destruction of themselves and their social realities. Such immense destructive scenes, climactically concluding *The Tommyknockers*, offer generically conventional, SF-apocalyptic versions of the Gothic deaths of writerly desire and of authorship that King figures most powerfully in *Misery*.

5

Misery's *Gothic Tropes*

'I felt that blank incapability of invention which is the greatest misery of authorship, when dull Nothing replies to our anxious invocations. *Have you thought of a story?* I was asked each morning, and each morning I was forced to reply with a mortifying negative.'[1]

Misery is, unsurprisingly, everywhere in Gothic writing. Mary Shelley's recollections, in 1831, of the origins of *Frankenstein* alert us to one dimension, perhaps the major one for any surface reading, of the particular 'misery' of Stephen King's *Misery* (1987) and of his Gothic writing more generally. This is the haunting authorial horror graphically explored in King's novel, the horror of the potential failure of authorship, the closure of creativity and of that excessive, potentially endless but mechanical, uncontrollable writerly over-production that concerns novels like *The Tommyknockers*. *Misery* addresses also the unavoidable *end* of narrative continuity, a fear that haunts King's works (from *The Shining* to 'Secret Window, Secret Garden' to *Bag of Bones*) as a dark potential, an excessive inversion or negation of his own excessive productivity. The terror of ending and specifically of the ending of writerly productivity is also, of course, an externalisation of the writer's fear of death, of the closure of all narrative with the death of the author. It is balanced by the writer's desire constantly to begin, to generate new narratives or to restart or continue existing ones as repeated confirmations of life and the creative drive. Shelley goes on in her 'Preface' to assert the interconnection of beginnings and pre-existing states in terms that (like King's problematic beginnings) both assert and deny the priority of origin:'Every thing must have a beginning [...]; and that beginning must be linked to something that went before'.[2] *Misery* enacts this double imperative in its concerns with beginning again and its familiar and overt derivation from previous narratives, including the narrative of its author's life, his fame and his entrapment in the trappings of that fame. As we have seen, the characteristic mode of operation of King's Gothic (and *Misery* is no exception) tends to be combinatory rather than innovatory, regenerative rather than generative.

Misery's examination of Shelley's 'dull Nothing' (her version of what would now be called 'writer's block') and its particular enactment of her 'mortifying negative' adds a specific intensity to the familiar Gothic tropes of writing and the writer. It informs a novel deeply concerned with narrative, with human endings and beginnings and with the potential and real falsenesses of both. It reinvigorates the Gothic trope of confinement (a particular kind of 'mortifying negative') through scrutiny of the imperative to write and compromises this imperative through an examination of the difficulties of writing to order and of overcoming the potential inhibition of writing by physical and mental suffering, of overcoming internal and external blockages to the flows of writing. One of *Misery*'s metaphors for this is the roadblock: 'when you were writing a novel you almost always got roadblocked somewhere' (*M*, 133). It is a metaphor the novel also uses to describe its central female character: 'There was a feeling about her of clots and roadblocks rather than welcoming orifices or even open spaces' (*M*, 8). *Misery*'s analysis of writer's block may also be its analysis of a term implicitly (if only by beginning rhyme) connected to 'misery', misogyny. The apparent inevitability of both in King's fictionalisations of the life of the (male) writer hasn't escaped the novel's critics. The double, contradictory movements articulated in the connection between the two in asserting the male author's right to write and to resurrection will shadow the discussion of the novel below.

The plot of *Misery* is simple. Paul Sheldon, an immensely success-ful but artistically frustrated author of popular pastiche Victorian romances involving the character Misery Chastain (whom he has killed off in a forthcoming final *Misery* novel), suffers a disastrous car crash. He awakes in agony, his legs severely broken, entrapped in the house of his self-proclaimed 'number one fan', the deranged nurse and unconvicted murderer Annie Wilkes, who proceeds by torture and coercion to force him to write to order and expressly for her a new novel, *Misery's Return*. The surname 'Chastain', as Clare Hanson notes, connotes a variety of contradictory meanings – chas-tise, chaste, chastened, chain, stained – each of which opens the space of a different modality of generic analysis, from romance to Gothic, as well as a series of gender-specific connotations of moral character.[3] Part of *Misery*'s agenda is the covert exploration of these generic and gender-oriented spaces. The novel, in effect, explores another version of what King has called, referring to *Carrie*, 'Planet Female' (*OW*, 53). For all its emphasis on male creativity, *Misery* is deeply anxious about male fantasies of *female* creativity, of woman's power to create. Paul dreams of Annie repetitively reciting narrative begin-nings in a surreal parody of his predicament:

> *Once upon a time,* Annie was calling. *Once upon a time it came to pass. This happened in the days when my grandfather's grandfather was a boy. This is the story of how a poor boy. I heard this from a man who. Once upon a time. Once upon a time.* (M, 74, italics in original)

If, as we will see, endings present one set of problems in *Misery*, beginnings present another. To 'get started' (*M*, 78), to start up the writing-machine in order to overcome Shelley's 'blank incapacity' (and *Misery* offers an extreme version of such an 'incapacity' and of its consequent writerly 'blankness') demands a specific set of circumstances, which *Misery* establishes in the form of radical con-straints, producers (in every sense of the word) of authorial misery.

Misery is much concerned with the meanings of the word 'misery'. Four are listed in the *SOED*, the most important of which are 'wretchedness of outward circumstances; distress caused by priva-tion or poverty' and 'wretched state of mind; a condition of extreme unhappiness'.[4] 'Misery' is connected to the noun 'miser', suggesting a grim economy of suffering and its distribution. The word's meanings develop from a description of 'outward' condition to internalised connotations of grief and emotional pain, the primary meanings accruing to its frequent usage in canonical Gothic writing, for example in Shelley's *Frankenstein*, where it is frequently used to signify damaging, excessive emotional suffering. We learn, for example, that Victor's 'spirit had been broken by misery', and that, to Walton, he is 'a noble creature destroyed by misery'.[5] In *Dracula*, Dr Seward describes Harker's 'misery that is appalling to see', and, in the same chapter (indicating the extent of that novel's structures of doubling and identification) the word accrues, in Mina Harker's compassionate understanding and empathy for the vampire's suffering, double significance in relation to Dracula's effects and their causes in himself: 'That poor soul who has wrought all this misery is the saddest case of all'.[6] In King's own work, Carrie White's emotions comprise 'Wanting and hating and fearing . . . and *misery*' (*C*, 34; italics in original), and Jessie Burlingame, in King's later revision of *Misery*, *Gerald's Game* (1992), bemoans her *'general misery'* (*GG*, 87; italics in original) of privation, entrapment, relentlessly re-enacted trauma and physical suffering. *It* traces one etymological root of the word in citing Virgil: 'Quaeque ipse miserrima vidi, / Et quorum pars magna fui' ('and those terrible things I saw, and in which I played a great part') (*It*, 353). In *Needful Things*, multiple personal miseries compound and magnify the social suffering exploited by Leland Gaunt, such as the 'deep sick misery' (*NT*, 292) of Myrtle Keeton. 'Misery' thus signifies, in Gothic writing generally and in King's works specifically, a broadly conceived notion of internal and external 'suffering', and in particular a suffering that separates and isolates individuals, connecting them to kinds of loneliness or solitude characteristic of Gothic writing.

Buried alive: Misery *and the uncanny*

In Poe's 'The Premature Burial' (1844) the narrator alludes to 'the long and weird catalogue of human miseries', of which 'To be buried while alive is, beyond question, the most terrific'.[7] Magistrale has extensively explored Poe's influence on King (which we noted earlier in King's use of 'The Purloined Letter' and 'The Tell-Tale Heart'), arguing that, 'In Poe's tales of fantasy and terror confined atmospheric environments are representative of the narrator's or main character's circumscribed state of mind'.[8] King adapts this quality for specific purposes, such as the mock-comic near-suffocation of Frank Jewett, hiding behind a sofa in *Needful Things*, who momentarily remembers 'Edgar Allan Poe stories he'd read as a kid, stories about being buried alive' (*NT*, 523). Most critics who relate Poe's work to King's do so via such cues in the writing itself, for example the overt references to 'The Masque of the Red Death' in *The Shining* (Strengell notes, somewhat cursorily, that the story 'was inspiration for *The Shining* and is referred to in its climactic pages').[9] Premature burial, symbolic and fictional, is a key structuring motif of *Misery*, definitive of its particular atmosphere and central state of mind, which King extends from Poe and connects to an analysis of the novel's central anxiety, the death of the author. The 'miseries' of *Misery*, like those of Poe's story, are multiple, 'long and weird': miseries of incarceration, forcible constraint, pain, addiction, frustration, fear, mutilation and impending death, alleviated only by the singular hope of survival envisaged as a kind of resurrection. Premature burial affords a metaphor for the entrapment and symbolic destruction that Sheldon suffers; the possibility of resurrection symbolises potential escape from this suffering. Poe's story provides the frame and engine of the narrative Paul eventually writes to earn, Scheherazade-like, his 'freedom'. The text he produces, *Misery's Return*, is initiated by 'the monstrous idea' (*M*, 142) of the retrospective, revisionary revelation of the premature burial and subsequent resurrection of its eponymous character, a fictional device to resurrect both a series of novels and a writer's life. The novel reworks Gothic themes of death, burial and resurrection explored earlier in King's earlier novel *Pet Sematary* (which we will turn to later). It enacts in its structure the dependence on repetition that organises King's Gothic, and explores via the novel-within-a-novel conceit of *Misery's Return* the uncanniness of resurrection in order to examine the writer's suffering at the hands of his fans.

In *Misery* Paul Sheldon is effectively 'buried while alive' (as Poe carefully puts it, introducing duration and endurance into his formulation).[10] He is encrypted within a distorted and spatialised fantasy construction of himself, 'Alone in Annie Wilkes's house, locked in this room. Locked in this bed' (*M*, 41). 'Alone' perpetuates the experience of solitude established in *Carrie*; the repeated 'locked' echoes the confining non-productivity of 'blocked'. Paul's imprisonment is multiple: immobilised by his broken legs, entrapped in the bed, the room, the house and the isolated locale of 'Sidewinder, Colorado' (*M*, 6) (the same state in which Jack Torrance and his family find themselves entrapped in the Overlook Hotel in *The Shining*), he is effectively dead to the outside world. He imagines his crashed, abandoned car covered by snow from the road clearance vehicle which 'entombs' it (*M*, 60). His incarceration is, furthermore, in some senses a symbolic 'death', a situation he fears will culminate in another, 'real', burial. He imagines Annie killing and burying him following the completion of his new novel, 'just as wild dogs begin to bury their illicit kills after they have been hunted awhile' (*M*, 64), 'a hasty interment in the back yard' (*M*, 72). Being metaphorically buried alive, it seems, is for Paul Sheldon merely a prelude to being buried, alive or dead, for real; he suffers in his live burial a living death, entrapped within the claustrophobic fantasy world of his captor. The novel he eventually writes, *Misery's Return*, imagines a live burial as its own escape from the fictional dead-end of the death, in the previously final *Misery* novel, of the eponymous character Misery Chastain. Her live interment is imagined, in Sheldon's popular romance, in Poe-esque terms: 'It sounds as if she were still alive down there and tryin' to work her way back up to the land o' the livin', so it does' (*M*, 141). Nicholas Royle's essay 'Buried Alive' explores the symbolic force of Poe's 'The Premature Burial', relating its complex connections to Freud's theorisations of the 'uncanny' in terms of 'an uncanny intertextuality, a catacomb-effect of voices'.[11] Tracing this intertextuality through English literature, Royle cites, among other texts, Milton's Samson, 'who experiences "a living death, / And buried: But, O yet more miserable!"'[12] Being buried alive is, for Freud, 'the crowning instance of uncanniness': as Royle unselfconsciously glosses, in live burial, 'Finally one gets to be His or Her Majesty: a coronation fit for royalty'.[13] We will return later to the connotations of 'Royalty' in *Misery*, but we need first again to explore Freud's definition of the uncanny, which affords initial ways of thinking about the Gothic elements of *Misery*.

Freud famously defines the uncanny as 'that class of the frightening that goes back to what was once well known and had long been familiar'.[14] This definition effectively accounts for uncanniness in the narrative of *Misery*, which enacts its protagonist's return to that which was 'once well known' and 'familiar' in its relating the writer's efforts to escape from and his enforced return to his familiar, habitual generic output. The double meaning of 'uncanny' as Freud outlines it – 'it belongs to two sets of ideas [. . .] the one relating to what is familiar and comfortable, the other to what is concealed and kept hidden'[15] – further reinforces this sense that *Misery* exemplifies the expression of the uncanny in King's writing. Sheldon's plight revolves around his forced return to writing 'what is familiar' (if not wholly comfortable) while being simultaneously 'concealed and kept out of sight', as if Sheldon himself – the author-surrogate – were the novel's locus of the uncanny. Freud also offers 'severed limbs, a severed head, a hand detached from the arm' as examples of the uncanny.[16] The violent severance of a limb is the central event of physical horror in *Misery*, as Annie 'hobble[s]' (*M*, 244) Paul by amputating one of his feet as punishment for his exploring her house: 'She picked up his foot. Its toes were still spasming. She carried it across the room. By the time she got to the door they had stopped moving' (*M*, 247). Narrated in short declarative sentences, this is an event that returns us to an extreme form of misery as singular and intense agony, the sheer physical pain suffered by Paul, 'who shrieked and writhed in the charred and blood-soaked bed, his face a deathly white' (*M*, 248). But it is also a repeated event, as it is later revealed that Annie has also cut off one of Paul's thumbs, forming a pair of amputations he compares to the typewriter's missing letters (to which we will return): 'and, really, what was a missing n compared to a missing foot and now, as an extra added attraction, a missing thumb?' (*M*, 280). The gradual dismemberment of Paul renders his body increasingly uncannily deformed and mutilated. This locus of physical horror in *Misery* is reworked from the auto-cannibalistic short story 'Survivor Instinct' (in the 1985 collection *Skeleton Crew*). 'Autocannibalism' (*M*, 363) is furthermore the word Sheldon uses at the end of *Misery* to refer disparagingly to the possibility of writing a book based on his experiences, suggesting King's awareness of how the writer's body (as well as the body of works he produces) is symbolically implicated in the processes of writerly production.

But it is through the metaphorical potential of the uncanniness of premature burial that *Misery* most firmly establishes its version of the Gothic uncanny. Paul's incarceration in Annie's house produces both his sense of 'anger that she could actually kidnap him – keep him prisoner here' (*M*, 31), and the series of escapist (and misogynist) fantasies that fuel his writerly imagination. It is, like the situation of Scheherazade, to which the novel frequently alludes, an imprisonment without apparent end. Paul imagines, late in the novel, another res-urrection, that of the state trooper murdered by Annie. 'He kept seeing the trooper coming back to life – *some* sort of life [. . .]' (*M*, 310; italics in original). Such fantasies of resurrection clearly represent Paul's sense that he too retains '*some* sort of life'. They indicate the blurring of feared premature burial and desired resurrection with which *Misery* deals. They perpetuate, in their enactment of the non-finality of Gothic versions of death, the apparent endlessness of Paul's predicament, investing it with the Gothic characteristics of repetition and return we have seen throughout King's writings. Premature burial likewise repudiates the conventional 'ending' associated with death, implying a doubling of that ending ('false' burial followed inexorably by 'real') that introduces another of Freud's categories of the uncanny, that of the double. Doubling indeed organises the relation between different modes of the word 'misery', and thus the structure and dynamics of King's novel.

The misery of Misery

Misery offers its own gloss on its own name, reflecting its title in its theme and its content. Etymologically the word derives from Latin *miseria*, meaning 'wretchedness' (as in the quote from Virgil cited above).[17] Its connotation of physical rather than emotional pain develops specifically in American usage in the 1820s. The novel, covertly referring to itself as well as to Sheldon's novels and to his experience, elaborates the word's double nominal reference: 'As a common noun', Sheldon speculates, 'it meant pain, usually lengthy and often pointless; as a proper one it meant a character and a plot, the latter most assuredly lengthy and pointless, but one which would nonetheless end very soon' (*M*, 260). 'Misery' evokes a kind of pain and suffering, both emotional and physical, which is thus also connected by Sheldon to temporal 'length' or duration (suggesting also the 'endurance' buried in Poe's 'buried while alive') and, while 'pointless' 'as a common noun', nevertheless implies 'as a proper one' an ending which is, in the narrative, imminent. Often lacking a 'point', 'misery' is unending yet finite, its end always impending. Such nominal and durational confusion suggests a way of reading *Misery's* relentless pathologising (evident in its revision of the oppositional relationship 'writer–reader' as 'patient–nurse') of writing and the writer and their relations to reading and the reader, in terms of endings and their impossibility. Endings conflict also with the infinite task of writing, the demand inculcated by the setting of writing, *Arabian Nights*-like, as a task to be completed and yet sustained and prolonged, stretched into an indefinitely deferred future resolution (deferred at least as long as the writer's life) in the (non-)closure of the narrative. The finite, overdetermined restriction of *Misery's* social world – reduced effectively to two people, a parodic human social relation, a pre-nuclear family – contrasts with the infinite and unanswerable ethical demand that the novel seems to imply is the duty of the writer to his readers. In the absurdity of *Misery*, its grim Gothic humour and sadistic gallows torture, King's work suggests comparisons with that of Beckett. Such echoes are implicit in the (non-)ending of *The Unnameable*: 'you must go on, I can't go on, I'll go on'[18] or, more pertinently, in Hamm's mock-tragic opening oration in *Endgame*: 'Can there be misery – [*he yawns*] – loftier than mine?'[19]

Endings and endgames, we can speculate, conflict with the infinite, unending relations to otherness that King's Gothic establishes and that *Misery* fantasises, in its construction of excessive dependencies and demands, as relations overridingly of 'shame' and 'guilt', gratefulness and 'ingratitude'. 'The Premature Burial' offers a particular expression of gratitude that resonates with *Misery*: 'That the ghastly extremes of agony are endured by man the unit, and never by man the mass – for this let us thank a merciful God!'[20] When, at the novel's end, genuine writerly inspiration does come, Paul finds himself able to write again, 'in gratitude and in terror' (*M*, 369), balancing what Annie earlier perceives as his 'ingratitude' (*M*, 70). 'Gratitude' and 'terror' define the Gothically inflected ethics of *Misery*, but they also delineate the writer's relation to writing as the novel comprehends it. The novel's oscillation between Paul's final 'gratitude' and his earlier 'ingratitude', his recognition and refusal of some kind of debt to Annie ('My payment for nursing you back to health!' (*M*, 69)), constitutes a major dynamic of their relationship. Gratitude and ingratitude, as Chris Baldick notes, are important and potentially monstrous emotions in *Frankenstein*, specifically in relation to that novel's imagining of the father–child relation as 'an unexpected turning against one's parent or benefactor'.[21] *Misery* reconceives them in terms of mother–child dependencies, but also in relation to notions of freedom, suggesting a link between 'gratitude' and 'gratis' that the novel exploits.

The endlessness of 'misery', evident in its connection both to the duration of endurance and to the false ending of premature burial, is thus also its relation to the unending demand of the reader and of writing, a double demand endured by the writer, and one with which King's novel is expressly concerned. 'THE END' (*M*, 307; emphasis in original), 'the most loved and hated phrase in the writer's vocabulary' (*M*, 341), signifies here a variety of endings: of the novel *Misery's Return* (latest in a series already ended by *Misery's Child* but resurrected anew, now, in the narrative of *Misery*, implying not the ending of the series but its continuance); of the relationship (dependence, contestation, agon and agony) between Sheldon and his captor, and potentially of the lives of them both; the end, too, of *Misery* for the novel's reader and of the 'misery' of popular authorship, its predictability, its oppressive repetitiveness and its overwhelming readerly demand, for the author Stephen King. 'I'll write THE END, and you'll read, and then *you'll* write THE END, won't you?' (*M*, 307; italics and emphasis in original), Paul tells Annie, declaring his particular comprehension of what John Fowles calls, in *The French Lieutenant's Woman*, 'the tyranny of the last chapter, the final, the "real" version'.[22] Fowles's novel famously offers alternate endings in an attempt to undermine this 'tyranny', to free the text from the demand of closure. *Misery* strives instead to resist the possibility of an alternative ending, imposing its own version of authority on a singular comprehension of narrative closure, that involving the writer's victory over the reader. For Sheldon, the struggle is one involving the author's authority, a struggle over who, author or reader, has the power to 'write' the ending and therefore assert their own 'tyranny'. 'THE END' becomes a kind of performative, an authorial assertion of closure that the novel delays, defers, exploits and resists in its repudiation of the reader, awaiting 'THE END' on its own terms.

Fowles figures twice in *Misery*; his *The Collector* (1963) is alluded to first by Paul, who 'found himself wondering dourly if she had John Fowles's first novel on her shelves' (*M*, 177), and then as an epigraph to 'Part Three', which quotes part of Miranda's narrative. Fowles's novel, for which King wrote a critical introduction in 1989 (*SW*, 339–52), suggests an analysis of how *Misery* enacts King's Gothic in order to connect ethical and artistic concerns. *The Collector* (which may have donated to King the name Annie, a nod to Frederick Clegg's 'Aunt Annie', who 'always said nurses were the nosiest parkers of them all')[23] famously documents a narrative of captivity, eventual death and the sinister threat of a repetition, in a form that allows space for two competing voices or discourses, those of male captor Clegg and his female prisoner Miranda. Miranda also perceives her incarceration as a kind of premature burial: she calls her prison 'this crypt-room', 'this foul little crypt', suggesting both burial and her encryption in the dialogic contest of voices of the novel.[24] *The Collector* counterpoints two incommensurate discourses, that of the captor and that of the captive. Its narrative emphasises the distinctions between them, undermining the assumption that the one conventionally privileged by class and education – in this novel that of the captive – will triumph over the other.[25]

In *The Collector*'s clash of discourses, the other – Clegg's discourse – dominates absolutely over the privileged, that of his female captive, annulling it, drowning it out and eventually reducing it to indeterminate sounds that prelude her death from pneumonia. The irony is that Miranda's discourse remains the weaker in terms of power, dominated and disempowered by Clegg's, despite being clearly privileged in terms of complexity, subtlety, aesthetic and ethical sensitivity and rhetorical persuasiveness. Through this clash, Fowles's novel analyses the ways in which language effects and perpetuates kinds of domination that undermine and compromise ethical demands in monstrous ways. *The Collector* has clearly influenced King's construction of the monstrosity of discursive oppression in *Misery* and also, paradoxically, his version of the monstrous-feminine. As Hanson notes, 'There could hardly be a clearer image [. . .] of the feminine as monstrous' than that of Annie's potential as castratrix in the novel.[26] Miranda's language in *The Collector* articulates one kind of demand, explicitly connecting injustice to a non-feminine monstrosity: 'I demand to be released at once. This is monstrous'.[27] She later reformulates this demand and metaphor as a fairy-tale, an allegorical expression articulated through her own impersonation of Scheherazade: 'Once upon a time (I said, and he stared bitterly at the floor) there was a very ugly monster who captured a princess and put her in a dungeon in his castle'.[28] King's novel translates this fairy-tale, reversing the gender roles, into the incarceration of a male writer by 'this monstrous woman' (*M*, 108) in 'the monster-woman's house' (*M*, 35), but the basic structure of his novel leans heavily on Fowles's, not least, again, in its exploitation of the suffering implied by the word 'misery'.

The word 'misery' and its derivative 'miserable' echo throughout Fowles's novel, always in Miranda's narrative, and usually referring to her captor. She calls Clegg a 'Miserable creature'; adjectivally she describes his 'miserable, wet, unwithit life' and condemns 'miserable people like you who don't believe anything'.[29] But she also prays to God to help 'this misery who has me under his power', before including herself in the prayer.[30] Miranda's awareness of the potentials of the word 'misery' in defining both the other person and her relation to him, rather than simply describing her own position, indicates that she is capable of placing Clegg's needs before her own. It expresses at this early point in her suffering a complex ethical awareness (implicit in the complexity of her language) of the other and of their needs; later, as she dies, she utters the final acknowledgement of the other: 'I forgive you'.[31] *Misery*'s revision of the relation explored in Fowles's novel offers no such ethical balance. King reverses the gender relations, making the prisoner male and the captor female and monstrous; his novel allows space for only one voice, that of the male prisoner, to be heard fully; and although the woman speaks (and speaks first), her speech is represented through the prisoner's

perception of it. In her limited speech, however, we find the complexities of *Misery* embedded, and those complexities relate to King's
Gothic sense of writing and of the writer's predicament.

Annie's speech

Misery presents, in its first, twelve-word, sixteen-syllable-long, haiku-
like chapter, a singular voice. Inarticulate, or rather misheard, this
voice is typographically represented by 'words' containing a surfeit
of u's and n's:

> *umber whunnnn,*
> *yerrrnnn umber whunnnn*
> *fayunnnn*

These sounds: even in the haze. (*M*, 3; italics in original)

Linda Badley rightly asserts that these 'first lines' 'can be comprehended
only when read phonetically: they must be pronounced and heard'.
'Such typography', she argues, 'replenishes the one-dimensional,
enclosed medium of the printed page.'[32] It does so by inserting the
reader actively into the text. The act of reading and the potential
hazards of misreading and over- or under-reading are, of course,
central to the narrative of *Misery* and are foregrounded at its opening.
Phonetically approximate and deictically proximate ('*These* sounds')
to the narrating consciousness, these lines (which echo the inarticulate
noises made by Fowles's Miranda just before her death) assert also
an odd primacy that momentarily overrides that consciousness,
excluding it and replacing it, momentarily but before it begins, with
another voice. This opening voice, not the voice of the narrator but
apparently reported by that voice, asserts its primacy over the narration through the words '*umber whunnnn*', the novel's first words and
first utterance that must later be decoded as 'number one', belatedly
recognised. They present as the opening of that apparent primacy
an initial absence, a missing first letter, the n of 'number'. This
incomplete and unopened primacy is, we later realise, that of self-
definition. The speaker defines herself, nominating her fan status as

definitive of her identity and elevating that identity above all others and specifically over that of the narrating voice. In doing so she establishes, initially, a specific kind of relation to her addressee, privileged, prioritised, self-elected, a relation that he (and we) must, first, decode ('These sounds' describes them, without decoding them, or even defining them as words) and must then learn to interpret.

For all its apparent orality, the text ensures that the act of reading is thus also deeply and doubly structured into the opening words of *Misery*, the reading of the transcribed utterance, and of the other through their acts of speaking and their utterances. This opening emphasises the act of reading and its effects, as the reader is required to perform the decoding that they demand. That reader remains aware that the deixis expressed in the narrational 'These sounds' locates them as proximal to a perceiving consciousness through which, it transpires, we will in turn perceive most if not all of the subsequent events but which remains in third-person, further refracted through a narrating consciousness. The representation of dialect discernible in 'These sounds', in the clearly oral accentual twang of *'fayunnnn'* for example, expresses other aspects of the identity of the subject who speaks them (her regional origins, and perhaps her class). Its translation and interpretation will be the tasks of the subject (in the narrative) who hears, as well as of the reader (of the narrative) who reads. The complex, proliferating relation between the two, repeatedly redefined as the novel progresses, constitutes the entire narrative of *Misery*.

The primacy established by 'these sounds' at the novel's opening is furthermore separate from the bulk of the narrative, isolated up front as an inscribed oral preface to a text already characteristically prefaced by multiple writings. These include a dedication, an acknowledgements page, a further prefatory page that offers only two words, 'goddess' and 'Africa', a further page of (medical) acknowledgements, and an epigraph quotation of Nietzsche's famous warning (in *Beyond Good and Evil*) about looking into the abyss.[33] As with *'Salem's Lot*, we enter the world of *Misery* through an emphatically *written*, overtly textualised series of spaces, here fragmented, 'shattered' (*M*, 6, 12, 43), like the legs of the novel's main protagonist. Such an entry is appropriate for a text so powerfully concerned with the mechanics and effects of writing. The excessive, non-grammatical, unpunctuated u's and n's of the first, tiny chapter (Kathleen Margaret Lant calls them, wrongly, 'meaningless letters on the page')[34] clearly signify the momentary collapse of language and its representational function into a 'haze' of indeterminate sounds and meanings, or perhaps the winding-up of words, a preparation for a beginning, like the repetitive, stuttering '*Rurr-rurr-rurr*' of the haunted car in *Christine* (*C*, 34; italics in original).

They also return to assume significance in relation to some of the novel's key motifs, particularly the 'Royal' typewriter that is central to the novel's action. The typewriter is both a machine for writing and, eventually, a murder weapon. It is a machine that, like the novel's opening 'word', 'has a missing n' (*M*, 67), and eventually drops its t and e as well (*M*, 251, 257). This writing-machine's output eventually resembles the novel's opening lines in its demands on the reader – 'For a mome   h   hr   of h m' (*M*, 257) – suggesting the writer's corresponding reduction to a similar inarticulacy. The brand-name 'Royal' connotes, of course, specific kinds of regal authority, not just the 'crowning' and 'Royalty' of Freud's uncanny that Nicholas Royle notes, but also that of the author 'King', present also in *Misery* as 'King of Pain' (*M*, 42), as 'King Kong' (*M*, 63) and (echoing Carrie's 'White House') as 'Ronald Reagan in *King's Row*' (*M*, 43). It also invokes, perhaps, the '*deus ex machina*' (*M*, 170; italics in original) noted in one of the novel's many meditations on the dramatics and dynamics of fiction (the connection between authorship and godliness is, of course, another key theme of *Misery*). To confirm the centrality of this machine to the novel's structure, the typewriter's missing n, e and t can spell out also the 'net' that has disastrously enmeshed the protagonist of *Misery* in the world of his 'number one fan'.

These two characters (accompanied by the characters missing from the typewriter) constitute the novel's principal society. *Misery* enacts a Gothic drama of confrontation between them in which each assumes a variety of roles in relation to the other, from patient and nurse and writer and reader, to prisoner and guard and, eventually, victim and murderer. King's radical and pointed reduction of the social world of *Misery* (preceded in the oeuvre by the sprawling *It* and *The Tommyknockers*, and followed by *The Dark Half* and *Needful Things*, all novels that extend their social fields well beyond the minimalism of *Misery*) effects a dramatic intensification of his Gothic's extended concern with the relation of the self to the other. *Misery* is initially concerned with the writer–reader relation, with the acts of creating and consuming in which each engages. It addresses the alarming tendency for such a fundamental opposition to collapse in on itself, the necessity of writing becoming simultaneously that of reading and vice versa and for readers to become writers and vice versa, each reflecting and inverting the other, like so many n's and u's. In a short piece about the writing of *Misery* King asserts that 'In a lot of my other books there are characters who are writers but the books are not about writing; *Misery* is'; but he also notes that this novel 'would turn the thumbscrews on the reader's sense of attention. Move the reader, but hurt the reader at the same time' (*SW*, 331–2). The intended suffering by torture of *Misery's* reader would here seem to mimic that endured by the writer within the novel. Each seems, in the author's imagination, potentially inter-changeable, as is implied from the novel's outset.

If the n's and u's in the novel's first chapter work pre-emptively within this collapsing opposition between readers and writers to alert us to the written-ness of *Misery* and to its being read, the first 'word', '*umber*', incomplete '*number*', suggests a different network of meanings that structure the novel. It denotes a dark colour, burnt umber, again echoing *The Collector*: Miranda imagines her painted garden 'as something very special, all black, umber, dark, dark grey, mysterious angular forms in shadow [. . .]' (her surname, we recall, is 'Grey').[35] In *Duma Key* (2008), King's 'American primitive' painter, Edgar Freemantle, 'sketche[s] the kitchen' with his 'Burnt Umber' (*DK*, 159, 509). This dark 'burnt' colour foreshadows the double textual immolations, the burning books, that frame the novel – the burning, enforced by the reader, early in his incarceration, of the manuscript of Paul's breakaway novel *Fast Cars*, and his revenge (but fake) burning, at the novel's climax, of what Annie thinks is the manuscript of *Misery's Return*, the novel she forces him to write. An umber-bird, the dictionary also informs us, is an African relative of the stork; it may be the 'rare bird with beautiful feathers – a rare bird which came from Africa' (*M*, 64) which Paul remembers seeing as a child in Boston Zoo (*M*, 33) and a symbol of freedom with which he clearly and repeatedly identifies in his imprisonment.

Such potential meanings indicate that Annie's phonetically rendered speech (and she is, in these early pages, an 'unseen voice' as well as a 'warder' (*M*, 5)) foreshadows much of importance in the novel. This speech initially defines her in relation to the novel and its symbolic structure; it both identifies her and reduces that identity to a figure standing for a hierarchised type ('number one fan'), only later (*M*, 6) supplemented by a proper name. As an articulated utterance it insists on the materiality of writing and reading, enforcing a concentrated act of reading to decode it, inspiring the novel, just as her breath, giving Paul the kiss of life, but like a 'dank suck of wind which follows a fast subway train' (*M*, 5) and reminiscent of the 'Wind in and out of unwholesome lungs' of T. S. Eliot's *Burnt Norton*,[36] literally 'inspires' him, reviving him so he can produce more writing for her. His 'resurrection', the novel's first ('Whew! That was a close one!', Annie breathes (*M*, 6)), is also a return of the body to its mechanical, unaided activities, to breathing 'as it had been doing his whole life without any help from him' (*M*, 5). The reader, like the author, may in this sense also be a kind of '*deus ex machina*', exhaling into the machinery of the writer and the text her revitalising demand for continuity, perpetuation, unending *Misery*.

The ostensible 'orality' of the novel's opening is thus, rather, its (re-)initiation by breath and inspiration of the 'machine' of writing and its textual productivity, its generation of meanings, intertextual connections and symbolic, writerly meanings. It foreshadows the fragmented text that the novel's protagonist will type, and he and his reader will supplement, by handwritten n's, e's and t's. Both author and reader become, in the process, perverse kinds of 'writing-machine'. *Misery* is King's definitive, pessimistic statement on the reduction, by market forces and audience desire, of author to 'shitty writing machine' (*M*, 173). This connection between writing and excretion, here also an abjecting excrementalisation of the writer himself, is commonly made in King's critical and fictional work. 'Writing shit always made him thirsty', we're told of Mort Rainey in 'Secret Window, Secret Garden' (*FPM*, 315). Rainey's writer's block leads inexorably to a bumper sticker he remembers reading: 'CONSTIPATED – CANNOT PASS' (*FPM*, 316). *On Writing* is replete with excrementary imagery connected to writing: 'Sometimes', King opines, echoing Hemingway, 'you're doing good work when it feels like all you're managing is to shovel shit from a sitting position' (*OW*, 55). In relation to style, he advises the aspiring writer that, 'you'll never say **John stopped long enough to perform an act of excretion** when you mean **John stopped long enough to take a shit**' (*OW*, 88; emphasis in original). And discussing the childhood memories of 'the jungle' that form one source of 'the Barrens' in *It*, he recalls: 'we were deep into the mysteries of this cool new playground when I was struck by an urgent need to move my bowels' (*OW*, 14), an adventure that ends with King 'enchanted by the idea of shitting like a cowboy' (*OW*, 14).

Writing itself, in *Misery*, is however less a 'constant secretion' or an excretion and more a punitive, enforced exercise in pointless, undesired repetition that ambivalently affords also a kind of salvation, the potential of another kind of repetition-as-resurrection and (a key word in the novel, as it is in *The Collector*) 'survival'. Paul thinks of 'mere brute survival' (*M*, 45) and of 'the survival instinct' (*M*, 66); Miranda commands herself – '*Survive*' (italics in original).[37] *Misery's* version of the popular romantic novelist's output is a cloying, sickly sweet, minimal and unhealthy parody of artistic creation, a parody from which its author is seeking to escape – 'survive' – into another space of writing, a different discursive frame, that of literary production. Annie 'resurrects' Paul by giving him the kiss of life. In this act, the novel's version of the genre of romance is 'inspired' by breath tainted with the 'dreadful mixed stench of vanilla cookies and chocolate ice-cream and chicken gravy and peanut-butter fudge' (*M*, 5), just as Annie imagines Paul has thought of the character Misery Chastain and then '*breathe[d] life* into her' (*M*, 22; italics in original). The narrative is initiated by this tension between male writerly productivity and female invasive orality (and King's metaphors for the process of life-saving revolve around a kind of reverse rape, the male author 'being raped back into life by the woman's stinking breath' (*M*, 7), as the text misogynistically expresses it). It establishes, too, a series of oppositions that resolve themselves into familiar Gothic doublings: victim and monster, (male) writer and (female) reader (but also writer-becoming-reader and reader-becoming- writer), inspirer and inspired, inside and outside, constraint and freedom, repetition and difference – all combine to elaborate the novel's ideological concern with the differences between unwholesome popular and vigorous literary writing.

Paradoxically (and symptomatic of the confused ideology of King's Gothic), Sheldon's new *Misery* novel, echoing Bobbie Anderson's machinically produced novel early in *The Tommyknockers*, is 'the best of the *Misery* books, and maybe the best thing I ever wrote, mongrel dog or not' (*M*, 345). Popular fiction produced in these absurdly adverse circumstances ironically becomes something like a version of the literary. Produced *in extremis*, *Misery's Return* bears the traces of genuine suffering ('misery') which, Paul thinks, elevate it. Early on in its production Paul recognises that it is a different kind of novel: shifting from the conventional romance formula of his previous work, incorporating his own Rider Haggard-influenced fantasies of Annie as *She*-goddess, *Misery's Return*, he quickly realises, will be 'a gothic novel, and thus [. . .] more dependent on plot than on situation' (*M*, 181). More specifically, it becomes a kind of Oriental Gothic, a narrative that displaces its action to increasingly exotic territories in order to dramatise fantasies of escape from the demands of the reader. 'The challenges were constant' (*M*, 181), he thinks, reminding us of the demand of Annie, 'that Victorian archetype, Constant Reader' (*M*, 71). If writing presents 'constant' challenges, so too does reading; Annie's role in *Misery* is that of the reader. Elsewhere in King's work, the 'Constant Reader' is the object of apparently sincere authorial gratitude, for example at the end of the 'Introduction' to *Everything's Eventual*: 'You most of all, Constant Reader. Always you' (*EE*, xvi). To read Annie as 'Constant Reader' is to begin to comprehend the significance of reading, and thus of writing, and thence of the infinite relation between the two, in *Misery*.

Resurrecting the author

One of the concerns of *Misery* is with what it calls 'radical reader involvement with the make-believe worlds the writer creates' (*M*, 274). Annie's real reading, her 'radical involvement' in the world of the writer rather than her passive, pseudo-addictive consumption of his works, begins with a chance encounter with the author as needy victim of his car crash, an encounter that invokes recognition: 'I thought you looked *familiar!*' (*M*, 17). She reads his name on his driver's licence, but dismisses it: 'I thought, "Oh, that must be a co-incidence"' (*M*, 17). Such statements construct her as a reader who recognises but refuses the significance of pattern, and fails to see patterns of significance. Her interpretations accommodate but miss the importance in narrative and fiction of coincidence, repetition, insistence, patterning elements of the aesthetic dimension of writing. Not quite condemned to the *mis*ery of *mis*reading (though she is emphatically '*Miss* Wilkes, if you don't mind' (*M*, 324)), Annie's read-ings are nevertheless restricted by the demands of credibility, hence her refusal of the 'dirty *cheat*' of resolving cliffhanger endings by obviously changing them (*M*, 124; italics in original). She is, Paul realises, exemplary of 'Constant Reader's flat, uncontradictable cer-tainty' (*M*, 123). Thus, she can inculcate shame in the author who tries to cheat her readerly expectations: 'He understood, and was amazed to find he was ashamed of himself. She was right. He *had* written a cheat' (*M*, 123; italics in original).

If *Misery* constructs the process of reading as a coercive demand (expressed in Annie's 'coercing permission to read the manuscript of *Fast Cars*' (*M*, 31)), it also maps through this coercion the various ways that Gothic tropes mobilise a critique of writing as constraint, perversion, aggression, and its relations within Gothic worlds to misogyny, power and death. Deeply structured by the tropes of con-finement and escape, *Misery* enacts a *mise en scène* crucial to a com-prehension of King's Gothic: the writer as prisoner, trapped within a world drastically redefined by his own work and its consumers. The psychosis of the reader fantasised in *Misery* is a coded version or inversion (and, increasingly, a perversion) of that of the author. Authorship is the condition of being bound, in a relationship that is unanswerable and infinite, irresistible, to a demand to produce writing. This is the coded message of texts like 'On Becoming a Brand Name' (*SW*, 39–70), *On Writing* and King's other ostensibly critical detours into extended autobiography. The writer's life, com-modified as narrative, becomes a written product, and control over it requires increasing levels of distorting assertions of authorial power.

Annie's literalism is one source, in *Misery*, of the gradual empower-ment of the reader, an empowerment the novel struggles to resist and eventually violently overcomes. Her involvement editorially and materially in the production of *Misery's Return* prematurely enacts the empowerment of the reader, as George Landow describes it in relation to the advent of hypertext, which 'permits readers to read actively in an even more powerful way, by annotating documents, arguing with them, leaving their own traces' in the objects of their acts of reading.[38] These interactive privileges, which effect trans-formations in the text consumed and make consuming a kind of production, are precisely those Annie achieves (and Paul, under duress, concedes) through her privileged, direct involvement in the writerly process. Her contributions to the writing of *Misery's Return* involve 'arguing' with it (and forcing the rewriting of its initial open-ing draft), 'annotating' (by inserting the typewriter's missing letters) and 'leaving her own traces' across the novel's textual surface. These traces include her name, inscribed into the first draft of the text as that of the nurse (*M*, 115) and her symbolic presence in the new novel's uses of the 'Bee-Goddess' and its 'great dark stone face' (*M*, 256). She is also overtly present in King's early working title for the novel, *The Annie Wilkes Edition*.[39] Her reading, in effect, determines a significant proportion of both novels, Sheldon's and King's, their direction and identity. She imposes her 'rules' of writing on the writing of *Misery's Return* (although, importantly, we never read the world through her eyes): 'Realism was not necessary; fairness was' (*M*, 130).

At the same time, Annie's reading relies initially upon her recog-nising the author's authority, the position of authorial power that she will begin almost immediately to undermine by asserting her own authority as reader. This process initiates a critique of that kind of reading that relies on the author's authority, a critique which becomes also a critique of conventional authorialism, a questioning of the centrality of the author in determining the meanings in the text. Such a critique leads in turn to Paul's deeper, more nuanced comprehension of the demands of the kind of reader Annie represents, of the complexity of her readerly desires and of her understanding of what narratives should do. As a reader she is structured by desire and its deferral: 'I want to find out for myself. I'm making it last' (*M*, 20), she states of reading *Misery's Child*. In the same conversation she asks Paul's 'permission' to read the manuscript of *Fast Cars*: 'And if I read it? You wouldn't mind if I read it?' (*M*, 21). Her reading of *Fast Cars* condemns its lack of '*nobility*' (again, perhaps, a sly nod to King himself) and its 'profanity' (*M*, 24; italics in original): 'Animal times demand animal words' (*M*, 25), she concedes. Annie's apparent perception of the worlds of Gothic and romance as (in Paul's comprehension) 'perfectly real' (*M*, 71) is constructed in *Misery* as a limitation on her reading ability. Yet it is echoed by Paul's faith that *Fast Cars*, his new non-genre novel, is somehow more effective, more true (but, potentially, equally deserving of another kind of recognition and fame: '*You may just have won next year's American Book Award*' (*M*, 16; italics in original) he remembers thinking on its completion). 'The subject dictates the form', he claims, in response to Annie's complaint that 'It's hard to follow. It keeps jumping back and forth in time' (*M*, 24). *Fast Cars*'s apparent formal experimentalism (its modernism, perhaps) rests uneasily with the reader familiar with the generic predictability of the *Misery* novels. As *author* (rather than victim), Paul's hatred of her centres on this set of comments. He condemns her for the crucial fact that she should 'find the nerve to *criticize* the best thing that he had ever written' (*M*, 31; italics in original).

The horror of Annie the reader, then, resides in the potential for her to become Annie the *critic*, her potential to read critically and even symbolically. She partially fulfils this potential through her insistence that Paul burns 'a few of the single pages' of the manuscript of *Fast Cars* 'as a symbol of your understanding' (*M*, 51). Yet Annie's 'rules' and her critical comments result in Paul writing a new kind of text, *Misery's Return*, a text marked by difference: 'It's not like any of the other *Misery* books', Annie remarks; 'This one was different', Paul thinks: 'this time he had been able to at least generate some power' (*M*, 159). A change of genre leads to (re-)generation of the 'degenerate [...] popular fiction' (*M*, 272) of the *Misery* novels. The novelty of the new novel (prefiguring the trope we have seen in the later novel *The Tommyknockers*) is its 'generation' of 'power', although where that power resides is ultimately the concern not of Sheldon's *Misery's Return*, but of King's *Misery*. Annie the reader is thus also Annie the critic, a critic whose judgement and whose capacity to judge are repudiated by the author. Her reading of *Misery's Child*, and specifically of the death of Misery at the end of that novel, further involves critical judgements that challenge the author's pre-conceptions of reading. Unconsciously paraphrasing the kind of assumptions about authorial power critiqued by Roland Barthes in 'The Death of the Author'[40] (and, incidentally, promoted by King himself: 'Being a writer is sort of a godlike function, in a way, and that's kind of fun', he told Matt Schaffer in 1983),[41] Annie asserts that,

> *a writer is God to the people in a story, he made them up just like God made US up and no-one can get hold of God to make him explain [. . .] but [. . .] God just happens to have a couple of broken legs and God just happens to be in MY house eating MY food and . . . and . . .* (M, 40; italics and emphasis in original)

By eventually killing Annie off, King's novel clears the space for the resurrection of the author-God Barthes famously claimed must die in order to liberate the reader. The author's fear of that liberation is the engine of the horror of *Misery*. In a graphic and violent reversal of Barthes' famous dictum, *Misery* demands and acts out the death of the (popular) reader as the precondition for the (re-)birth of the (literary) author.[42]

This (re-)birth is the novel's central resurrection, the one of which all the others are symbolic versions. In broad allegorical terms, what seems to have been prematurely buried in *Misery* is a version of the author as God. The novel enables and enacts the resurrection or exhumation of that prematurely buried God. *Misery* is a grand, Gothic assertion of the author's miraculous endurance beyond his own historical death. The novel's repetition at the beginning of its final section of its opening representation of Annie's slurred speech (M, 361) asserts an assimilation and a survival. Wrested from being owned by the woman who uttered them, 'These sounds' now 'belong' to the writer and are integrated into the writer's structuring of his narrative, rendered as significant repetition rather than simply repeated. Orpheus-like, the resurrected 'author-God' has been re-assembled bodily, with 'a custom-made prosthesis' (M, 361), and is armed with a new novel – *Misery's Return* – but is again in the thrall of writer's block: 'he had begun to wonder if there ever *would* be a next book' (M, 362; italics in original). His writerly existence seems, at this point, to be posthumous: '*This is what it's like after the end*' (*M*, 364), he thinks:

> *This is why no-one writes it. It's too fucking dreary. She should have died after I stuffed her head full of blank paper and busted pages, and I should have died then too. At that moment if at no other we really were like characters in one of Annie's chapter-plays — no grays, only blacks and whites, good and bad. [. . .] This . . . well, I've heard of denouement, but this is ridiculous.* (*M*, 364; italics in original)

The author's posthumous existence 'beyond' the narrative of *Misery* and of *Misery's Return* (and beyond *The Collector*: 'no grays' eliminates characters like Miranda Grey) is the concern of these final pages, which are replete with imagined resurrections and exhumations of both author and 'Constant Reader'. 'Annie rose up from behind the sofa like a white ghost' (*M*, 364), Paul imagines; 'The *writer's scenario* was that Annie was still alive' (*M*, 365; italics in original), he thinks. Annie may be 'in her grave', but 'like Misery Chastain, she rested there uneasily. In his dreams and waking fantasies, he dug her up again and again' (*M*, 366).

The writer's eventual 'resurrection' — his return to writing and the return to him of writerly inspiration — will replace these imagined resurrections of the demonic reader. It marks the end of *Misery* and of the misery of writer's block to which *Misery* has responded so graphically. As Roland Barthes remarks of Proust's *Á la recherche du temps perdu*, 'the novel ends when writing at last becomes possible'.[43] Such imagined returns both frame and express the writer's own desire for resurrection. They articulate in a series of Gothic images the novel's effort to imagine the writer's resurrection from his premature burial within a fictional world, constructed and (as the novel violently puts it) 'hobbled' by reductive readerly expectation (*M*, 248). That *Misery* imagines such a resurrection at the cost of such violent destruction of a feminised readership indicates the extent to which the novel ultimately conforms to the limits of the genres on which it depends. Nevertheless, the complexity of its analysis of reading and writing opens the space for analyses of the dimensions of King's Gothic, and indicates ways in which King's focus on writing and its effects extend and enforce those dimensions.

6

Gothic Time in 'The Langoliers'

☙

'They must have been ghosts, I said, "I wonder whence they dated?"'[1]

'The present is [...] a rip in the infinite beginninglessness and endless fabric of existing. The present rips apart and joins together again; it begins; it is beginning itself. It has a past, but in the form of remembrance. It has a history, but it is not history.'[2]

Time machines

One of the texts most frequently alluded to in King's works (and one largely unnoticed by critics) is H. G. Wells's short novel *The Time Machine* (1895). Many of King's narratives draw, directly or indirectly, on the basic premise of Wells's tale, suggesting that King is well aware of the Gothic potentials of a conceit – time travel – that is generically, for Wells, an originary science fiction motif. In *Christine* (clearly a novel about an uncanny, Gothicised kind of time travel) Arnie becomes a 'marvellously resurrected time-traveller' (*Ch*, 192). In *It*, another novel of symbolic (and, in one sequence, literal (*It*, 742–6)) time travel, Eddie Kaspbrak travels back to Derry on a train which he thinks of as '*a time machine*' (*It*, 110; italics in original), and the narrator compares Ben Hanscom to '*Wells's Time Traveller* [. . .] *falling with a broken rung in one hand, down and down into the land of the Morlocks'* (*It*, 174; italics in original). Larry Underwood, walking in the darkness of the Lincoln Tunnel in *The Stand*, imagines 'the Morlocks from the Classic Comic version [. . .], humped and blind creatures coming out of their holes in the ground' (*St*, 296). *Bag of Bones* tries to explain its hauntings by *'spiritual time travel'*: '*I've discovered the secret of time travel*', Mike Noonan thinks, '*It's an auditory phenomenon*' (*BB*, 349, 113; italics in original). Quite apart from 'The Langoliers' (1990), King's time-travel novella which we will analyse below, the other narratives in *Four Past Midnight* draw heavily on Wells's tale. In 'The Library Policeman' Sam, escaping from the library which, 'bulking all around him, was his time machine', feels 'like H. G. Wells's Time Traveller'; in 'The Sun Dog' Kevin tries to make sense, in Wellsian rhetoric, of the photographs his camera keeps producing: '*They say for us time is the fourth dimension, and we know it's there, but we can't see it*' (*FPM*, 715, 808; italics in original).

The Time Machine is one of the sequence of Wells novels that, famously, define the generic features of science fiction, but it also draws heavily on the Gothic tradition. Kelly Hurley notes it in her discussion of British *fin-de-siècle* Gothic writing.[3] Roger Luckhurst devotes several pages to scrutinising the 'sublime terror and awe' of the novel's closing pages, as well as its 'riven and contradictory' ideological messages,[4] its desire both to despise, in good Gothic fashion, 'a wretched aristocracy in decay'[5] and to protect it from the even more horrific degeneracy of the proletarian Morlocks. Wells's text is replete with Gothic imagery, not least the Morlocks themselves, whose appeal to King's writerly imagination surely resides not merely in some residual class identification, but in their functional Gothic connotations and activities, such as their nocturnal cannibalism. They first appear in Wells's novel as 'ghosts' in the 'ghastly half-light' of dusk, a darkness that to Weena (the Eloi who befriends the Time Traveller) is 'the one thing dreadful'.[6] Ghosts recur throughout Wells's tale. A sceptical viewer of the experimental model Time Machine asks 'is this a trick – like that ghost you showed us last Christmas?'[7] The model Time Machine itself, disappearing into the future, 'was seen as a ghost for a second perhaps'.[8] The Time Traveller, returning at the end of the text to the world of the year 802,701, is momentarily seen by the narrator as 'a ghostly, indistinct figure', a 'phantasm' which 'vanished as I rubbed my eyes'.[9]

This Gothic trope indicates how Wells's novel is concerned with the ghostly implications of time travel, its invocation of the spectral and the uncannily surviving. It draws for its imagery on contemporary scientific and entertainment technologies of magic lanterns, phenakistoscopes, praxinoscopes and other early proto-cinematic devices. Its Time Traveller is himself a strange kind of ghost, an anachronistic figure from the ancient past (that is, Wells's contemporary) surviving uncannily into the distant future and returning 'ghastly pale' from that future to the present to recount his tale with only 'the ghost of his old smile'.[10] This coalescence of the Gothic trope of the spectral with the science fiction trope of time travel is the initial generic space of King's Gothic vision of time. Where Wells uses time travel to articulate a contradictory and restricted but highly productive and suggestive class-bound vision of future society,[11] King's references to it tend to focus on the Gothic potentials of time travel itself and on the iconography of the Morlocks and their connotations of repression, ghost-inhabited darkness and the horror of cannibalism. In doing so he connects his writing to the inscription in generic traditions of an extended analysis of the time of a vision of democracy to come – 'Communism', in Wells's Time Traveller's vocabulary[12] – a spectre of particular kind of social organisation, of 'a communism [. . .] still to come beyond its name'.[13]

Jacques Derrida draws indirectly on Wells's returning Time Traveller in a chapter entitled 'The Phantom Friend Returning (in the Name of Democracy)' in *The Politics of Friendship*, where he describes the time of the contemporary. Derrida offers the unthinkability of a time that would belong in some way fully to the contemporary. Such a time would be constituted only in the impossibility of its presence, thinkable instead in its endless displacement into a temporal eventuality that is potentially deranged and deranging:

A time said to be contemporary [. . .] would be anything but contemporary – anything, except proper to its own time. It would resemble nothing, nor would it gather itself up in anything, lending itself to any possible reflection. It would no longer relate to itself. There would, however, be absolutely no indifference; it *would not be* – in other words, it would not be *present* – either *with* the other or *with* itself. Should it present itself, should it with some word, say 'I', its speech could only be that of a madman; and if it described itself as living, this would again be – and more probably than ever – a sign of madness. (Italics in original)[14]

The time of such a democracy would 'remain without relation to any other, without attraction or repulsion, nor living analogy'.[15] Such a time, improper and unimaginable (indescribable, unwriteable), circulates around the difficulty (mapped elsewhere in Derrida's discussion of Emmanuel Levinas)[16] of describing such concepts while necessarily using the verb 'to be'. It indicates the complexity of thinking the temporality of the contemporary, and particularly of the contemporary Gothic, with all its difficult and specific relations to tradition and the survival out of time of the past: 'a time out of joint', Derrida insists.[17] Within its strange logic of phantoms returning within a contemporary, such a time implies a dislocation of selfhood and of subjectivity, a derangement of the senses, an irredeemable fracturing of the social with which the Gothic text is surely concerned. In *The Time Machine* the inscrutability of such a time is indeed figured as the partially illegible text of a future only partially decipherable: 'Suppose you found an inscription, with sentences here and there in excellent plain English, and interpolated therewith, others, made up of words, of letters even, absolutely unknown to you?'[18] Derrida's time suggests, too, the connection between the contemporary and death; 'absolutely no indifference' indicates absolute *différance*, the 'tomb of the proper in which is produced, by *différance*, the *economy of death*'.[19] The unknowability of such a contemporary, its absolute resistance to the order of time that facilitates knowledge, is one concern of Stephen King's novella 'The Langoliers'. As one character puts it late in the narrative: 'It all comes back to time, doesn't it? Time . . . and sleep . . . and not knowing' (*FPM*, 279).

'The Langoliers'

Halfway through 'The Langoliers', King's theoretically and philosophically suggestive novella of unwilling time-travellers, deranged stock trader Craig Toomy, displaying all the 'signs of madness' Derrida associates with this unthinkable anachronistic contemporary, searches in a deserted airport office 'for a weapon – something sharp. His hand happened almost immediately upon a letter-opener' (*FPM*, 193). Toomy's compulsive habit, signifier of his psychotic disconnection, is to shred pieces of paper, pages of magazines and books, into long strips, at one point 'dismembering the in-flight magazine' (*FPM*, 93), at another (crucially, in this narrative of a lost plane and its passengers) a 'stack of lost-luggage forms' (*FPM*, 203). This metaphor for destructive obsession suggests, in King's moral universe, a telling disregard for the sacredness of the written text, but also offers a clue to the processes of destruction with which this novella is in part concerned. Toomy is clearly no reader or writer. In the anti-democratic, self-oriented 1980s ideology he embodies and which the novella critiques he is a doer, 'a can-do type of guy' (*FPM*, 87), and his psychosis prohibits him from any accurate interpretation of events and their consequences. His ideology, an absolute narrative revealed as absolute fantasy, effectively imposes a course of action, a demand for a progressive, linear movement forwards, a figure of a lifetime fixed from childhood through to death, from which he is unable to deviate. His letter-opener is used, a few pages later, to murder a fellow-traveller.

Toomy evinces an excessive liking for 'The familiar accoutrements of white-collar America' (*FPM*, 192–3): paper, letter-openers and other signifiers of the burdensome anti-aesthetic textuality of bureaucratic postmodernism (and eventually, moments before his death, he hallucinates, through a telepathic intervention to which we will return, 'a long mahogany boardroom table', on which 'At each place was a yellow legal pad' (*FPM*, 234)). These paraphernalia are, like the 'calmness' Toomy feels when sat 'behind a desk', conduits for the novella's analysis of the insanity of capitalism (*FPM*, 193). He critiques its singular inappropriateness and potentially lethal connection to administrative violence and its negation of the (impossible, unthinkable) time of democracy, even within the bizarre, Gothic contexts his narrative elaborately constructs. Toomy's fantasy, dependent on his absolute obeisance to the Law of a particularly draconian Father, is of a world managed by oppressive, capitalised, simplistic paternal clichés. Examples of these pepper the narrative as simplistic decrees ('THE BIG PICTURE', 'LYING DOWN ON THE JOB' (*FPM*, 166; emphasis in original)) that define a world in which desire and potential are parcelled up and delivered on time, a world in which he, too, will (in his fantasy) be delivered on time and as pre-arranged to his crucial board meeting in Boston. No matter that his trade is (as the narrative quickly reveals) fraudulent, a fiction within a fiction. In his insanity ideology overrides sense, an illogic that makes him paradoxically indispensable to his fellow travellers in ways that only one of them can foresee, and which again paradoxically fulfils the inexorable democratic logic and its impossible time that concerns 'The Langoliers'. The German-sounding word 'Langoliers' connotes ideas of time and delay: *lang*, 'long, of time or a journey', *langsam*, 'slow', *langweilig*, 'boring', 'taking a long time'. In the narrative constructed by his father's 'pressure' the Langoliers figure Toomy's childhood horror, the imaginary monsters that 'prey on lazy, time-wasting children' (*FPM*, 78, 79). They exist to punish Toomy's infant 'time-wasting', as his father calls it, in the paternal voice we hear repeatedly defining Toomy as a failure. Like everything in this narra-tive, the Langoliers are doubled; they exist also as monsters consuming the last remnants of the decaying present, literalising the novella's Gothic vision of time as that which ultimately consumes everything, even what seems to survive time itself.

Toomy is a male, adult, unsympathetic version of Carrie White, an abused child who lacks only Carrie's psychic powers (which appear elsewhere in 'The Langoliers') and so survives into some kind of compromised adulthood. His own psychological condition, a consequence of his subsequent oversubscription to an aggressively capitalist ideology, is analogous to that of the time represented in the novella, a time '*deranged*, both out of order and mad'.[20] His mad-ness, a consequence of his disastrous mismanagement of an inter-national fund transaction, is characterised in part by his 'unsettling look of blankness' (*FPM*, 82). This look doubles the madness or 'derangement' of the 'dead blankness' (*FPM*, 59) of the past, suggesting that one allegorical dimension of 'The Langoliers' concerns a specific mirroring, the doubling in individual consciousnesses of internal and external worlds and of imagined and real monsters. Toomy is thus a central character through whom the relays of doubling and repetition function throughout 'The Langoliers'. His ostensible moral backsliding complements the temporal slippages explored in and structuring the narrative. His internal condition reflects the external

situation, as his madness presents a similar hurdle to the other characters as the insane world and time in which they find themselves.
His name, inscribing into the text Derrida's 'tomb of the proper' of
différance, homonymically implies his initial connection to impending
mortality; this name also resonates, as we will see, in relation to the
novella's ideological concern with self and group.

Toomy's murderous letter-opener symbolically undoes the parcel
– the narrative and its actants, his memories and desires and their
potentials – and its contents, which constitute the themes and events
of 'The Langoliers'. A murder weapon linked to a postal system, it
figures, as a motif of destiny and of the letter's destiny to be received
and ripped open, this narrative's concern with the past as a kind of
death and with its persistence in the 'post', the delayed, tardy time
of postal delivery and deliverance. 'The Langoliers', emphasising this
teleological drive, this quick establishment and sustaining of narrative
suspense, uses devices derived from the thriller genre – not least a
strange nod to James Bond in its British character, Nick Hopewell
– that organise the narrative's relentless teleology. It links this teleology
with another order of destination, that of an apocalyptic sense of
time running out, that King's Gothic configures, via a series of stra-
tegic metaphors of deliverance and delivery, as a drive towards a
salvational resolution of narrative suspense, in which apocalypse is
(in Hollywood style) both 'Now' and temporally delayed, averted,
refused and finally evaded. In his 'Note' to 'The Langoliers' King
mentions the 'apocalyptic feel' (*FPM*, 14) of the text, which he links
to another generically similar novella, 'The Mist' (*SC*, 21–134). This
apocalyptic dimension is, as we will see, a product in part of a chain
of metaphors on which the narrative relies. But it also locates 'The
Langoliers' within a Cold War historical and ideological context of
potential nuclear wars, of international capitalist and other empires
and of the early days of global terrorism (the novella was published
in the wake of the Lockerbie plane crash of 1987). This context, at
the time of its publication in 1990 (and thus after the events in
Eastern Europe of 1989), was already quickly becoming historical,
an index of the disastrous fading of the presence of the present into
the past which is the text's main intellectual conceit.

Destinerrance

'The Langoliers' describes the struggle to survive of a group of over-night airline passengers who awaken, a short time into Flight 29 from Los Angeles to Boston, to find that most of their fellow travellers, the whole crew and, indeed, the entire population of the world have disappeared. Only those who were awake on the flight have vanished, leaving traces, uncanny and sometimes abject prosthetic remainders (watches, surgical pins, pacemakers, wigs, dildos), as reminders of themselves. The sleepers, including, of course, a writer, 'author of more than forty mystery novels' (*FPM*, 60), whose deductive skills make him the detective of the narrative, survive, to awaken in a strangely different world. Sleep and awakening thus frame the narra-tive, implying a sustained nightmare scenario of narrative suspense derived in part from Hitchcock. As the survivors struggle to com-prehend their predicament, it becomes apparent that their flight has unwittingly entered a 'time-rip' and become displaced in time into the past. In order to return to the present they must return through the 'time-rip' before the world of the past is consumed by the rapidly approaching creatures named 'the Langoliers', who constitute this novella's figure of monstrous horror, its version of Wells's Morlocks.

Characters thus awaken into a condition of horror, the origin of which sleep has enabled them to evade, a horror (a kind of non-existence, or a movement into a world of non-existence) which persists as a kind of nightmare. The writer in the group, Bob Jenkins, christens the moment of temporal dislocation 'the Event' (*FPM*, 119), inviting a consideration of how a notion of the 'Event' marks the passage (or otherwise) of Gothic time. Gilles Deleuze, analysing Stoic philosophy in relation to Lewis Carroll's nonsense texts, iden-tifies 'two times, one of which is composed only of interlocking presents; the other is constantly decomposed into elongated pasts and futures' (Deleuze, 1990: 73).[21] The narrative structure of 'The Langoliers' counterpoints these two times. A breach in the interlocking structure of the former, the familiar, sequentially ordered time of everyday mundanity and linear temporal progression, results in an errant movement into the latter, the unfamiliar, decomposing/elon-gating (non-)time of the past. 'Constant decomposition' is the con-dition of time in the bulk of the duration of King's narrative. The future, repositioned as a present to which the survivors struggle to return (in what is now problematically the future of the narrative's teleology, the resolution towards which it drives), exists only as an absent presence, a temporal condition to be attained, in effect a future-present to come. In such an experience of time, Deleuze argues, 'the event has no present. It rather retreats and advances in two directions at once, being the perpetual object of a double question: What is going to happen? What has just happened?' (Deleuze, 1990: 73).[22] This is precisely the uncertain situation of 'The Langoliers': the double non-presence of the 'Events' (the passages through the 'time-rip') of the narrative, and of the present to which the characters must return, leads to a disconcerting double movement in which the regression of the past is experienced in terms of narrative progression. The narrative imports into the impossible backsliding of time ('What has just happened?') the forward impetus of narrational teleology ('What is going to happen?').

In this world the time, like Craig Toomy's mental state, is truly Gothicised, 'out of joint'. 'The Langoliers' conforms to the Derridean 'spectrality effect' which, David Glover argues, is characteristic of a Gothic vision of modernity: 'the distinction between the various modalities of time becomes notoriously blurred, disturbing the reader's confidence in the vivid, transparent immediacy of the present and disrupting its orderly relations between past and future', troubling 'the linear succession of a before and an after'.[23] Temporality becomes definitive of an experience of alienation that is both material and psychological, a 'wandering away from the present' (*FPM*, 221) that is also a kind of errancy or error, a consequence of a drastic mistake within which the bulk of the narrative is located. The survivors must firstly comprehend and then respond to this mistake. It is an error that is perceptually evident, and much of the narrative involves deductive perceptual processes of working it out. The blind girl, Dinah, says of the world they wander into, 'It's really wrong here', and Bob Jenkins urges people to correct their 'error of perspective' (*FPM*, 117, 134). The errancy of error implies, in this context, a movement from an allotted path, a straying, a movement also connected to the notion of an 'errand' (and one such errand, the carrying back to the present, by Lauren, of a message of reconciliation from Nick Hopewell to his hitherto estranged father, provides a key element of the narrative's closure). The error here is ultimately an error of movement in time, a movement backwards that results in the experience of a temporal dislocation.

These insistent metaphors of error and perspective suggest the novella's efforts to express in language and narrative codes its concerns with time. 'The Langoliers' is at every level a narrative about time and how to survive it, about the time of the present and of presence within that present, about how the present may persist as the past, about (as we will see) how the future may present itself to us in coded forms as dreams or fantasies, about being and failing to be on time and about the errancy apparently consequent on time's failure and the failure to keep time, its loss. This errancy is understood and theorised by the survivors variously as (early in the narrative, when no answers are yet forthcoming) the potential destruction of the world by nuclear holocaust, and (much later) as 'navigational error' or the mistake of non-comprehension, the failure to recognise 'Something wrong. Or out of place. Or lost. Or forgotten' (*FPM*, 265, 262–3). King's novella (like *The Tommy-knockers*) clearly draws on conventional science fiction motifs. Its plot is characteristic of a *Twilight Zone* episode and, like Vonnegut's Billy Pilgrim in *Slaughterhouse 5*, its characters have 'come unstuck in time';[24] in *Duma Key*, Edgar's daughter, under the influence of his paintings, seems 'strangely unfixed in time' (*DK*, 456)). They find themselves trapped out of their own time, in a time 'out of joint' with their present. They, not time, are at a loss. They become the uncanny remainder of a present; they are what is wrong, out of place, lost, forgotten. They are ghosts of the future (and then, in that future, of the past), displaced out of their time, uncannily removed and recurring. The novella scrutinises the meanings of the economics of temporality, the connections of value between 'wrong' and 'out of place' and 'lost' and 'forgotten', that such rhetoric involves. It explores the difficulty of expressing in language (and particularly in the language of popular fiction) the temporal disjunctions its narrative involves. Time's out-of-placeness, a metaphor for the novella's predicament, draws on a rhetoric of the spatial; the other options here suggest different conditions of incorrectness or inaccuracy, loss and forgottenness, conditions germane to a psychoanalytic understanding of the human subject situated in time, but also implying the postal analogy with which this discussion began.

Everything in the narrative tends towards the tension between a temporality subject to a trauma (a puncture or punctuation) that is both absolute (a loss) and yet reversible (out of place, therefore potentially replaceable), and a sequence of events within, consequent on and leading on time (punctually) towards that trauma. The sequence demands a different narrative *telos* within which the absolute/reversible tension organises itself. Everything points towards an unaccountable loss or displacement (hence the importance of Craig Toomy's accounting frauds), a drastic failure of a system of circulation. The failure has culminated in one package or parcel, an aeroplane containing twelve survivors, a biblical number that heralds the importance of angel-messengers in this novella's apocalyptic vision, being misplaced, lost or forgotten. Errors of potentially immense magnitude ('Some sort of accident', possibly 'a nuclear war' (*FPM*, 58)) and confused destination ('Then what *is* our destination?' (*FPM*, 59)), combine with errors of judgement and desire to produce a Derridean sense of *destinerrance*, a '*dispatch for which there is no self-presentation nor assured destination*' (italics in original).[25] 'Destinerrance', a neologism conceived in part to account for the excess of Cold War visions of nuclear apocalypse, would name, Derrida argues, a failure that 'no longer gives us even the assurance of *a sending* of Being, of *a* gathered-up sending of Being'. It invites, instead, 'randomness', '*some* sendings, many sendings, missiles whose destinerring and randomness may, in the very process of calculation and the games that simulate the process, escape all control' (italics in original).[26] Destinerrance is, then, a form of mis-sending, a failing structure of delivery and receipt, an effort to think the possibility of failure within a temporising system of sendings, transmissions and deliveries. In this system one element (at least: 'How many other planes do you suppose went through?' wonders Nick (*FPM*, 266)) has gone astray, become lost.

'Destinerrance' expresses well the novella's apocalyptic sense of temporal dislocation, couched in late 1980s Cold War iconography, and its location within King's concerns in this text with the time of writing and with writing's relations to time. Its double valency (linking it to the Gothic doublings that again dynamise King's narrative) produces an oscillation of conflicting effects (destiny and the possibility of erring from it, error and its inevitability affirming destiny), enabling a reading of 'The Langoliers' that accounts for the productive conflict between its temporal and narrative logics. Derrida argues in the 'Preface' to *Of Grammatology* that,

> The age already in the *past* is in fact constituted in every respect as a *text*, in a sense of these words that I shall have to establish. As such, the age conserves the values of legibility and the efficacy of a model and thus disturbs the time (tense) of the line or the line of time. (Italics in original)[27]

King's novella, working within the confusing tenses of such statements, explores the consequences of conceiving of the past as a textual recording gradually (and then suddenly) being erased. It explores also the consequences of the disturbance and then severing of the 'line of time' which it scrutinises through a concern with (grammatical) tense and (narrative) tension and their displacement and return. Such movements organise the narrative, just as they disorganise its logic and, potentially, its grammar: 'Time-travel plays hell on the old verb tenses, doesn't it?' remarks Nick (*FPM*, 253).

In 'The Langoliers' the past becomes a particular kind of text destructured and made partially illegible (like the text of the future that Wells's Time Traveller tries to interpret) by the relation between tense and tension. As tenses fail, so tension tightens, transforming the past into a dead letter, a shattered text, a wholly errant destiny declining into unthinkable nothingness, contrasting with the potential double-message of Flight 29 and its temporarily errant destiny. Itself a parcel of time inscribed with signs of movement and intent, signs repeated for emphasis by the text – 'Along the fuselage, the words AMERICAN PRIDE were written in letters which had been raked backward to indicate speed' (*FPM*, 100–1, 287) – Flight 29 contains within it also a further set of messages inscribed in human and social desires and in the allegorical potential of sacrifice as the bearing of a message, symbolically expressed (as we will see) in the most conventional of apocalyptic messengers, the angel. Destiny, destination, error and errancy of the letter and its non-destination, confused with the strange tenses of inheritance and the impending repayment of what is due: such are the strange, anachronistic temporal logics that organise 'The Langoliers'.

Time out of joint

King writes of the stories in *Four Past Midnight* that they concern themes including 'Time, for instance, and the corrosive effects it can have on the human heart. The past, and the shadows it throws upon the present – shadows where unpleasant things sometimes grow and even more unpleasant things hide ... and grow fat' (*FPM*, 7). Time's materiality as a ground of experience, and the sense of imminent, destinerrant threat it invokes in Gothic texts, are primary concerns of many of King's works. *It* constructs extensively at formal and thematic levels a strong 'sense of time [. . .] as something real, as something that had unseen weight [. . .] time as something that would eventually bury him' (*It*, 278). Time's paradoxical constitution within and through the conditions of human experience – memory and desire, anticipation and fear, persistence and return – is a recurrent concern of King's versions of the Gothic, which rely on a double sense that time passes (human beings grow older, retaining somehow something of their pasts) and that time is fixed (the 'something' they retain persists in unchanging, remembered, sometimes externalised or symbolised forms). Time is thus experienced as double and doubly experienced: mobile and fixed, proceeding and remaining, en-countered within and without and sometimes oddly doubled or enfolded (in 'Secret Window, Secret Garden' Mort experiences 'a weird feeling that time had somehow doubled back on itself' (*FPM*, 396)). If Gothic time may be a version of time 'out of joint', in the sense that historical sequence is unhinged by the logics of haunting and of spectrality that mark the Gothic text, it is often, in King's revisions of Gothic, double- or multiple-jointed, twisted in many different directions. This many-jointed temporality is furthermore explicitly linked to the written-ness of the Gothic text, to writing's peculiar relation to temporality. Gothic writing embeds within its own script the ambivalence of Gothic time, its static motion, its persistent erasure and return, its archaic decline and its youthful rejuvenation.

Set mainly in the depersonalised social spaces of airplanes and airports, 'The Langoliers' manifests, of course, the alienating de-temporalisation or disjointedness characteristic of jetlag and the experience of air travel across time zones. It thus exploits a peculiarly modern form of disorientation, consequent on the international structure of time difference. 'The time difference [*décallage horaire*] is in me, it is me. It blocks, inhibits, dissociate, arrests – but it also releases, makes me fly',[28] writes Derrida, summarising the sensory disorientation of time difference within the delays and relays of the international transport system. King's characters, 'blocked' and in-hibited' in their temporal disjunction, find themselves marooned in a world of the 'strange' (*FPM*, 116) where entropy accelerates, time slows down and the void of nothingness, the total and horrific aporia of history as mass forgetting, is made real. This spectral world of muffled, flattened sensory experience is gradually decoded by the characters as an 'out of joint' world of the immediate past. 'It feels as if we're out of step [...] with everything' (*FPM*, 156), says Bethany. Brian Engle, late in the narrative, thinks of how 'things were so badly out of joint' (*FPM*, 252). This 'out of joint-ness' connects the novella to *Hamlet* (and, in another Shakespearean echo, the notion of a 'time-rip' echoes Macduff's being 'untimely ripp'd' from his mother's womb (*Macbeth* V. viii. 16))[29] and to a Gothic sense of the written-ness of tradition. It recurs at key points in King's writing. In *The Dark Half*, Thad, about to embark on the 'automatic writing' that connects him with George Stark, experiences the error it implies, 'That feeling that things were out of joint, that things were wrong and going wronger all the time' (*DH*, 278). In *Needful Things*, Alan Pangborn feels 'that there was something badly out of joint' in Castle Rock (*NT*, 633). '*Salem's Lot*, Ben Mears thinks, 'had the wrong name. It ought to be Time' (*SL*, 130–1). Undergoing the 'alien ritual' of confession that makes him feel 'out of joint with his time' (*SL*, 368), Ben experiences the interconnections of disrupted time and the written: 'he could almost see the word "vampire" printed on the black screen of his mind, not in scare movie-poster print, but in small, economical letters that were made to be a woodcut or scratched upon a scroll' (*SL*, 367–8). Ben regresses mentally through historical modes of representation from movies to handwritten scrolls, the mind moving from 'screen' to an older form of inscribed surface.

Being 'out of joint' in King's works connects a sense of temporal dislocation to the strange time of writing, the time of 'a disjointed or disadjusted now'.[30]

The word 'Langoliers' suggests the 'lingering' of delay and temporal displacement, imagining the remainder of the past and its decline into nothingness as a process of destructive consumption, the decay of time beyond memory into the horror of non-existence. The world of the present lingers, in the narrative, within the past. Signifiers of its affect – the fizziness of beer, the flavour of sandwiches, the flammability of aviation fuel – wane perceptibly as time fades. To account for and comprehend this waning, 'The Langoliers' offers a structure of doubles and repetitions characteristic of dream logic and inviting a psychoanalytic reading that emphasises the differences between the time of the past, the 'imaginary' or dream-space of sleep through which characters travel and the 'symbolic' world of the present to which they return. Sleep also implies the absence of experience, the impossibility of direct encounter with the potentially disastrous event of transition. Maurice Blanchot writes of the disaster that it 'always takes place after having taken place', so 'there cannot possibly be any experience of it'.[31] The double disaster of 'The Langoliers' confirms this assertion. No one can experience the passage through the 'time-rip' and live, so no experience of it is related in the narrative. It happens twice, both times within and outside the narrative frame, a doubled ellipsis that the narrative both evades and relies upon, a doubled delivery (a sending and a return), effecting a delayed consequence that takes place outside the narrative frame and yet constitutes it.

S(c)ent in the post

We can interpret 'The Langoliers' as both a tale lost in the post and a tale of being lost in the post, a purloined (or at least misdirected) postcard or undelivered parcel stranded in the dead letter office of the past, enfolded in a 'time-rip' and then ripped open by a madman with a letter-opener. King's writing draws again on the circulatory metaphors that organise Poe's 'The Purloined Letter' to offer a complex, dense, doubly enfolded meditation on the Gothic potentials of disrupted temporality, revising the Gothic haunting-from-the-future motif used by, amongst others, Dickens in *A Christmas Carol* (1843). Its characters and the plane in which they fly constitute the contents of a parcel of time displaced into another time that is wholly *other*. They are lost in the temporal post, a 'post-' (posthumous, post-rational, possibly post-apocalyptic) which is revealed to be a pre-, a version of time-before, and then becomes truly a post-, a time-after, before returning to the presence and substance of a now. The novella handles this movement against and within the sequentiality of narrative time by deploying a rhetoric of the oneiric to metaphorise its derangement of the senses. 'The Langoliers' is a truly Gothic night-mare-text. The survivors (and uncounted numbers are lost, awake at the undisclosed moment of the 'event') awake into a nightmare. 'I keep thinking this is a dream', says the man Toomy will murder, 'I keep thinking this is the worst nightmare I've ever had but I'll wake up soon' (*FPM*, 174). Through a series of deductive manoeuvres of which Poe would have been proud, they work out both their predicament and a means of escape from it. Death characterises this nightmare world of 'dead blankness' (*FPM*, 59) and lost messages forbidding communication: in this world the phones are all 'dead' (*FPM*, 120), Craig Toomy's deranged mind imagines the 'dead voice' of his father (*FPM*, 123), and Dinah screams that this is the world in which '*We're all going to die*' (*FPM*, 128; italics in original). Symbolic presence has been erased, leaving only a persistent after-image, a spectral version of being fading into senselessness, in the process of and on the verge of disappearing into nothingness. Kant's three modes of the object's existence in time, permanence, succession and simultaneity, are replaced here by their Gothicised counterparts, transience, regressive repetition and anachrony.[32]

So much of 'The Langoliers' is concerned, through this Gothic-isation of time, with human senses. Dinah, blind since birth, has a 'radar sense' (*FPM*, 27) or 'sixth sense' (*FPM*, 124) that compensates to an extent for her blindness, alongside touch and her superb hear-ing. At the moment of her death she reveals that she 'saw through Mr Toomy's eyes' (*FPM*, 255), an act of empathetic identification that places her alongside Sue Snell as an empathiser. Crucially, sensory perception is foregrounded in Brian's struggle to remember the name and scent of his dead wife's perfume (*FPM*, 21). King's 'Note' to 'The Langoliers' emphasises the novella's origin in an image, of 'a woman pressing her hand over a crack in the wall of a commercial jetliner' (*FPM*, 13), which he reworks into Brian's dream. Sleeping and dreams, with their distorted sense of time, are pivotal to a narrative that begins with Brian arriving as an exhausted pilot after a shaky cross-Pacific flight into Los Angeles airport, intending to 'sleep for fourteen hours' (*FPM*, 15). In the brief interlude between this arrival and his departure on the flight for Boston (and 'The Langoliers' is deeply structured by the logic of arrival as prelude to departure and departure as a form of arrival) he is informed, seemingly incidentally to the narrative, of the death of his ex-wife, Anne, whom (in an apparently gratuitous piece of misanthropy and misogyny) he once hit. Later, asleep on the way to Boston and troubled by his inability to remember the perfume she wore, he dreams of Anne, 'dressed in the dark-green uniform of an American Pride flight attendant';

> Her hand was pressed against a crack in the fuselage. [. . .] A fold appeared in the back of her hand, mimicking the shape of the crack in the fuselage. It grew deeper as the pressure differential sucked her hand relentlessly outward. [. . .] Yet, Anne went on smiling. *It's L'Envoi, darling*, she said as her arm began to disappear [. . .] (*FPM*, 28; italics in original)

'*L'Envoi*' offers a clue to the text's postal logic, a thread the novella only picks up near the end. The French word for 'sending' or 'something sent', 'package' or 'parcel', (from the verb *envoyer*, 'to send', 'to dispatch', 'to forward'), '*L'Envoi*, names the half-remembered, half-forgotten scent ('perfume [. . .] fragrance', insists the narrative (*FPM*, 20)) Brian struggles to name and whose name is provided by his unconscious prevision of the impending rip in time. The word suggests something endlessly sent but never received, a message delayed in the post, demanding a response forestalled, something, like the name of the 'perfume', 'maddening': 'It danced just beyond his grasp' (*FPM*, 21). '*L'Envoi*' encrypts the narrative's coded theme, confirming its concern with dreaming and sending, the dreamt and the s(c)ent, leaving in question only the nature, cause and consequence of the sending of which we read. Unable to recall a scent, Brian Engle awakens with his fellow travellers, having been sent, letter-like, into a dreamlike world that refuses the senses.

King's vision of Gothic time eschews (at this stage) the 'gross-out' (*DM*, 40) level of horror, offering instead the past as a dulled and dulling blankness, a chill, senseless, fading world, a sending into the past which is also a sending into a scentless world: 'it has no smell, no taste' (*FPM*, 108). From there, we return to a contemporary world of presence and the present that bombards the senses with scents: 'Smells suddenly struck Brian with a bang: sweat, perfume, aftershave, cologne, cigarette smoke, leather, industrial cleaner' (*FPM*, 297). At this moment of the return of scent and of the sent, the novella deploys its postal simile:

> *I am going to see the moving present lock onto this stationary future and pull it along, the way hooks on moving express trains used to snatch bags of mail from the Postal Service poles standing by the tracks in sleepy little towns down south and out west. I am going to see time itself open like a rose on a summer morning.* (*FPM*, 297; italics in original)

– or like an envelope delivered on that summer morning, finally reaching its destination after such Gothic delays. This crucial passage embeds the structure of the postal system, collection and delivery into the novella's conceit of temporal dislocation, offering a tiny allegory of American modernity as a product (at last) of postal efficiency.

Rips, strips, cracks, folds, différance

Metaphorical 'bags of mail' – the passengers of Flight 29, the flight itself and the future they briefly arrive into – indicate also the textual density and complexity of 'The Langoliers'. Brian Engle's dream, a message from the unconscious to be deciphered, suggests that the 'crack', the 'fold' and the 'differential' will saturate King's narrative with potential meanings. Engle's dream 'crack' figures the 'rip' in time through which the airplane has travelled. This 'crack' also represents division and the temporal and social in-between-ness or disconnection consequent upon it. The 'crack' and the 'fold' are dream-figures of metonymic correspondence and of the time-rip itself, the 'crack' into which the characters and their airplane are 'folded' like a missive by the narrative. This space of enfoldment is inaugurated in the scream of Dinah, the blind girl who awakens first, the sound of a vocalised rip to which the other characters awaken, an audible 'crack' that disrupts sleep and invokes the fragmentation and disorder of temporal displacement: 'But the scream went on, ripping across the air, darkening as it came, and everything began to break up' (*FPM*, 34). The scream is an auditory echo and a prefiguring, an echo of the 'event' that prefigures the disappearance of reality into 'senseless chunks of emptiness' (*FPM*, 242) with the arrival of the Langoliers. It reverberates symbolically back and forth across the times that the narrative relates. The narrative space opened up by this auditory 'crack' figures the threat and the strangeness of Gothic time, in which the irrational holds sway. On hearing this scream, Brian 'felt his entire structure of organised thought begin to slide slowly toward some dark abyss' (*FPM*, 57). In this moment the un-canniness of the narrative situation is established. It is a moment of multiple significance: the moment of a belated intellectual appre-hension of an uncanny event that has always already repeatedly taken place, in the unconscious (Brian's dream of the 'crack' in the airplane fuselage), in Craig Toomy's childhood fears of the Langoliers and, within the narrative's own temporal structure, while the passengers slept. It is also a moment yet to come, in the future repetition of the act of flying through the time-rip for a second time. Gothic time is thus predicated within, between and belonging both to an always-already-preceding singularity and to a yet-to-come repetition.

Cracks, rips and folds indicate how the text codes its vision of the erasure of the world of the past as a kind of text awaiting in-scription and decoding. In devouring the remainders of history the Langoliers leave 'a world of scrawled black lines' (*FPM*, 242), as if time were a tabula rasa on to which the destruction of the past is inscribed, leaving not a text but the blank, black nothingness of unbeing, an uncanny reversal of writing's calling into being of the non-existent. The actions of the 'Langoliers' are analogous to (but reverse) that of the writer. Where writing fixes the luminosity of experience into a text of 'scrawled black lines', their 'rolling up' of 'narrow strips of the world' (*FPM*, 239) imitates Mr Toomy's habitual tearing of strips of paper as an act of destruction, a further 'ripping' of time and text: 'The strips reminded him of Craig Toomy: *Rii-ip*' (*FPM*, 246–7). Strips and rips, paper and black lines mirror each other as ground and figure or figure and ground, comprising a metaphor of writerly creativity re-imagined momentarily in the temporal logic of 'The Langoliers' as utter destruction. The un-canniness of Gothic time is an effect of and is made effective in an image of inscription in which 'the timekeepers of eternity' (*FPM*, 243) record their annihilation of the remainders of time. Time itself is implicit in these strips, which echo the 'time-rip' that dislocates the characters from one time-stream or time-frame to another. The 'time-rip' opens furthermore the space of the impossibility of being, the non-being of the contemporary. Bob Jenkins, perceiving their impending return to the present from the future into which their second entry to the time-rip transports them, cries 'Quickly! [. . .] We can't be here. It's going to happen soon – at any moment, I believe – and we can't be here when it does' (*FPM*, 295). He expresses the coded truth of the mobile, destabilising anachronisms of Gothic time, which disallow the possibility of 'being' or of presence, rendering instead a world of prohibited being, of unbeing comprehensible only through injunction and belief. From this world the characters can rejoin the symbolic world of the present and of presence only through the uncanniness of repetition, entering into 'the moving present' as it 'locks on to the stationary future' (*FPM*, 297).

In 'The Langoliers', then, temporal linearity is absolute but bi-zarrely confused. The present slides along the scale from past to future, along the chain of *différance* that presents itself precisely as the condition of both temporisation and spacing. This *différance*, a condensation of the 'differentials' noted earlier, is integral to the plot of 'The Langoliers'. In the future, at the end of the narrative, one character realises this: '"Something's different," Albert said suddenly. [. . .] "Something's changed. I can't tell what it is . . . but it's not the same"' (*FPM*, 289). The narrator glosses this, echoing Brian's failure to 'grasp' the name of the perfume, as 'Some essential difference which he could not quite grasp' (*FPM*, 289). Eventually this difference is revealed, bizarrely, to be *sameness*: 'I know what's different! Look at the plane! *Now it's the same as all the others!*', cries Albert (*FPM*, 292; italics in original). Returning to the present involves re-encountering the temporal and sensory sameness that has eluded the narrative, a sameness that re-establishes a strange kind of conformity with which, in these closing pages, the survivors rush to catch up. Difference, at the narrative's end, is difference from the difference of the decaying past, the difference of a contemporary time in which '*the same*' marks differentiation.

A temporal comprehension of this 'difference' resides in the sliding, differential time-frames of 'The Langoliers', suggesting its connection to *différance* as 'the temporal and temporalising mediation of a detour' which is also 'a temporalisation and spacing, [...] space's becoming-temporal and time's becoming-spatial'.[33] The difficulty of 'telling' or 'grasping' the 'essential difference' of the contemporary that Albert perceives is precisely what ultimately concerns the text. King's narrative seeks ways of addressing a series of questions that confront the contemporary Gothic writer. These include how the Gothic text might convey, within the tenses and temporalities of language and narrative, its sense of time's difference from itself and the time of that difference, as well as the kinds of spacings – social, subjective, perceptual – that these differences imply, the weirdness of anachronism, the strange imminence of that which survives and lives beyond and outside its time and which yet threatens, in the future, to return. What might be the 'essential difference' between past and future within the mobile experience of the present and of 'presence' (with all the spectral undertones that word carries)? How might the present be presented within this differentiation, and how might it differ in turn from what precedes and succeeds it? And, ultimately, what are the political implications of the possibility of Gothic time, of imagining Gothic temporality?

The ghost of Democracy to Come

The recurrent figure of this final political question of the social implications of Gothic time, a figure again asserting the primacy of Gothic over science fiction codes in King's writing, is the ghost. 'The future can only be for ghosts. And the past', asserts Derrida.[34] The ghostly world of 'The Langoliers' offers a past made 'present' – represented – in the act of its writing, but, within that writing, always already in the condition of fading away into nothingness. But it is the characters in 'The Langoliers', rather than this world, who are (like Wells's Time Traveller) the ghosts, anachronistic but possibly divine, at least angelic – as the novella's imagery insists – trespassers from the present, both belated and tardy, messengers and messages of an apocalyptic vision of utter destruction bringing with them human strife, social disorder and murder. Ghosts and angels interchange throughout 'The Langoliers'. Dinah, in the light from the windows, appears 'ghostlike and eerie' (*FPM*, 125), and Toomy, humming to himself a line from a Nina Simone song, 'Just call me angel . . . of the *morn*-ing, *ba*-by' (*FPM*, 193), sees her as an 'Angel', 'like the ghosts in the story about Mr Scrooge' (*FPM*, 234). 'Are you an Angel?' he asks her, in the last stages of his hallucinatory insanity – '*Yes*, the glowing girl replied' (*FPM*, 231; italics in original).

As an 'Angel' she doubles Brian Engle (*Engel* is the German word for angel), the airplane pilot and other, more instrumental salvation of the survivors. The group's re-emergence into the world of the present at the narrative's end is also a confirmation of their own return, initially appearing within a world of spectral presences (rather than presence), which itself solidifies from spectrality into a kind of reality: 'He saw a ghost-father leading two small ghost-children, and through them he could see more ghosts sitting in their chairs, reading transparent copies of *Cosmopolitan* and *Esquire* and *US News & World Report*' (*FPM*, 298). Brand-names and the act of reading thus characteristically signify the return to the symbolic contemporary world of media and mediation, of trade and commerce. The child who sees the survivors materialise calls them not 'ghosts' but 'New people!' (*FPM*, 298), misreading them by signifying their appearance as new. The child wrongly complains, 'But they weren't there *before*' (*FPM*, 299; italics in original) when 'there' is, of course, precisely where they *were*. Heralds (as everyone is) of survival from the past into the present, yet paradoxically *returning* to their *own* time, the survivors re-enter the world feeling 'reborn [. . .] new and fresh and unmarked by the world' (*FPM*, 300), that is, as tabulae rasae, blank pages awaiting the inscription of the 'scrawled black lines' of Gothic time. This 'Ghost-effect'[35] is a product of the excess of presence, the sensory intensity of the world to which they return, that the survivors re-discover after the sensory dullness of the past.

Gothic time is thus effected within a doubled, mirrored structure of temporal dislocation. The passengers become ghosts in relation to the temporality of a present which to them appears momentarily ghostly. The past into which they are displaced is a past of decay, persisting posthumously and temporarily. The persistent crisis within this past is furthermore always an economic crisis in time and of time. '*Time is short*', screams Toomy (*FPM*, 115; italics in original), and Brian thinks of trying to reason with a madman as 'time-consuming' (*FPM*, 159), a figure of all the processes of action, waste, delay, deferral and displacement both resisted and necessitated by their predicament. 'Consuming' time is what they are condemned to do by the narrative's logic, in their efforts to escape being consumed in that logic by time, in imitation of the Langoliers, who also consume time and the world of remainders left in its wake.

The anachronistic time of the past in 'The Langoliers' is balanced in a further doubling by the presence within it of '*our own time*' (*FPM*, 177; italics in original), contained in the airplane in which they are travelling. This raises within the novella's play on temporality and dislocation the urgent question of ownership: how can a group of people *own* time? Such a profoundly political question is explored through the text's aforementioned concern with self-sacrifice for the good of the group. It interrogates the demand of democracy through more complex doublings, in which, in simple narrative logic, the saving of time is also the saving of the group, and concomitantly the expenditure of time is an expenditure implicitly of a member of the group (and therefore a threat to the constituency of the group). This logic of investment and sacrifice would be familiar to Toomy, the novella's figure of its dangers. The symbolic function of Dinah, blind and yet possessing by virtue of her telepathic 'sixth sense' insights that far exceed the ethical horizons of the other characters, is crucial here. At the point where Craig Toomy tries to kill her, she angelically embraces him in an act of selflessness: 'She looked up from her darkness and into his, and now she held her arms out, as if to enfold and comfort him' (*FPM*, 181). In this act (echoing the 'folding' of which Brian Engle dreams) Dinah momentarily becomes the 'Angel' that Toomy perceives her as. She offers herself as part of a double sacrifice (Toomy is the other part), guaranteeing the survival of the group. In doing so, she becomes the message that she has already envisioned. Her self-sacrifice reveals the contents of '*L'Envoi*', of that which has been sent. Dinah's understanding of the necessity of Toomy is also her awareness of her own role within the novella's symbolic economy. She recognises the transactional significance of him, his name and his narrative function within the logic of sacrifice that group survival demands.

Toomy's name is not only redolent of the tomb; it implies also his own symbolic role within the social economy that 'The Langoliers' counterpoints with its dislocated temporal economy: he is too much of the 'me' and the 'my', the 'me too', rather than the 'we' and the 'our', the social identity which, in the novella's nascent group ideology, is what is demanded by circumstances. Brian makes the correct linguistic and ideological amendment when Nick asks him 'What now, Captain?' His self-correcting reply, 'You tell me. Us' (*FPM*, 115), momentarily but decisively shifts the emphasis from the needs and position of the individual to those of the group (a group, furthermore, encoding its own symbolic value as a metonymy, despite Nick's presence, of the US). Nick's response to Toomy's stabbing of Dinah expresses the ambivalent liberal position between these extremes. Typically unethical, as might befit a character whose symbolic power resides outside US jurisdiction (Nick is an agent of 'Her Majesty' with a past record of questionable political and military actions, which ironically qualifies him as a 'hero' (*FPM*, 58)), it nevertheless cements the link between the economies of time and sacrifice. 'I almost hope she's dead, God help me. It will save time if she is' (*FPM*, 186), he argues, implying the necessary trade-off between individual death and increased chances of group survival, a balancing of accounts that structures the novella. He redresses this by his own self-sacrifice, becoming 'Nick, who had died so the rest of them *could* be here' (*FPM*, 294; italics in original). Dinah recognises that their 'need' for Toomy outweighs any desire for retribution for his murdering her. She also acknowledges the need for her own death, and foresees the need to sacrifice Toomy as a distraction for the first Langoliers, thus enabling Flight 29 to take off and saving the rest of the group. A logic of exchange – a stabbing for a sacrifice, an ethical retribution for group survival – is thus established within the atemporal world of the novella, a logic balanced by the need for a further, selfless, willing sacrifice, that of the Englishman Nick, signifier of old Empire values and ethics, to allow a symbolic seven American survivors to travel back through the time-rip into the present.

'The Langoliers', then, offers, amid all its temporal complexity and speculation, a Gothic parable of time running out, perhaps for a particular ideology, that of 1980s America. Its message is simple: group survival overrides and demands sacrifices from the individual. But this sits uneasily alongside its critique (through the figure of Toomy) of 1980s capitalism (with all its speculatory energy, its fragile basis on unstable fiscal futures and ideologically motivated socio-economic sacrifices of jobs, industries, histories and traditions) and its valorisation instead (through the actions of Dinah and Nick) of an old, genre-bound ethic of self-sacrifice, connected to ideologies of messianic evangelism and imperial power. It concerns the representation of a Gothic experience of time through metaphors of the postal system, sendings and returns, ghosts and angels, doublings and repetitions, and through these figures with a particular partially historicised experience of destinerrance which offers a fragmentary critique of Cold War apocalyptic visions. It represents the most sustained engagement in King's oeuvre with the *différance* of Gothic temporality and with the encoding of that *différance*, via echoes of and borrowings from *The Time Machine*, as a vision of Gothic time's fatal difference from itself. In this difference the Gothic text of the past persists as memory and representation, and, as material object, is shredded into nothingness by the Langoliers. The next chapter will extend this discussion of Gothic dimensionality, turning to the construction of place in King's writings and focusing on *The Shining* as its example text.

7

'This Inhuman Place': *King's Gothic Places*

જી

'Immense hydroptic hedges, trees which were never quite straight and each day succumb a fraction more to the damp, persistent winds; the gravel path is an old contessa, all pallor and cobwebs, moving among her hump-backed entourage here in the garden. [. . .]

The house has abandoned nurseries and sad kitchen maids, it cowers behind rusty ivy and the quiet tread of spiders; a child's face, pale and plump, presses against a high window.

Clearly, something interesting is about to happen.'[1]

Gothic place

Stephen King's Gothic is firmly located in specific topoi, landscapes and geographies rooted in authorial experience. Place is a dimension of his work that tends to encourage biographically focused criticism. His home state of Maine and fictionalised versions of many of its towns, shops, streets and institutions provide the settings for the bulk of his writing and act as defining features of his work. Critics were quick to latch on to the significance of this geographical dimension, as indicated by many of the titles of early critical works on King (*Landscape of Fear*, *The Gothic World of Stephen King*; and, punningly,

Kingdom of Fear:The World of Stephen King). In these settings, individual places assume deeper symbolic significance within the contexts of specific narratives. Places like the 'White House' in Chamberlain in *Carrie*, the town of Castle Rock in many narratives and Derry in *It* assert the importance of a Gothic sense of place to the effects achieved in King's works. In some cases, as scrutiny of pre-published drafts of novels reveals, place names and locations have changed in order to reinforce the biographical 'authority' of the text. The location of *Carrie*, for example, was moved from Massachusetts to Maine in response to a memo from King's then editor Bill Thompson.[2]

King's writings exploit the Gothic potentials of place in a variety of ways. In *It*, for example, a characteristic troping of place as allegory of internal, psychological conditions and traumas is clearly deployed. The next chapter will explore some aspects of this troping in relation to that novel's contribution to King's analysis of the monstrous other. But *It* points also to a key feature of King's uses of place, in which places both identify with and become identified with character and with groups of characters. King's Gothic adapts and extends a deliberate confusion of internal, character-psychological or group-dynamic features with external, spatial/topological features. Such confusion is structural to the Gothic genre's extension and complication of notions of sympathetic background. Place constitutes (as we will see) both a complex form or expression of otherness and a territory in which otherness may reside. It both contains and fails to contain otherness. King's analysis, in early novels like *Carrie* and *'Salem's Lot*, of the failure of social fabrics and of neighbourliness, and of the monstrosities of violence and anomie that lurk within them, is one aspect of this double effort and failure, an aspect that lends his strain of Gothic its particular social force and which locates place as its fulcrum.

Critics like Slavoj Žižek have noted this force. Using *The Shining*, on which this chapter will concentrate, to illustrate his discussion of theoretical constructions of the 'Neighbour' as other, and specifically of the Lacanian conception of the 'Thing' as 'the monstrosity of the Neighbour', Žižek writes:

> One should hear in this term [the Lacanian 'Thing'] all the connotations of horror fiction: the Neighbour is the (Evil) Thing which

potentially lurks beneath every homely human face, like the hero of Stephen King's *The Shining*, a gentle failed writer, who gradually turns into a killing beast and, with an evil grin, goes on to slaughter his entire family.[3]

While the theoretical gist of Žižek's argument may be useful and its exemplification in King's novel appropriate, his misreading of *The Shining* is remarkable. Not only does King's hero fail to 'slaughter his entire family', but he is hardly 'a gentle failed writer' either. Žižek is clearly drawing here not on King's novel, but on Fredric Jameson's more thoughtful observations on Kubrick's film version of *The Shining* (1979). Jameson writes, of Kubrick's Jack Torrance, played by Jack Nicholson, that he is 'someone who would like to *be* a writer' and that the film's narrative (not the novel) 'is the story of a failed writer' (italics in original).[4] King's writer, in contrast, has already experienced some success. Failure lies ahead of him and is, in fact, deeply linked to this novel's construction of the Gothic resonances of place in relation to narrative potential (its destination, as it were) and to the act of reading.

Desire and its failure within the structure of the nuclear family organise psychoanalytic readings of *The Shining*, but such readings tend to overlook or underplay the importance of place in the novel, constructing it as a simple variety of 'haunted house' tale. Hoppenstand and Browne argue, with some accuracy, that 'The Overlook Hotel [. . .] is but merely the vehicle' for the novel's analysis of family breakdown.[5] Nevertheless, they ignore how *The Shining* condenses a series of key tropes of place that recur throughout King's Gothic writing and which centre precisely on the topography of subjective surface and depth (that which 'potentially lurks beneath') that Žižek deploys. These tropes range from the uncanniness of place to its destructuring intervention in the establishment of subjectivity; from place as symbolic resonance to place as textualised repository (like the 'library' metaphor used to describe Sue Snell's mind as *Carrie* 'reads' it); and from place as potential escape to place as geographical restriction or constraint. The play of place as topos and language as *tropos* (or 'turn', the deviation of language from literal to figural meanings) also marks the narrative construction of place in Gothic ways. It always involves also subjective movements through or across place, a movement analogous to the reading eye scanning a page, leading inevitably to displacement, as topology demands accounting for in terms of troping. Place, in other words, is never merely place, never simply the setting for action. Like writing, it always signifies beyond itself. Part of that signification takes King's specific places away from their overt, biographically bound functions and into the tradition of Gothically inscribed places from which they take their origins.

King owes debts to the New England Gothic tradition, particularly Hawthorne and Lovecraft, in describing his landscapes. Many critics have enumerated these debts. Rebecca Janicker's careful reading of *Pet Sematary* relates that novel usefully to regionalist traditions of American writing, drawing on Allan Lloyd Smith's reading of American Gothic's historical differences from European Gothic traditions, constructing a text-world which, Janicker argues (*pace* Freud), is 'hauntingly familiar' and simultaneously 'utterly unknown'.[6] Janicker draws on work by Tony Magistrale, who also links *Pet Sematary* with American Gothic traditions, noting the similarities between what Louis Creed and Hawthorne's Young Goodman Brown 'uncover in the wilderness behind their respective communities'. For Magistrale, what is uncovered in the woods is 'a reflection of the self's essential darkness and the human affinity to sin'.[7] This is a version of the basic Gothic mechanism of place: human psychology is mirrored by environment, so that environment is invested with psychological depth and symbolic force (and mirroring, as we will see, is definitive of the functioning of place in King's Gothic). Place becomes a figure of self, a kind of reflection of an ego projected outside of itself into landscape. In a modernist twist on this mechanism, Angela Carter notes that 'Since Lovecraft's geography is that of dream, it has the uncanny precision of dream'.[8] The 'uncanny precision' achieved in King's texts depends, rather, on a more documentary form of realism than the surrealism of dream (projections of the ego rather than, as Carter implies, the id), but the effects are comparably unnerving. For example, *Bag of Bones* blurs the relation between dream and reality. The novel explores narrator Mike Noonan's experience of 'the peculiar cross-pollination between [his] dreams and things in the real world' (*BB*, 74–5). This is, for him, profoundly disconcerting and culminates in a loss of self which is also a loss of the self's place: 'I had lost my place in things and couldn't find it again' (*BB*, 75). At its strongest, in novels like *'Salem's Lot* (a text named after its central place, unlike most of King's novels), King's realism achieves through such 'cross-pollination' a powerful Gothic uncanny effect. It inscribes place as an arena into which the ego's desires are actively or otherwise displaced and within which they are disordered, (de)structured and redirected by conflicting dialectics of familiar and strange, internal and external, intrusive and extrusive.

Intrusion, a figure of violent or disruptive displacement, is a process central to an initial understanding of King's use of place, suggesting that if place is textualised in order to invite readerly scrutiny or interpretation, it also invites, in that textualisation, violent distortion or misreading. Figures like Leland Gaunt (in *Needful Things*) and Kurt Barlow (in *'Salem's Lot*) intrude destructively from indeterminately external non-places (geographically and historically distant, exotic, alien) into the spaces and lives of small-town America. These intrusions invert their familiar structures of secrecy and concealment (gossip, private affairs, domestic abuses and internal family conflicts offered as acceptable products of the *heimlich* dimensions of the home's privacy) and turn them into *unheimlich* threatened and threatening places. In *'Salem's Lot* the violent intrusion of Barlow into the Petrie family's domestic space, 'a totally illogical invasion' (*SL*, 393) that immediately results in the absolute and irreversible disruption of that family space as he murders Mark's parents, marks also a shift in the narrative, an irruption of the figural power of the Gothic into the family and its spaces. This intrusion figures in turn the novel's entire theme. Its force echoes throughout the oeuvre: a phrase from this scene, 'Then a shadow had moved in the kitchen' (*SL*, 393), might act as a metonymy for the basic construction of place in King's Gothic. When, early in *Misery*, Paul Sheldon understands Annie as 'a pair of fingers poking into his mouth' (*M*, 9), we understand, in a similar way and through an analogous metonymy, that this physical intrusion of one metonymised figure into another is also, in the novel's sexual politics, a violation of his body, an organism already metaphorised as a place, the metal pilings Paul remembers from his childhood visits to Revere Beach ('Revere' implies, perhaps, the repetition of dream or reverie, drawing suggestively on Carter's point about Lovecraftian landscapes). Paul's first question to Annie enquires of place: 'Where am I?' (*M*, 6), siting location as fundamental to his sense of self, but also implying the centrality to King's Gothic of the self's experience of displacement or misplacing as an intrusion.

Allegorical of body and mind and of their interrelations in spaces, place involves siting and locating Gothic events – placing them – in literal and metaphorical senses, giving the genre the geographical or architectural contexts within which Gothic effects become conventionally significant and generically familiar. 'You've been here before', announces the title of the prefatory and concluding sections of *Needful Things* (*NT*, 11). This allusion to the reader's experience of déjà vu indicates that the resonance of King's Gothicised places resides partly in their insistent, disturbing familiarity to a reader already 'placed' within the genre. It reconstructs the reader as rereader, already complicit in its meanings, already familiar (even *over*-familiar, in the logic of excess on which King's works rely) with the generic map and already structured by the self-conscious repetition of its revisiting and rereading (as in the returns and revisitings that structure the opening of *'Salem's Lot*). King's Gothic achieves other surface effects through its grounding in worlds and contexts reliant on the familiar, popular-cultural and consumer-society references and namechecks that constitute what Magistrale calls 'minute and accurate descriptions of American society', but which are, nevertheless, 'superficial landmarks'.[9]

The relationship between site and locale, between the specific point in space – a particular house, a specific street – and its immediate environment and between the sense of place as a text and its being read by the experienced reader, structures the resonances of place that the writings generate. 'You know the important features of its *mise en scène*', writes Eve Kosofsky Sedgwick of the Gothic, drawing like King in *Needful Things* on the reader's complicit familiarity with the genre: 'an oppressive ruin, a wild landscape, a Catholic or feudal society'.[10] These 'features' work internally: Marshall Brown emphasises the Gothic genre's attention to 'the human inside of things' rather than its 'flamboyant – but silly – externals', and later, inverting this equation, he notes of the Gothic of *Frankenstein* that it 'is *in* our world but not *of* it' (italics in original).[11] In Gothic, 'things' may be internally 'human' (and, implicitly, the 'human' may be a 'thing', or a Lacanian monstrous 'Thing'), while the world may contain that which is not of it. Gothic place mobilises such disturbing, dislocating inversions and involutions. Patterned and regularised into familiar unfamiliarities by Gothic generic conventions, place is closely connected with memory as a kind of repetition that acts, in the case of the house, through what Gaston Bachelard describes as 'a simple localisation of our memories'[12] in the (dis)figured space of the domestically familiar. It works alongside other Gothic tropes to evoke the uncanny persistence of the ostensibly absent past, rendering spatially the internal processes of memorisation and recall. In *Bag of Bones*, Mike Noonan (like Jack Torrance in *The Shining* a blocked writer who finds himself an inhabitant of a haunted house) articulates this Gothic sense of place: 'I think houses live their own lives along a time-stream that's different from the ones upon which their owners float, one that's slower. In a house, especially an old one, the past is closer' (*BB*, 88). Persistence here is also proximity, a confusion of 'time-streams' that deploys Gothically inflected place-as-difference in order to assert an effacement of another, historical, form of difference.

Place is, then, closely connected with contradictory experiences of intrusion and extrusion. Gothic place is familiar and unfamiliar, affording comfort and discomfort, welcome and hostility. It seduces and repulses in paradoxically equal measure. It is thus allegorical, as its functions are rarely simply geographical or architectural, but are instead symbolic, concrete manifestations of psychological, emotional, or other abstract levels of experience. In its connection with and containment of the intimate, the enclosed, the secreted (effects exploited powerfully by King), place effectively indicates the interpenetration in Gothic modes of inside and outside, of concealed psychological depths in human minds and their unfolding, their manifestation outside themselves in the worlds they perceive and create. It is thus indicative of Gothic's efforts to express cultural anxieties of mis-placed-ness, of abjection and evisceration (the inside becoming outside) or of penetration and intrusion (the outside becoming inside). Place resides within both outside and inside and on the borderlines between the two. Its familiar/unfamiliar, canny/uncanny double structure effects its dynamic symbolic function in the Gothic mode.

The Marsten House in *'Salem's Lot* exemplifies these processes and connects King's Gothic again to the genre's earliest texts. Anne Williams echoes many other critics when she asserts that 'The imposing house with a terrible secret is surely one – possibly *the* – "central" characteristic of the category "Gothic" in its early years' (italics in original).[13] In his discussion of the Gothic archetype of the 'Bad Place' in *Danse Macabre*, King locates the source of this particular symbolic place in his own childhood: 'a decrepit manse on the Deep Cut Road in my home town of Durham, Maine' (*DM*, 296). He links this place to his reading of an article on haunted houses and to the third influence on *'Salem's Lot*, his 'teaching Stoker's *Dracula*' (*DM*, 296–8), in order to frame his creation of 'the fictional Marsten House, which stands overlooking the little town of Jerusalem's Lot' (*DM*, 298). The counterpointing here of the 'Marsten House' with the verb 'overlooking', foreshadowing the hotel in *The Shining*, indicates the extent of the affinity between and functions of the two fictional places. In *'Salem's Lot* the house evokes the hotel's name: 'you could look right down into the town proper', Ben thinks (we will return to that word 'proper'), an action he then imitates: 'He put his hands on the hood of his car and looked out over the town' (*SL*, 20–1). The uncanniness of such a place seems to reside partly in its menacingly spectatorial rather than spectral agency, displaced here on to the protagonist's actions. Danny Torrance intimates just such uncanniness in the Overlook Hotel's 'seeming to stare at him with its many windows' (*S*, 272). A building can only 'look out' or 'overlook' anthropomorphically, suggesting rhetorical intrusions and transformations of the uncanny, a humanising of the inhuman, already structuring King's Gothic sense of place.

King nevertheless disavows the centrality of the 'Marsten House' to *'Salem's Lot*, confirming Williams's assertion that the haunted house may be 'both "central" and unnecessary to Gothic'. Williams points out that American Gothic traditions in particular exemplify this 'paradox' in their obvious dearth of aristocratic, historically ancient buildings.[14] 'Boston', Eddie Kaspbrak thinks in *It*, 'is a sprat compared with London, an infant compared with Rome, but by American standards at least it is old, old' (*It*, 291). But *It* (if we exclude the 'house on Niebolt Street', a weak version of the motif (*It*, 365ff.)) lacks a haunted house in either Boston or Derry to concentrate this agedness. The novel relies instead on tropes of surface and depth, associating Gothic monstrosity with whatever lurks persistently in the sewers and tunnels beneath the town's surface, intruding from there into the banality of Derry life and ultimately locating its horror (as we will see) in a conventional, weakly Gothic construction of the monstrous-feminine. In a similar way King emphasises in *Danse Macabre* that *'Salem's Lot'* is a book about vampires, not hauntings'; the Marsten House is, he argues, 'really only a curlicue, the gothic equivalent of an appendix' (*DM*, 298). Yet we have seen how the novel draws heavily on textual 'hauntings' (internal and external) by Shirley Jackson's book, as well as by *Dracula* and other resources in the traditions of vampire literature, so that it is possible to read *'Salem's Lot* itself as an 'appendix' to an American(ised) Gothic tradition that Jackson's novel, for one, exemplifies. King's invocation, in arguing the secondary status of the Gothic house, of a logic of supplementarity, suggests the 'Bad Place' is both secondary to and equally central to the text. The action of *'Salem's Lot* depends upon the house, but the house is peripheral to its action, a mere adjunct. As 'curlicue' or 'appendix', the Marsten House is both an ornamental addition and a necessary supplement to the traditions of vampire narratives and haunted house tales into which King's novel inserts itself (perhaps as another 'curlicue', another supplement). It is a necessary element of the novel's textuality, its written-ness, establishing *'Salem's Lot* and its sense of place within the inscribed conventions of the Gothic genre.

The word 'curlicue' introduces another dimension to this supplementary logic, however. A curlicue is, the dictionary tells us, 'a fantastic curl or twist', alluding to a writerly or architectural flourish often consists of spirals or concentric circles. '*Nothing fancy. No curlicues. Right?*' Paul Sheldon admonishes himself over the writing of *Misery's Return* in *Misery* (*M*, 225; italics in original). In writing and in architecture a curlicue is a redundant flourish, an inscribed ornamentation added to but not essential to the building or the inscription it decorates. The metaphor links writing and the uncanniness of place, asserting in this double function the significance of place as a product of inscription within King's works. King's description of the 'Marsten House' links that place to the materiality of writing (a 'flourish' implicit too in his textualising description of the house as an 'appendix') and to another of his 'Bad Places', the double locale that structures *Pet Sematary*. Here, the 'Pet Sematary', comprised of concentric circles of graves indicating simple, childishly regressive historical movement, doubles the Micmac burial ground, itself 'just like the Pet Sematary' (*PS*, 327), configured like an inscription on the uncannily flat, page-like landscape. Louis sees 'some weird, flat-topped mesa, a geological anomaly', its 'flatness' 'so odd in the context of New England's low and somehow tired hills'. Later, he describes 'a gigantic spiral, made by what the oldtimers would have called Various Hands' (*PS*, 118, 327). The spiral form of the burial ground situates it outside the semi-official history of pet mortalities signified by the Pet Sematary's concentricity. It is, in contrast, a place belonging to prehistory ('the place is old', Jud warns Louis (*PS*, 121)). The key uncanny places of *Pet Sematary* are giant circles and spirals, 'curlicues' inscribed into the landscape of the novel's setting and yet marginal to the novel's apparent location within the stream of King's characteristic invocations of modern history as narrative, the history narrated with relentless sequentiality by Jud Crandall. They establish an uncanny and anonymous writing, an inscription of place, at the centre of the novel's Gothic events. As Jodey Castricano has argued, *Pet Sematary* offers a coded discourse on 'the remains' not only of Louis Creed's family, but also of the historical import of 'the Micmac Indian tribe' (*PS*, 10) and their burial practices, traces of which are marginal to and yet uncannily structure the novel's action and its geography.[15] Place is written into texts like *Pet Sematary* as an expression of and product of writing itself, at once supplementary to and fundamental to the Gothic logic of the specific text.

Inhuman place

'*This inhuman place makes human monsters*' (*S*, 137, 186; italics in original). The reiterated present-tense refrain of *The Shining* (1977), heard but not understood by Danny Torrance, the telepathic child of this novel, indicates the importance of place in King's Gothic writing. The play of 'inhuman–human' and the repeated placing and displacing of the human within that relationship express a complex comprehension of place in relation to the human, offering one entrance into *The Shining*'s analysis of Gothic place. This analysis is dependent on a kind of delayed decoding, as Danny's interpretations of his paranormal (and normal) perceptions gradually develop in complexity and accuracy as the novel progresses. Understood as a specific form of context containing and making manifest the traces and effects of time, place acts verbally on (and thus locates) the human. In opening the space of the human to its effects, place transforms what it means to be human. In doing so it becomes uncanny, a version of the 'inhuman'. It becomes both not-human (outside of human bounds) and literally 'in-human', located 'within' the human. It 'makes' the human, creating in its externalising effects the subject's sense of itself *as* subject. This self-reflexiveness implies a distancing of the self from itself in the moment of self-recognition, symbolised in the psychoanalytic concept of the mirror stage, the moment of the child's misrecognition of its mirror image as itself. It inscribes human subjectivity with a particular kind of uncanny geometry, rendering textually and historically the notion of the 'inhuman' as something residing uncannily within the space of the 'human' and within the persistence of a conception of 'human'. It also 'makes' the human monstrous. '*It's the inhuman monsters that I fear*' (*S*, 214; italics in original), as one of the novel's disembodied, ghostly voices puts it. Itself a manifestation of the monstrously inhuman persistence of the past within the hotel's Gothic echo-chamber, this voice expresses the self's fear of a hidden, threatening place within itself.

Place engages furthermore in the act of 'making' 'human monsters'. It has an effect upon the people who encounter it which is both formative and deforming, integral to the manifold processes of becoming-monstrous that concern King's Gothic. In *Pet Sematary* Louis is drawn to the Micmac burial ground: 'It's an evil, curdled place', Jud warns him; 'It has a power' (*PS*, 243). In King's Gothic, place is an aspect or a face of the 'inhuman'. In its most powerful forms it works to transform the 'human' into the 'monstrous' ('curdled' implying the horror that is 'blood-curdling', resituating place and its uncanny effects within the symbolic body). In relation to place the inhuman is a product of transformation, a consequence of a 'making', a process on the other side of a becoming-inhuman. Place, like writing, exerts 'power', constituting a textualised emanation of the powers of history, a spatialisation of historical force, a 'curlicue' bound to power as it interacts with the potentially uncontrolled and dangerous energies of human desire. In a novel like *The Shining* place is a particular kind of desiring-machine. The novel's figure for the destructive potential of that desire is not a flying saucer buried in a forest, but an ancient boiler hidden in a hotel basement. The 'inhuman', a product of the effects of particular kinds of place, is also the result of the 'becoming-monstrous' driven by this machine. The deformations of desire in *The Shining* relocate the inhuman within the human via processes of reading and writing, asking questions of how Gothic interprets place, and how Gothic belongs to its sense of place.

Jean-François Lyotard's discussion of the relations between human and inhuman in terms of belonging and the notion of the 'proper' offers some leverage on the functions of the 'inhuman' in *The Shining*. Lyotard asks, 'What if what is "proper" to humankind were to be inhabited by the inhuman?'[16] This is a form of the central question of *The Shining* and of Gothic more generally. The uncanny, residing within the homely or familiar – the family, the father, the son, the domestic space – belongs within this space and simultaneously subverts it, subtly altering its dimensions. Lyotard's 'inhuman' is furthermore predicated on the condition and effects of what he calls 'writing at a distance', a condition which fundamentally calls into question humanity's relation to a broadly conceived technology.[17] Technology, Lyotard suggests, will enable survival, but what survives will no longer be human. The distanced communication facilitated by the telegraph (as a metonymy of modernity's transformations of communications) refracts the temporal extension of life, so that technology (including technologies of writing, which Lyotard refers to as 'telegraphy') changes what constitutes life, what it means to be *human*, by inserting into the paradigm of humanity such *inhuman* extensions.

The cohabitation of the human and the inhuman within the same temporality (but distanced from each other, delayed) affords a powerful metaphor for the functions of the monstrous in King's Gothic. Clearly, the recurrent trope of telepathy (discussed above in chapter 2, and developed in *The Shining* as the titular theme of the novel) enacts a version of Lyotard's 'writing at a distance' and constitutes a figure for how inhuman qualities reside within and transform the human. Telepathy situates the uncanny firmly within the human mind but constitutes an excess to the mind's actions and to its knowledge, a communicative reaching-out beyond the scope of conventional communication media. It invites forms of knowledge of the other and the self inaccessible to conventional media. In telepathy the inhuman can be known: 'There is uncanny knowledge', as Nicholas Royle puts it, a knowledge central to telepathy, as it is, Royle argues, to narrative fiction in general.[18] The problem of *The Shining* centres on the processes of reading and interpretation through which this knowledge may come to be understood, processes connected in the novel's language to the Gothic functions of place.

Bad place

King's discussion of what he calls 'the Bad Place' (*DM*, 296ff.) draws heavily on the Freudian uncanny, locating the 'Bad Place' initially within the confines of the familiar domestic space signalled by the house, a domestic space transformed into a 'Bad Place'. He introduces the uncanny sense of the confusion of interior and exterior when he writes in this passage of horror fiction's 'cold touch in the midst of the familiar' (*DM*, 299). He elaborates this intrusive uncanny sense by turning to history, arguing that 'the truest definition of a haunted house would be "a house with an unsavoury history"' (*DM*, 300). 'History' here stands for that which intrudes from the external, excluded world of the social into the private, domestic space implied by the house. It also implies that which persists, intruding into the present from beyond the temporal boundaries of its own proper time. This specific sense of history as localised, confined to geographically and architecturally limited spaces and seemingly disconnected from a wider social sense of shared, public history because the house implies familial rather than wider social groupings, is key to King's conception in *Danse Macabre* of the 'Bad Place' archetype and to his inflection of the rhetoric of place with that of temporality. 'The past', he argues, identifying another unwarranted intrusion characteristic of the uncanny, '*is* a ghost which haunts our present lives constantly' (*DM*, 298; italics in original). The potentially conflicting tenses of this sentence gesture towards the difficulty of articulating a Gothic sense of place as something separate from time. In Gothic writing, place is usually imbued with the extra dimension of the temporal. It is simultaneously residue and repository, record and repetition of past moments. It expresses Gothic's awareness of the uncanny persistence of the traces and effects of history. As King puts it: 'The haunted house tale demands a historical context' (*DM*, 300). This 'context', however, is resisted by the mythology of the house on which King's description relies. History is not so much 'context' as that which intrudes into and deforms the domestic space of the house, turning the (implicitly 'Good') place into the 'Bad Place'.

History's intrusion into the present in Gothic writing is a version of the intrusion of the inhuman into the space of the human. The interiority into which the historical moves is revealed as illusory, a mythical effect of representation. Mark Wigley, glossing Derridean deployments of the figure of the house, argues that, 'The sense of interior is actually an effect of representation. It is produced by what it supposedly excludes'. Wigley glosses this sense via Freud's uncanny:

> In this structural slippage from *heimliche* to *unheimliche* that which supposedly lies outside the familiar comfort of the home turns out to be inhabiting it all along, surfacing only in a return of the repressed as a foreign element that strangely seems to belong in the very domain that renders it foreign.[19]

This doubling inversion characterises King's versions of the uncanny domestic place, connecting them to the dynamic of human–inhuman. For King's Gothic, human (and inhuman) inhabitings of place inculcate the drive to monstrous inhumanity, opening the space of the human to the intrusions of the (repressed and returning) monstrous, turning the human itself into a kind of place. In *The Shining*, Jack's atavistic regression to alcoholic psychopath effects the return of the excluded or repressed past within the family triangle. His volatile, fragile mind is, furthermore, figured in the novel through a variety of initially *heimlich* spaces that become increasingly *unheimlich* and yet reside relentlessly *within* the ostensibly familiar, public-cum-domestic, spaces established in the novel. Such internalised external spaces (hotel bedrooms, the wasps' nest placed in Danny's room and the boiler room) enact the involution of Gothic place, its internalisation within the psyche and the damaging consequences of this improper resituation *within* of that which should be *without*. The uncanny space becomes in this process a new form of property, a reworking that links Gothic space to anxieties of ownership and property-dispossession (the Torrance family move to the Overlook in part because Jack needs the work and the money) and to the notion in *'Salem's Lot* and elsewhere in the Castle Rock novels of 'the town proper'. But in 'making human monsters', the hotel and the novel enact another kind of transformation, a double movement invited in the phrase's ambiguity: human monsters are made/humans are made monsters. *The Shining* enacts in form and content the 'proper' condition of humanity as a dramatic impropriety, its 'proper' condition transformed into its improper inhabiting by the inhuman, or its becoming the property of – possessed by – the inhumanly monstrous.

Placing and playing in The Shining

The Shining relates the incidents befalling a family wintering out in an isolated and haunted resort hotel. The Torrance family, fatally fractured (like Danny's arm, broken by his father in a drunken rage) by paternal violence and alcoholism, apparently fall victim to the hotel's resident spirits. Its history, a condensed, selective version of post-war American histories of wealth and corruption, scandal and destruction, partly pieced together by Jack, reawakens in response to the telepathic abilities of five-year-old Danny Torrance and to the desires of aspiring playwright Jack Torrance. The family name implies 'torrents', 'torrid', 'trance', 'rants', all terms that resonate with the novel's action. Gothic criticism is, furthermore, haunted by this novel's rhetoric: Fred Botting writes of the critic of Gothic as 'a forensic examiner of the excluded, but no less significant, patterns in which meanings are produced, circulated and, even, *overlooked*', and goes on immediately to discuss 'The *torrent* of criticism defining, extending and celebrating Gothic fiction and film' (my italics).[20] Such unconscious wordplay is available to any careful reading of *The Shining*, confirming that the surface meanings of this text are worked by subterranean forces, just as the hotel is animated by the buried desires of the ghosts of its dead inhabitants.

The intentions and failings of writing are both the absent centre and another crucial engine or driving force of this text. A short sequence in the novel, just after Danny returns, unaccountably injured, from Room 217, exemplifies the textual playfulness offered by writing's centrality to the novel. Jack's play, '*The Little School*', with which he struggles and which he inevitably fails to complete, symbolises the kinds of transformations with which the novel is concerned: 'He had begun with one play and it had somehow turned into another, presto-chango' (*S*, 243), 'another' in which, in a mirror-like inversion of the plot of *The Shining*, Jack finds himself writing of 'this monster masquerading as a boy' (*S*, 243). As Jack ponders his doomed play he's forced also to address Danny's catatonic seizure: he 'wondered if it hadn't been a piece of play-acting' (*S*, 244). Wendy's anxiety about Danny is extensive: 'I worry when he goes out to play', she tells Jack (*S*, 245). Anxious that Danny has been assaulted by someone unknown intruding into the hotel, she attacks Jack, not for wasting time writing, but for *reading*: 'And you . . . you're sitting there reading your *play*!' (*S*, 244; italics in original).

The interplay between nominal and verbal meanings of 'play' indicates how the novel addresses and perverts issues of playfulness, particularly in the relation between father and son. Jack's (un)written play is a figure not so much of his writerly creativity or power (its plot ramifications baffle him, its characters are undeveloped, it peters out into irresolution: from the novel's outset this is a doomed drama, like the family drama *The Shining* enacts), but of the hotel's desire to 'play' with him and his family. 'Play', in all its rhetorical complexity, is central to the novel which becomes through this verbal play a veritable Gothic playground. Danny, asked early on by his mother whether he wants to spend the winter in the hotel, replies 'Nobody much to play with around here' (*S*, 19). Jack, deploying lay psycho-analysis to explain Danny's condition to Wendy, reassures her: 'Games, little games. Conscious on one side of the net, subconscious on the other' (*S*, 248). The Overlook even features a *mise en abyme* of itself, a model hotel in a 'playground', 'a playhouse that was an exact replica of the Overlook itself' (*S*, 69), later described as 'the play-Overlook' (*S*, 267). 'Playhouse' ambiguously implies both a toy house and a setting for a performance, perhaps of the novel's deeper drama, the text that remains unwritten by Jack but is instead scripted in the hotel's history and inscribed in the documents that fill its basement, but which he is unable to read properly as an account (textually comprised of 'ledgers' and 'invoices' (*S*, 146)) that will demand both telling and settling.

This account initiates another play on words, instigating a potential narrative, the hotel's biography, which relies on Jack's 'shining' (*S*, 146) his flashlight on the boxes that contain it in order to expose and set in motion its own desiring machine. In the documents Jack reads the hotel is 'this shining, glowing Overlook' for which 'The future lay ahead, clean and shining' (*S*, 148), a hotel built on land funded by a company called 'Colorado Sunshine, Inc.' (*S*, 151). *The Shining* here asserts in reiterating its own name its own unconscious, inserting itself into its narratives for Jack to read and, simultaneously, to fail to read. *His* unconscious insists instead on taking the shine off such a potential future through insistent recollections of phrases from Poe's 'The Masque of the Red Death' (*S*, 148), itself 'a gay and magnificent revel' of playful denial that inserts another Gothic reading, overlooking the reading of the history of the Overlook.[21] In this extended wordplay text becomes performance, a Gothic manifestation and playscript becomes scripted Gothic melodrama, a Poe-esque playing to the death, a fatal toying-with.

Play is indeed integral to the text's reliance on the play of signs and significations as encodings of its overt significances. It implies a perverted *jouissance*, or verbal playfulness, evident in *The Shining*'s textual play on its own name and on the word 'play' (a play picked up on by Kubrick's famous, infinitely repeated, 'All work and no play makes Jack a dull boy'). These significances are excessively perceptible but virtually meaningless to Danny, who can perceive the signs – 'NO SWIMMING. DANGER! LIVE WIRES' and, importantly, 'THIS PROPERTY CONDEMNED', alongside the recurrent and baffling 'REDRUM' (*S*, 35; emphases in original) – but can't fully read or understand them. Danny's learning to read, and his learning to interpret the signs the hotel presents to him (as well as the language of traumatised adulthood that echoes in the minds, if not the speech, of his parents) is one way in which King emphasises the necessity of reading in, and learning how to read, such a Gothic place. Place, *The Shining* implies, is a product of a specific readerly sensitivity, an alertness to the Gothic semiotics of space as features ('landmarks', in Magistrale's word) to be read. The novel offers a remarkable analysis of the ways in which a Gothic comprehension of place demands the coalescence of the geometries of space, subjectivity and textuality through the prevailing metaphor of a historically palimpsestic notion of haunting. This coalescence produces in turn the specifically Gothic dynamics of haunting characteristic of King's writings, a haunting which is textually rooted, generically conventional, traditionally located and formally structured by repetition and insistence. The palimpsest is a key image here. *The Shining*'s metaphor for a Gothically haunted sense of place is clearly palimpsestic, an image of overlaying textualised pasts and of overlooking their coexistence, enacting the narrative's definition of the haunted hotel: 'It was as if another Overlook now lay scant inches beyond this one, separated from the real world [. . .] but gradually coming into balance with it' (*S*, 319). This simile, reiterated through the novel, demonstrates the novel's Gothic conception of place as a textual product, the effect of a complex form of intertextuality.

This is evident most powerfully in the passage in the novel where the hotel seems to 'come to life', a passage worthy of quoting at length:

He could almost hear the self-important *ding! ding!* of the silver-plated bell on the registration desk, summoning bellboys to the front as men in the fashionable flannels of the 1920s checked in and men in fashionable 1940s double-breasted pinstripes checked out. There would be three nuns sitting in front of the fireplace as they waited for the check-out line to thin, and standing behind them, nattily dressed with diamond stick-pins holding their blue-and-white figured ties, Charles Grondin and Vito Gienelli discussed profit and loss, life and death. There was [*sic*] a dozen trucks in the loading bays out back, some laid one over the other like bad time exposures. In the east wing ballroom a dozen different business conventions were going on at the same time within temporal centimetres of each other. There was a costume ball going on. There were soirées, wedding receptions, birthday and anniversary parties. Men talked about Neville Chamberlain and the Archduke of Austria. Music. Laughter. Drunkenness. Hysteria. Little love, not here, but a steady undercurrent of sensuousness. And he could almost hear all of them together, drifting through the hotel and making a graceful cacophony. In the dining room where he stood,

breakfast, lunch and dinner for seventy years were all being served
simultaneously behind him. He could almost . . . no, strike the *almost*.
He *could* hear them, faintly as yet, but clearly – the way one can hear
thunder miles off on a hot summer's day. (*S*, 320; italics in original)

This remarkable passage demonstrates King's debts to modernism.
Not coincidentally, its theme – the palimpsestic co-presence of the
various moments of the hotel's history – is mimicked formally in
the writing's reliance on the great palimpsestic text to which King
frequently refers, T. S. Eliot's *The Waste Land*. Later in *The Shining*,
King alludes to *The Waste Land* while citing the conclusion of
Frank Norris's *McTeague*: 'handcuffed to a dead man in the wasteland'
(*S*, 355). But here, as the hotel awakens, King offers a résumé of
echoes of Eliot's poem and of its fractured, faded grandeur and moral
emptiness in order to establish a textual provenance for the temporal
and spatial simultaneities of his own novel. The discussion of 'profit
and loss' echoes Eliot's Phlebas the Phoenician in 'Death by Water',
who, 'a fortnight dead, / Forgot [. . .] the profit and loss'. 'The
Archduke of Austria' echoes Eliot's narrator 'Marie', 'staying at the
arch-duke's / My cousin's'. 'Little love, not here, but an undercurrent
of sensuousness' might summarise the moral tone of Eliot's entire
poem; and the 'thunder' heard 'miles off on a hot summer's day'
reprises Eliot's 'What the Thunder Said'.[22] *The Shining* offers in such
passages and in its repeated allusions to other writings (most notably
'The Masque of the Red Death', which provides the longest of the
novel's epigraphs) its own self-reflexive textuality, its drawing on
literary tradition, as a version of its own palimpsestic vision of Gothic
place.

Reading the Overlook

The Shining centres, then, on characteristically Gothic questions of
writing. It interrogates what it means to belong to a textualised,
narrated history and what kinds of ownership (or possession) seek
to transcend or survive that history; how property, in such possession,
becomes improper, and possession fractures into forms of dispossession;
and how what is inherited, in Gothic fictions, is the textual residue

of the past, ghosts as 'pictures in a book' (*S*, 85) as Hallorann, himself telepathically gifted and a witness of these 'pictures', tells Danny. The past, as 'pictures in a book' which come alive, takes on an uncanny life that links this novel to the oldest Gothic conventions. As many critics have noted,[23] *The Shining* reworks *The Castle of Otranto* and its sense of Gothic place (Wendy jokes that eating in the Overlook Dining Room is 'like having dinner in the middle of a Horace Walpole novel' (*S*, 159)). What Clare Hanson describes as *The Shining's* 'complex and shifting meaning'[24] is structured in part around a series of unanswered and ultimately inconsequential questions: why does the hotel want Danny? Why are particular moments in its history re-enacted and not others? What is the symbolic force of these specific moments? What causes the hedge animals to come alive?

These questions both belong to and are marginal ('curlicues') to the novel's thematisation of Gothic concerns. What tends to disappear in critical readings of the novel is the hotel itself. Recent criticism, focusing on the novel's dubious sexual politics and the mechanisms of repression that (in a curious mixture of the self-conscious and the self-blind) it deploys, glosses the hotel in conventional ways. Valdine Clemens reads the hotel as 'the traditional Gothic symbol of a haunted past' which 'represents the failure of the American dream since World War II' and 'the failure of the original promise of the City on the Hill, the dream of America's Puritan forefathers'.[25] Linda J. Holland-Toll's Bakhtinian reading of the novel describes the Overlook as 'a *polyphonous* repository of the darker aspects of carnival' (italics in original),[26] while Strengell relates the Hotel to 'the ruined castle of Gothic literature with its labyrinthine corridors, forbidden rooms, rattling chains (in the elevator shaft), and ghosts'. In her reading, Jack 'succumbs to the evil spirit of the hotel, which works through him to get hold of Danny'.[27] She later echoes King's own description of the hotel as 'a kind of symbol of unexpiated sin', 'the house-as-psychic-battery' (*DM*, 298; Strengell writes that 'the haunted house is turned into a kind of symbol of unexpiated sin').[28]

Strengell, like most critics, offers little comment on the naming of the hotel. Joseph Grixti at least notes that 'its name and high position suggest that, like the similarly placed vampire mansion in *'Salem's Lot*, it too has spent many years looking down at all the "peccadilloes and sins and lies" of the people living beneath it'.[29]

Hanson, whose Freudian reading summarises much of significance in the novel, is more alert to the potentials of the hotel's name: 'We may never overcome these terrors; we may remain always "overlooked"', she argues of the novel's reliance on images of death.[30] Most critics note the connection between the material space of the hotel and the psychic space of Jack's mind. Steven Bruhm's persuasive account reads the hotel in relation to 'Gothic's long association with male homosexuality' and notes that 'the ghosts of the Overlook gradually invade and penetrate Jack's identity' in ways similar to Gothic's 'penetration' of conventional histories and discourses, returning us to the dynamic of intrusion that is central to King's Gothic conception of place.[31] External place is reified in such readings as the internalised place of psychological processes. Each becomes interchangeable with the other, so that Jack's disordered psyche mirrors the decadent, atemporal disorder of the manifestations in the hotel, which again reflects back to Jack his own desires and frustrations. This is the confusion of internality and externality central to the experience of Gothic place: dislocating, disorientating, disturbing.

The Overlook Hotel itself is a strangely indeterminate presence in *The Shining* and in its critics, a presence lacking in actual presence as if the novel and the tradition of readings it has inspired had overlooked its own central metaphor. The reader gets no full description of it, no writerly establishment shot (unlike Kubrick's film, which exploits to the full the uncanny potential of such shots). Danny's psychic powers preview the hotel only as 'Another shape, looming, rearing. Huge and rectangular' (*S*, 35), alongside the unidentified monster and unintelligible signs he repeatedly presages roaming its corridors. Seen for the first time by Wendy amid the literally breathtaking landscape of Colorado, the hotel is merely 'the hotel. The Overlook' (*S*, 64), named but unelaborated by any description ('no curlicues', again) that might elucidate details of form or style or indicate an architectural notation of menace. Glimpsed by Danny as they approach it, it offers only 'its massive bank of westward-looking windows reflecting back the sun' (*S*, 64). The hotel, mirror-like as its new inhabitants gaze at it, resists their gaze, offering itself as a non-place, inviting comparison with Michel Foucault's concept of a particular manifestation of place as a 'the utopia of the mirror', a 'placeless place', a reflection of real social space.[32] A 'placeless' mirror, the Overlook Hotel exists paradoxically in this novel of Gothic place as a non-place in which social and historical traces reside or are stored but also distorted, wrenched out of synch and relocated into alternative narratives of Gothic horror – 'pictures in a book' (*S*, 85), as Danny tries to make sense of his previsions. Botting, paraphrasing Foucault, argues that such a 'utopic' non-place is 'intermingled with a heterotopic form', different kinds of places in which conventional cultural values and structures are (in Gothic texts) inverted, distorted. In Gothic generic terms, 'mimesis finds itself distorted by the fanciful effects of romance'.[33] 'Distortion' is a way of comprehending the structures of projection (of the present on to the past, the absent on to the present) that Gothic exploits. In this reading, the Overlook offers a utopic mirror of the present of the novel, redefining that present by inserting intrusively into it its own historically stored horrors.

The lack of rhetorical elaboration of the hotel marks it as significant by default. In its apparent verbal anonymity it becomes a specific place demanding a specific kind of representation, the place of the uncanny: 'the dark and booming place where some hideous figure sought him down long corridors carpeted with jungle', as Danny tries to word his visions (*S*, 64). 'Some hideous figure' neatly describes the novel's confluence of the topological and the tropological in placing its Gothic place, figured through extended allegorical motifs like the wasps' nest Jack disturbs under the hotel's roof shingles (*S*, 101) or the figure of Tony, Danny's alter ego (a prevision of an older self, suggesting that selfhood itself is palimpsestic, constituted of temporally differentiated layers of simultaneous being). Another such figure can be found in Jack's memories of the childhood optical illusion that reveals the image of Christ's face, a 'jumble of whites and blacks, senseless and patternless' (*S*, 262), an unreadable sign that figures in its desperate symptomatology the loss of faith implicit in Jack's failed writing and in his failure to resolve into a coherent text the narratives that the hotel presents to him. Such recurrent figures establish the novel's conspicuous and self-consciously overt allegory. Each stands in turn for the central process of interpreting or reading the hotel as a kind of text, a task undertaken primarily by Danny.

The Shining, we might argue, is about the consequences of failing to read properly. Adults and children are equally culpable in this failure. Jack cannot read his own demise, Wendy 'had never been able to read [Jack] very well', whereas 'Danny could' (S, 181), but of course Danny cannot yet 'read' in the literal sense. Danny's learning to read (and to write: 'he could now write about three dozen words on his own' (S, 117)) is integral to the saving of his and his mother's lives. The moment at which this embedded allegory of reading surfaces in the novel's textuality is also the moment of a mirrored recognition and transformation, a moment of learning-to-read properly:

> The light was coming from the bathroom door, half-open. Just beyond it a hand gangled limply, blood dripping from the tips of the fingers. And in the medicine mirror, the word REDRUM flashing off and on.
> Suddenly a huge clock in a glass bowl materialised in front of it. There were no hands or numbers on the clockface, only a date written in red: DECEMBER 2. And then, eyes widening in horror, he saw the word REDRUM reflecting dimly from the glass dome, now reflected twice. And he saw that it spelled MURDER. (S, 286–7)

Leaving aside the dubious optics of this scene, it is clear that Danny's new reading skills motivate the novel's resolution. Steven Bruhm connects the repeated mirroring of the word 'REDRUM' to one of the novel's central uncanny conceits, Danny's telepathic apprehension of it, experienced as a reversal: "MURDER' on the mirror of his unconscious'.[34] No one in the novel has so far decoded RED-RUM, 'that indecipherable word' which, the novel tells us, Danny 'had seen in his spirit's mirror' (S, 37), not even the child psychologist Edmonds to whom Danny is taken after his early seizure. Danny's parents, baffled by it, also cannot explain the words 'the shining': 'Doesn't matter', says Edmonds, incorrectly, neatly embedding King's critique of psychology (S, 144). REDRUM mirrors MURDER, the unreadable mirroring the unthinkable, establishing mirroring at the novel's unstable centre and affording a mechanism to think the relation between 'inhuman place' and 'human monsters'. Danny's mind, in which the mirroring is prefigured, becomes the space in which decoding and interpretation constantly take place. The novel's figure for this privileging of the child's mind (again, a central trope in King's Gothic mythology of innocence) centres on another kind of reading, remembering. Danny triumphantly remembers 'What his father had forgotten' (*S*, 400), the hotel's boiler, overheating and approaching explosive potential, an apt metaphor of the pent-up tensions and repressions that constitute and motivate Jack's transformation into 'inhuman monster'. The narrative conceit of the son remembering what the father has forgotten locates *The Shining* within the Gothic tradition of narratives of inherited legacies and their uncanny returns. But the novel's figures for this revolve around 'inhuman' or prosthetic technologies of reading, from Jack's reading of the hotel's history to Danny's learning to read books and minds and Hallorann's reading of Danny's thoughts. In this sense, *The Shining* mobilises a Gothic sense of place in order to construct an extended allegory of how to learn to read Gothic tropes.

Tropes, topiary

This emphasis on the reading of Gothic tropes is most clearly evident in the function of the ornamental hedge animals, particular kinds of 'curlicue' and therefore of place within the novel's action and agents of some of the novel's most uncanny moments. The hedge animals are first encountered after the discussion of the game of American croquet or 'roque', a word to do with 'play' which Danny cannot read but misunderstands as a *place*. The animals are very specifically located during the family's first tour of the hotel: 'Beyond the path leading to *roque* there were hedges clipped into the shapes of various animals' (*S*, 68; italics in original). Wendy names this place for Danny: 'That's called a topiary' (*S*, 68). The topiary, an unfamiliar word italicised by Danny's point of view, leads in turn to another beyond ('The playground was beyond the *topiary*' (*S*, 69; italics in original)), which prefaces yet another and another and another: 'Beyond the playground there was an inconspicuous chain link security fence, beyond that the wide, macadamised drive that led up to the hotel, and beyond that the valley itself, dropping away into the bright blue haze of afternoon' (*S*, 69). At one point on a progression of seemingly endless visual and spatial displacements into 'haze' (echoing the 'haze' through which Annie speaks in *Misery*), the topiary marks a process of displacement or deflection of the gaze that mirrors that of the hotel itself, a liminal place at once determinate and indicating or leading towards that which is already 'beyond' itself, both attached to and separate from the hotel, the 'beyond' of the inhuman towards which both Danny and his father are drawn. The topiary is also, of course, indeterminately placed in other ways, being neither animate nor inanimate, still nor moving, its indeterminacies embodying the functions of horror in *The Shining*.

Unaccounted for by the narration, omitted from Kubrick's film version, peripheral to the hotel's locale and yet central to the experience of three of the novel's limited society (for these animated animals attack Dick Hallorann, too), the hedge animals offer clues to the interconnections of place, reading and the inhuman within *The Shining*'s version of Gothic. Located significantly (in the novel's play on 'play') near the hotel's 'Playground' the animals seem to come alive, moving uncannily at the fringes of Jack's vision: 'Yes, there was something different. In the topiary' (*S*, 195). The hedge animals' behaviour conforms to Freud's noting, *pace* Jentsch, of a key example of the difference of the uncanny, the uncanniness of 'the lifeless bear[ing] an excessive likeness to the living'.[35] This uncanniness resides in part in the topiary animals' disturbing resemblance to domestic pets: Danny thinks that the lion 'looked like a great big housecat that was having a good time playing with a mouse before killing it' (*S*, 272). They combine into a single repeated trope the elements of play and place that structure *The Shining*. Their uncanniness resides in their apparent ability to move, that is, to displace and resituate themselves. Jack, thinking he has hallucinated their movement, sees with relief that each has returned to its original location: 'The lions, rooted into place, stood beside the path' (*S*, 197). Likewise, the word 'topiary' enacts the mobility of language, as Jack and Wendy play a game of suggestive puns: 'I used to trim a lady's topiary', says Jack, gently exploiting Danny's naive credence (*S*, 68). Embedded in the etymology of the word 'topiary', meaning '*Gardening*. Consisting in clipping and trimming shrubs', lies the Greek root *topoi*, 'place'.[36] The word 'topiary', like the hedge lion, is literally 'rooted into place' and yet uncannily mobile, suggestively ambiguous. The function of the hotel's topiary, this etymology suggests, is to constitute the mobile relationship between inhuman place and its human monsters, monsters that signal or warn (as monsters do: 'monster' derives partly from the Latin *monstrum*, 'a divine portent or warning')[37] of the borders or limits of the human. This borderline or liminal function is encoded in the novel's description of the hedge animals at its climax: Dick Hallorann, driving his snowmobile through a blizzard to attempt to rescue the Torrance family, encounters, 'limned in stark black and whites', what he thinks is 'some hideously huge timberwolf', which he then recognises as a 'hedge lion' (S, 377–8).

The hedge animals, then, establish the novel's analysis of place in relation to questions of the human and the inhuman, the liminal ('limned') spaces between them, and the functions of place in encoding such spaces in Gothic texts. Above all, they offer a configuration of the monstrous other that remains unaccountable in the novel's evasive narration, a monstrosity that simply exists. Their monstrosity is signified through a particular rhetoric that establishes in King's works a series of tropes of otherness. As 'inhuman monsters', their otherness is marked in particular ways that link them to different versions of the monstrous other in the oeuvre. Dick Hallorann sees in his encounter with the animated monstrous hedge lion something that 'he recognised': 'Its features were a mask of black shadow and powdered snow, its haunches wound tight to spring' (S, 378). Jack, trying to clip the inanimate hedges, 'touched up the rabbit's "face" (up this close it didn't look like a face at all, but he knew that at a distance of twenty paces or so light and shadow would seem to suggest one; that, and the viewer's imagination)' (S, 192). And when he first apprehends their movement, he sees other faces: 'The hedge mouth yawned wider, the pruned sticks looked sharp and vicious. And now he fancied he could see faint eye indentations in the greenery as well' (S, 195). And Danny, pursued by the hedge lions, sees that 'The green indentations that were their eyes were fixed on him' (S, 271). The monstrosity of the hedge animals is, through this rhetoric of the paranoid gaze, related to the hotel's apparent spectatorial power. In King's Gothic, place may be that which, when gazed upon, seems to gaze back with its own face, a face that returns the gaze in an explicit series of challenges (the challenge of the in-human). The next chapter will explore the faces of King's human and inhuman monsters, central motifs of his versions of Gothic.

8

Facing Gothic Monstrosity

'I mean, it's like the monster rally. Everybody is there. I thought it would be a good one to go out with. Called *It*. I should call it *Shit*.'[1]

'I was appalled to see the inside of the facial mask, but I was far more terrified still of seeing a head bare and stripped of its face.'[2]

The Shining locates Gothic horror ultimately not in architecture or in the minds of its protagonists, but in the faces of monsters like the hedge animals, figures of a disfiguring horror, an otherness that Gothic writing constantly encounters and seeks ways of expressing. The limits marked by the hedge animals lead only to a series of 'beyonds' (*S*, 68–9). Their very mobility indicates the potential fluidity of this border, its ambiguous status within the Gothic text. For Michel Foucault, the modern conception of the monster emerges in the late eighteenth century within 'a "juridico-biological" domain', that is, as a discursive product of the confluence of legal and ana-tomical sciences geared around defining specific limits of behaviour, constitution, form, morality and other normalising qualities demanded by the emergent discursive paradigms of modernity. 'The monster is the limit, both the point at which law is overturned and the ex-ception that is found only in extreme cases', he argues.[3] Monsters appear at, signify and embody limits, indicating in their relation to the limit the existence of a prohibited 'beyond' (embedded in the monster's etymological origins as a warning not to transgress). This 'beyond' repeatedly seduces Gothic writing, articulating a demand to be faced up to and overcome to which Gothic responds. This chapter will explore some of the ways King's versions of monstrosity envisage this confrontation and response, moving from figures of the monstrosity of abjection to the faces King's works give to monsters and to the central motif of Gothic horror, the corpse in death and undeath. All are linked to the recurrent trope that disfigures King's Gothic, the insistent gendering of monstrosity as feminine.

The narrative drive of King's Gothic across limits towards this monstrous beyond reveals death as the experience that monstrosity repeatedly codifies. In King's Gothic death is monstrous, an un-representable, faceless otherness constantly threatening the teeming, contemporary, living world of his fictions. Yet King's writings repeatedly attempt to give a face to death, drawing on the resources of the Gothic tradition of monstrosity in their efforts to figure it. *It* (1987) is King's most sustained attempt to do this, an immense, plot-driven, symbolically confused novel that connects death to the recurrent border constructed in Gothic writing, that of the abject, the 'place of meaninglessness' from which subjectivity is spoken.[4] This crucial linkage is also a gendering of the monstrous, in which a complex interlinking of monstrosity, death, abjection and the feminine is repeatedly enacted in King's narratives. *It* reduces monstrosity to an ostensibly impersonal yet clearly neutered pronoun, signifying the linguistic exclusion of the monster from the possibility of subjectivity and the potential isolation of sub-jectivity from the possibility of being monstrous. In expressing the connection between monstrosity and non-subjective agency, the word 'It' figures the monster as absolute Other, encompassing the whole of what Jacques Lacan calls '*Das Ding*', the 'strange and hostile' 'Thing' that is 'the absolute Other of the subject'.[5] '*Das Ding*' figures the empty 'beyond' to which Freud alludes in *Beyond the Pleasure Principle* and towards which monstrosity moves in *The Shining*.[6] *It*, seeking a rhetoric to describe its own excessive monstrosity, initially offers that monstrosity as polymorphous and many-faced, but soon abandons the struggle to represent the un-representable that inaugurates the Gothic. It offers instead a bizarre compendium of monstrosity as a relentless, historically cyclical account of the transgression of the abject into the symbolic world of childhood. *It* attempts through its impersonal pronoun to express a trans-historical, transcendent notion of monstrosity that can only ultimately be expressed in historically specific forms, 'manifested' (as Douglas Keesey argues) 'in socially specific monsters'.[7] These are in turn compressed into a single, disturbingly obvious image of feminine monstrosity that is both a symptom of Gothic's familiar failure to transcend conventional gender codes and a marker of the limits of King's transformations of the genre. The abject 'beyond' of '*Das Ding*' that monstrosity signifies in *It* is symbolically reduced and simplified, connected to monsters associated with the world of adulthood, a world bordering childhood (which is, in the novel, itself gendered, a particularly *masculine* mythologisation of infancy), but also repressed by it.

We can also trace this conventionalisation of the potentially threatening monstrosity of *It* in the novel's concern with abjection. We have seen how King is often concerned with 'Writing "shit"' (*FPM*, 315). The immense temporal and textual territory of *It*, structured by excremental flows and blockages, offers figures of the novel's textuality and of its connection of monstrosity with an abjection explicitly associated with writing. 'It' speaks to Beverley Marsh and to others through the pipes and drains of Derry's sewage system. At one point, 'It' seems to be using a shattered lavatory as a means of access to the surface world. The children elected to combat 'It' build a dam in the Barrens, a deterritorialised and largely adult-free district of the town, whose name implies an anxiety about creativity. The dam leads to backed-up bathrooms further downtown, a material image of the novel's concern with linguistic flows and blockages and with language's struggle to articulate the anxiety about monstrosity that concerns the novel. The multiple functions of the word 'it', a word indeterminate because uncontainable within the novel's attempts to express its engagement with otherness, delineate the polymorphous complexity of the figures of monstrosity in this text. If childhood is innately mutable, so too is the monstrosity (and the language necessary to express that monstrosity) that threatens it. Each mirrors the other in an extended, generationally repeated confrontation, mapped by the movement of signifiers across the text.

It, *She*

A short passage from early in *It* demonstrates this process and its connection to the concern with writing that surfaces here again in relation to Gothic's figuring of the monstrous. Patty Uris has discovered her husband Stan, formerly one of the Losers' Club, dead in the bath, apparently a suicide:

> A drop of water gathered at the lip of the shiny chromium faucet. It grew fat. Grew *pregnant*, you might say. It sparkled. It dropped. *Plink*.
>
> He had dipped his right forefinger in his own blood and had written a single word on the blue tiles above the tub, written it in two huge, staggering letters. A zig-zagging bloody fingermark fell away from the second letter of this word – his finger had made that mark, she saw, as his hand fell into the tub, where it now floated. She thought Stanley must have made that mark – his final impression on the world – as he lost consciousness. It seemed to cry out at her: [Here the novel reproduces a handwritten scrawled 'IT!'. . .]
>
> Another drop fell into the tub.
>
> *Plink.*
>
> That did it. Patty Uris at last found her voice. Staring into her husband's dead and sparkling eyes, she began to scream. (*It*, 69)

Here we can see the symbolic density momentarily achieved in *It*, for all its sprawling inchoateness. Set in a bathtub, the writing emphasises the connection between monstrosity and the waste pipes, sewers and drains that simultaneously cleanse and signify the pollution of everyday urban life, implying a subterranean excremental culture evident in King's deliberate punning on 'it' and 'shit' implied in this chapter's epigraph, the implications of 'urine' and 'urea' in Stan's surname, and lurking within and intrinsically connected to the domestic space of the home. The word 'It' is connected to writing, moving in this passage between typeface and reproduced handwriting. In the slippage between the word referred to by the pronoun 'it' ('written it in huge letters', 'It seemed to cry out at her') and that word being 'IT' itself, we see the novel's linguistic positioning of its monster, both located in and 'outside' – referred to by – the text. 'It' returns encrypted in the passage, reversed in the word '*ti*les' (the surface upon which

'IT' is written'). Most forcefully, 'it' is embedded in the word 'wri*tt*en'.

This movement of 'It' across the text demonstrates the Lacanian 'agency of the letter in the unconscious'. The letter – in this case, the message Stan has left as 'his final impression on the world', which is also the novel's title – is, as Lacan asserts, 'the material support that material discourse borrows from language'.[8] 'It', both message and agent of horror, is presented as writing inscribed in blood on to the material surfaces offered up by an unbearably hostile world. 'It' signifies, in Lacan's sense, the movement of language along un-conscious threads of meaning. 'It' is both the letter's effect as Stan's suicide note and a linguistic coding of the Freudian 'id'. Freud takes this word from Nietzsche; 'it' translates the German *Es*. Freud's 'id', like King's monstrous 'It', is a monster that 'knows no judgements of value: no good and no evil, no morality'.[9] 'It' is the unconscious of the 'things', times and places of King's Gothic world, the 'Morlock' subterranean space that, as we saw in chapter 6, King borrows from H. G. Wells: 'It was the stink of the beast, the stink of It, down there in the darkness under Derry where the machines thundered on and on' (*It*, 79). The letters of 'It' and their fugitive, monstrous significances can be traced again across *this* sentence, reversed in the repeated 'st*i*nk' (which contains, too, the 'ink' with which 'It' is inscribed into the text), reiterated from the opening 'It' and implicit as blockage and release in the stuttering alliteration of d's and the echo of 'under' in 'thundered'. The Freudian motto 'Wo es war, soll ich werden' ('Where id was, there ego shall be')[10] effectively summarises the psychoanalytic trajectory undertaken by the children-becoming-adults of *It*. In vanquishing the monster, they enter a version of the adult symbolic world which they then, within that world's Gothic repetitive imperative, have to leave in order to repeat this action, rediscovering in doing so a trace, a belated resurrection, of the myth-ical power of childhood friendship, but one haunted by endlessly repeated 'its'.

'It' repeats, flowing throughout the novel and at the novel's source ('*all things flowed from It*', we learn (*It*, 990; italics in original)), binding in its mobile significatory function the monstrous thing to the impersonality of the world and inserting into that world the forces of the id, projections (like the historically located Hollywood monsters imagined and thus reified and experienced by the children of *It*) of ideology, of the social forces which structure desire and its frustration. In the description of Stan's suicide, 'it' works pronominally and intratextually to describe everyday things which then uncannily take on qualities associated with the monstrous 'It', the thing touched by the transformative agency of the unconscious, a facelessness given a multitude of faces. The water droplet which 'Grew *pregnant*' works through emphasis to prefigure the final confrontation with 'It', when the adults/children realise 'It's true horror: '*It is female, It's pregnant with some unimaginable spawn*' (*It*, 1030; italics in original). Coded by its author's conventional adherence to rather than transformation of (in this case, fantasy) traditions, King's monster, Strengell notes, resembles Tolkien's 'female monster'.[11] This 'It' links with all the other (neutral, faceless) uses of the word 'it' in the novel, a neutrality which shifts and collapses in the 'It' recognised in a crucial moment of gendered revelation by Beverley Marsh: 'It was true; childhood would end; she would be a woman' (*It*, 401).

Beverley's childhood insight exploits again the ambiguity of 'it' to indicate provisionally here a version of what Levinas would call the *il y a*, the 'there is' or 'it is' of impersonal agency, the 'it' of 'it's cold' or 'it's a long time'. Lars Iyer offers a useful gloss on this usage, describing the *il y a*

as the locus of an exposure, an opening to what Levinas calls existence in general, existence, as he puts it, *without existents*: the *il y a*. The *il y a* is not linked, unlike Heidegger's *'es gibt'* according to Levinas, to 'the joy of what exists' but to 'the phenomenon of impersonal being', or what he calls in another essay, 'horrible neutrality' (italics in original).[12]

Such 'horrible neutrality' is signified by King's use of the impersonal (or faceless) pronoun. Its full force is realised in the connection between the monstrosity intended by the word 'it' throughout the novel and the apparently 'neutral' usage of the same word in Beverley's moment of self-recognition. 'It' becomes not 'neutral' but 'horribly neutral', the neuter gender neutralised by the imposition of a recognition of inescapable gender-coding that marks Beverley as different from the other protagonists of the novel, and thus implicitly connects her ideologically to the female monster she and the others combine to fight. King's novel, hampered by its monstrous length and lack of narrative cogency, clearly resolves its monster, as King's works (from *Carrie* onwards) so often do, into a gendered, sexualised, *female* entity. This has also been a major concern of King criticism since Chelsea Quinn Yarbro's comments, in an essay published in 1985, on the 'lamentable flaw' in King's writing: 'It is disheartening when a writer with so much talent and strength and vision is not able to develop a believable woman character between the ages of seventeen and sixty'.[13] *Misery*, in German translation, was significantly retitled *Sie* (German for *She*), partially in acknowledgement of that novel's debt to Rider Haggard. We have seen how that novel locates horror in the invasive body and threatening demands of the adult woman. *Carrie* offers a double configuration of feminine monstrosity in the figures of the 'possessed' daughter and the possessive, insane mother. One of *The Shining*'s key images of horror is the living corpse of an elderly woman. *Bag of Bones* and *Duma Key* (2008), ghost narratives in conventionally Gothic mode, both rely on vengeful female ghosts as their sources of monstrosity. Such examples indicate that objects of horror in King's works are recurrently feminised for consumption by a male reader. For Beverley Marsh and the male protagonists of *It*, the horror of the end of childhood is, in the collective unconscious that *It* constructs, also the central horror that King's Gothic seems to indicate, a (child's, masculinised) horror of adult, female fertility. This gendered anxiety is also the major ideological failure of King's monstrous effort in this novel to codify monstrosity.

This ideological failure is palpable in King's works and marks another kind of limit (that of their political critique). Another insistently rhetorical strategy, connected to the difficulties involved in gendering objects of horror, involves giving a face to horror, a process linked to the envisaging of the object of horror in an effort simultaneously to assimilate it to the category of the human and to signify its marked difference from that category. Late texts, like *Duma Key*, confront further, repetitive configurations of the monstrous-feminine and its Gothic provenance in figures like Coleridge's 'Nightmare Life-In-Death', 'a baggy pallid thing, vaguely female' (*DK*, 409).[14] *Duma Key* seeks rhetorically to deflect such images on to the trope of the face as a metonymy of both suffering and horror:

'Those faces. Those screaming drowned faces in the ship's sunset wake' (*DK*, 373). 'Faces' return in this novel's reworking of imagery from *The Shining*, feminised again, as the 'pale horrors' of drowned twin sisters (*DK*, 264). In King's Gothic, the face, like these 'vaguely female' faces or the faces of the hedge monsters in *The Shining*, is potentially inhuman, a signifier of something other than humanity. It is both nominal and verbal in its linguistic function, both a visage and a facing-up-to that intermittently detaches the face of the monster from, but invariably returns it to, the conventional gender codes of King's Gothic. Faces signify a potent form of confrontation over, across and through the notional limit-function of monstrosity. King's Gothic demands that his heroes (often children, like Danny Torrance) face up to the face of the monster, and in doing so face down its manifestation as an internalisation in the form of the encroachments and intrusions that monstrosity enforces upon subjectivity. The Gothic monster, always a figure of death, is faced in and by King's writings in a double sense, confronted and rendered readable, located within the signifying system set in motion, as we will see, by the face. It is also, at crucial moments, conspicuously faceless or unfaced. Horror, King's works suggest, is a product of internalised encounters with the faces of a monstrous, often feminine, otherness which may also be faceless, encounters definitive of a momentarily stable but endlessly threatened, often masculine subjectivity.

For King, individuation – the establishment of the subject as separate agent – is a crucial product of the encounter with Gothic monstrosity, returning us to the word 'alone'. His critical writing conceives of this encounter in terms that echo Aristotelian notions of catharsis: 'Horror, terror, fear, panic: these are the emotions which drive wedges between us, split us off from the crowd, and make us alone' (*DM*, 26–7). 'Making us alone', the imposition by extreme emotion of solitude, signifies separation and individuation as well as the imposition of solitude within the collectivity implied by 'us'. Limits, splittings, agglomerations, concentrations, separations, margins, centralities and repetitive occurrences mark the different spaces occupied by monstrosity. 'Aloneness' sits uncomfortably amidst such contradictory movements and positionings. Being 'alone', Carrie White's lament that resounds throughout the oeuvre, is also for King the basic condition of horror, existing in productive tension with the individualism inherent in his American Gothic ideology and with the drive his work evinces towards a reliance on the group, the social, as a potentially effective form of resistance to the destructive forces of the Gothic. 'Alone' suggests, in King's versions of it, Gothic's construction of a drastic and sometimes irresolveable relation of separation between the subject and the social. King's writings are ultimately Gothic because of their deployments of constructions of monstrosity in order to enact, in facing up to them, particular kinds of becoming, concepts of agency and self-determination that simultaneously bind the subject to a sense of self and a sense of group identity. At the same time, his writings work relentlessly to differentiate the subject from the group, embodying within subjectivity a myth of heroic agency all the more powerful because of its location in childhood (in King's early, pre-1987 works) and its subsequent, reactionary dislocation (in works like *The Dark Half* and *Needful Things*) into figures of authority like the policeman and, importantly, the writer.

The failure to invent a novel form of monstrosity, a failure implicit in *It*'s eventual reduction of its polymorphous monster figure to a female, pregnant spider (an image surely borrowed as much from James Cameron's *Aliens* (1986), and laden with that film's anxieties about femininity and motherhood, as from Tolkien) is a key issue in *It*. King's novel accumulates and combines in the now familiar manner, generating a multifaceted monstrosity, rather than creating anew (just as *Danse Macabre* tends to summarise and anthologise instead of analysing and theorising), again conforming to the reading of King's Gothic fiction pursued here. Gothic monstrosity is a figure of otherness, but King's monsters figure versions of otherness that are uncannily familiar in their accretive, tradition-dependent construction. Through these monsters he constructs a Gothic world in which the encounter with otherness – our coming face-to-face with 'It' – is also an encounter with ourselves and with what we (already) know, that which we have read before and must now reread. It is this doubled, reflective conception of monstrosity to which we can now turn through considering the recurrent figure of the monster in *It*, Pennywise the Clown, a marker of the ambivalent status of adults in this text, both alluring and deceptive, masked, connected to an adult comprehension of 'play' unrelated to childhood versions of enjoyment. The key motif of the horror embodied in the clown can be read in his face. Extending this reading across the oeuvre will enable us to link, in one crucial scene in *Pet Sematary*, the horror of the face to the other insistent horror of King's writing, the regendering of the feminine as genderless, as 'it'.

Clown-face: facing horror

The clown presents a particular kind of monstrosity, a performance of the monstrous signified by its face:

> It wasn't make-up the clown was wearing. Nor was the clown simply swaddled in a bunch of bandages. There *were* bandages, most of them around its neck and wrists, blowing back in the wind, but Ben could see the clown's face clearly. It was deeply lined, the skin a parchment map of tattered cheeks, arid flesh. The skin of its forehead was split but bloodless. Dead lips grinned back from a maw in which teeth leaned like tombstones. Its gums were pitted and black. Ben could see no eyes, but *something* glittered far back in the charcoal pits of those puckered sockets, something like the cold jewels in the eyes of Egyptian scarab beetles. (*It*, 220)

The details here signify an abject, bodily located 'horror' associated with old age: 'bandages', 'split' skin, 'tattered cheeks', 'Dead lips' . . . each item offers a specific metonymy connecting sickness and horror, fear and death to the iconography of the face. Jean-François Lyotard writes similarly of another, real, aged face and its implication of uncanny immortality:

> The FACE, but not the countenance, is a landscape, several landscapes. A photograph of Beckett at eighty. An entire land parched with drought, the flesh defied. And in the wrinkles, in the creases where the pupils flash with anger, a cheerful incredulity. So the mummy is still alive. Just.[15]

Bill's brother Georgie, the first victim of 'It' in the novel's narrative, sees the same face, figured differently: 'The face of the clown in the stormdrain was white, there were funny tufts of red hair on either side of his bald head, and there was a big clown-smile painted over his mouth' (*It*, 25).

The horror connoted by the face changes according to the perceiver, suggesting that the face of the clown offers a text to be read or interpreted, a generator of different readings. The horror monster in *It* exists firstly and recurrently as such a face, or sometimes a 'Face': Henry Bowers, gazing in horror at the night sky, imagines that 'the face of the moon would turn into It's face' (*It*, 907) and 'a Face forming in lines of fire' (*It*, 928). The 'face' is the signifying aspect of the form 'It' assumes as 'bait': '*The fears of children could often be summoned up in a single face . . . and if bait were needed, why, what child would not love a clown?*' (*It*, 998; italics in original). But 'It' is also implicitly 'faceless': '*It had put on no face – It did not dress when it was at home*' (*It*, 998; italics in original). 'It' has many different faces, including the 'facelessness' that, as we will see, connects it to other forms of monstrosity in King's oeuvre. For Beverley Marsh, 'It' is a version of her father; her three-year-old neighbour inverts this image when he sees 'something terrible and inhuman in Mr Marsh's face. He had nightmares for three weeks after. In them he saw Mr Marsh turning into a spider inside his clothes' (*It*, 895). Facing 'It', the children/adults face up to – come face to face with – the 'inhuman' face of their own unconscious fears. As 'It' puts it, '*you meet Me face to face*' and Ben, revisiting Derry library as an adult, recognises this: '*I am a grown man, and I am face to face with my childhood's greatest nightmare. I am face to face with It*' (*It*, 1034, 540; italics in original).

The horror of the face and its demand to be faced up to are everywhere in King's writings. In *The Shining*, Wendy imagines a face in the window, 'a hideous white face with circles of darkness for eyes [. . .] the face of a monstrous lunatic' (*S*, 367), and Jack, at the end of his possession, becomes 'a strange, shifting composite, many faces mixed imperfectly into one' (*S*, 400). Dinah, in 'The Langoliers', imagining Craig Toomey's perspective on the group of survivors, thinks of 'evil faces, cruel faces', imagining 'her own face' as 'a piggish baby face with the eyes hidden behind huge black lenses' (*FPM*, 65). In *Misery*, Annie appears in a photograph, a 'blank, stonelike face' (*M*, 214); looking at Paul, 'her eyes burned black holes in her face' (*M*, 185). In *Needful Things* Leland Gaunt's face is a locus of horror: 'His face was a horror of eyes and teeth and blowing steam' (*NT*, 605). 'A horror story, the face is a horror story', write Deleuze and Guattari; 'It is naturally inhuman, naturally a monstrous hood'.[16] Their analysis of the signifying functions of the face explores its effecting of what they call 'faciality' ('*visagéité*'). The face signifies, but does so in complex ways. It marks a site of identity and difference, a place of movement and fixity. It conceals and reveals inner selves, hidden emotions, repressed desires, unconscious urges, functioning as surface and cover in relation to each. It confronts us, forcing us to face it and to face it out. King recognises this potential when, discussing the writing of *It*, he comments: 'When your face changes, what is inside your head changes too, but it doesn't happen all at once'.[17] The 'horror story' of the face (the phrase translates '*un conte de terreur*', literally 'a tale of terror'), is a major thread of the narrative of *It*. Deleuze and Guattari argue for a conception of the 'face' and 'faciality' as a signifying system 'engendered by *an abstract machine*', 'the abstract machine that produces faces according to the changeable combinations of its cogwheels' (italics in original).[18] This is another version of the 'Status Quo Machine' of *The Tommyknockers*, the 'machine' that engineers and enforces social and ideological conformity.

The face is the basis of and the product of a signifying system. In King's working over of facial imagery in *It*, the signifying system into which faces fit is that of Gothic horror, the horror of an other of many faces, but also of an other without a face. Ben's encounter with the clown's face signifies this 'horror' and does so, in the novel's telepathic logic, not according to conventional codes of signification (whereby 'clown' signifies 'comedy'), but, instead, in response to unconscious desires located in the viewer of the face and manipulated by 'It'. The monstrous face becomes in effect a screen on to which the perceiving subject unconsciously projects their fears, in the process redefining the signifying pattern of faciality. The movement of the face of 'It' from one incarnation to another, and the implication that the 'real' face remains both concealed within *and* revealed by these different faces or 'dress', suggests that the relation between the face and what it signifies is monstrously distorted in King's novel. Each child/adult reconnects 'It' to an image of horror and in doing so renders the monstrous other in a particular (usually Hollywood-derived) image. The innovative monstrosity of *It*, if it exists, may reside in this contribution to the line of Gothic monsters on which it draws, the implication that the face of Gothic monstrosity is a system of signification – of faces – through which otherness can be apprehended, attached to connotative meanings specifically Gothic in their functions. The Gothic face, *It* implies, is a monstrous version of the face of the other, lending King's Gothic faciality an ethical function which will be scrutinised below. This potential goes further: *It* implies in its coded anxieties about becoming adult that the children will also become versions of 'It', assuming, as they age into adults, the features of 'It'. As each enters, excrement-like, the sewage pipe in pursuit of 'It', Bill's mind evokes 'a vague circus image – all the big clowns coming out of the little car' (*It*, 964), an image that foreshadows the becoming-adult (in the novel's imagery, becoming-clown) of the 'Losers' Club', their potential monstrosity to themselves.

Richard Rushton has explored Deleuze and Guattari's conceptualisation of the face and its functions in relation to structures of signification. The face, he notes, both expresses and contains within it the signification of that which it may also conceal. Rushton situates the face as a link in a communicative chain, a stage in a process of communication:

> [. . .] the face is a link between a destination and an origin; the face arrives from somewhere and is on its way to somewhere else. As such, it is the phase of communicability between a here and a there. Rather than being the matter of communication – the what that is thought, said, or felt – the face establishes the prior level of communicability, the 'is it possible?' that precedes the what of thinking, saying, feeling. The face, therefore, sets in play the process of communication; it is the encounter prior to communication, but it is not communication as such.[19]

For Rushton, the 'face' is a 'phase' in a process of deictic movement, a relay or channel in the process of communication. It enables the communication of something to someone. Deleuze and Guattari situate the face at the intersection of the structures of *signifiance* and subjectification; the face works within a '*white wall / black hole* system' that corresponds to the written text, black marks on a white surface (italics in original).[20] *The Shining*'s 'hideous white face with circles of darkness for eyes' exemplifies this 'system' (*S*, 367). To connect the face with the process of signification introduces into faciality the metaphor of writing. The face's whiteness is like the page on which 'signs', the 'black holes' of *signifiance*, are 'inscribed'. In effect, the face is a version of (constructed by, constitutive of) the page. Faces, like pages, are inscribed with signs that generate meanings, products of the abstract machine of writing. The 'black/white' configuration of the face repeatedly finds its expression in King's Gothic as a sign of horror as transformation and of the written difference effected by that transformation.

Facing the Master

To take *'Salem's Lot* as an example: the face assumes a specific function with the emergence of the master-vampire Barlow. His attack on the Petrie family, focalised through Father Callahan, is described thus:

> He saw Mark trying to drag his mother through the arch which led into the living room. Henry Petrie stood beside them, his head turned, his calm face suddenly slack-jawed with amazement at this totally illogical invasion. And behind him, looming over them, a white, grinning face like something out of a Frazetta painting, which split to reveal long, sharp fangs – and red, lurid eyes like furnace doors to hell. (*SL*, 393)

Here, the faces double; the rational face of Henry Petrie, associated with the safely domestic space of the living room and of the human mind it represents, is transformed by the face it perceives intruding into that space. Its 'slack-jawed' look of disrupted domesticity contrasts with and responds to the 'grinning' of Barlow's face (like the 'clown-smile' in *It*), a metonymy of all he represents, resembling an image from the fantasy art of Frank Frazetta. Barlow's face is thus 'like' an art image, momentarily dissociated from its body. Deleuze comments on painting's ability to capture the two 'poles' of the face, its double potential to build up to a climactic expression and its presenting a 'receptive immobile surface'.[21] This suggests a double comprehension of the face as movement and as screen upon which becoming can be traced. The activity performed by Barlow's face – its 'grinning', echoing also the 'grinning' typewriter in *Misery* – is both a signifier of character and emotion and of Barlow's moment of triumph, his exercise of absolute power, the triumph of Gothic horror's other over the domestic banality of King's small-town world and the fulfilling of Gothic's promise of destruction. It also connotes the skull's grin, an index of the death with which the vampire is associated. The face becomes the potent, multivalent sign of vampirism, black holes on a white surface that reproduce themselves as the vampire plague proliferates. Thus, Marjorie Glick, resurrected as a vampire, presents as a face 'a pallid, moonlike circle in the semi-dark, punched only by the black holes of her eyes' (*SL*, 301).

At the same time his monstrous face is not the monstrous 'reality' of Barlow, whatever that may be. That 'reality' is refracted through the internal horror of Father Callahan, who recognises this face as that of 'his own personal bogeyman, the thing that hid in the closet during the days and came out after his mother closed the bedroom door' (*SL*, 394–5). The face as external feature is quickly transformed in the narrative into an internal, individuated structure of anxiety, the process of individuation of horror that mobilises *It*. It becomes a figure of a private trauma that redefines it and domesticates it within the personal *unheimlich* of Father Callahan's childhood. The face of horror becomes that which (as King argues) 'makes us alone'. Facing this face magnifies the alone-ness of the subject. In this incarnation in Callahan's childhood memories, Barlow's face ceases to belong to Barlow. It becomes instead a figure of a type, a Gothically fulfilled childhood fantasy of otherness and a figure in turn of the 'type' that returns repeatedly in King's writings, horror as a 'thin white face' or 'clown-white face', with 'eyes glowing and red' (*SL*, 395). This recurrent clown-face, exemplified by the face of 'It' as 'Pennywise the Clown', is King's master-figure of the unconscious horrors of childhood. It is also the horror-story face of Deleuze and Guattari: 'Clown head, white clown, moon-white mime, angel of death, Holy Shroud'.[22]

The face of the vampire is thus polymorphous, multiple in its significatory power. Through this symbolism King's writing establishes the communicative function of the face as a site of horror, specifically the horror embodied repetitively in his early fiction in the brutal, abusive father. At Barlow's death, his victims crowd around the remains of his corpse: 'You killed the Master', one observes, 'How could you kill the master?' (*SL*, 461). Barlow symbolises, in this novel, demonic paternity. He is the face of the Father-as-Other, the symbolic expression or surface manifestation of the Law of the Father. *'Salem's Lot* furthermore imagines his conflict with Ben Mears as a conflict of writers and of scripts. As Ben prepares to stake his body, Barlow's voice intrudes telepathically into his mind: '*Look upon me, scribbler. I have written in human lives, and blood has been my ink. Look upon me and despair*' (*SL*, 458; italics in original). Paternity, writing, and the power of the gaze combine here. The echo of Shelley's 'Ozymandias' (Barlow's 'me' substituted for 'my works', the vampire offering himself as his own author) situates Barlow in a Romantic tradition of faith in the enduring powers of the written word embodied in the script of the self, a scripted self displayed in the propensity of the face of horror to be 'looked upon', interpreted, read and faced. The link with 'Ozymandias' also marks the connection of the vampire's face with death and the facing up to death and the residual, hubristic desire for immortality that structures the Gothic. Barlow's demand – '*Look upon me*' – is the demand of the monstrous to be faced up to and, in the process, to become faced, rather than faceless. Barlow, of course, is a personification of the fundamental unrepresentable Gothic horror, death. Death, in being faced, becomes also the master trope of the monstrosity of otherness in King's writing, a monstrous otherness most graphically explicated in his novel of American ways of death, *Pet Sematary*.

Pet Sematary: *facing and unfacing death*

'He sat alone in the darkness, gazing at the dying fire, and seeing faces in it.'[23]

Pet Sematary is King's most powerful meditation on the horror of death and the deeper horror of resurrection. The novel offers, among many other readings, a detailed analysis of the family as a machine for denying the necessity of facing up to death. Family relations, robust guardians of convention at the novel's start (a structure King repeats later, less effectively, in *The Dark Half*), collapse into failed mechanisms for dealing with the absences caused by death. Parental and filial connections, and connections of love and trust, are strained beyond breaking point by death's demand to be 'looked upon'. This demand intrudes, along lines opened by encounters with the neighbour and the friend, into the spaces vacated by fractured family affiliations. King's analysis of the tensions encountered by the individual in his relation with family and society finds condensed expression in the novel's focalisation through Louis Creed, whose intimate, conflicting relationships with his family and his neighbours undergo a series of external-isations, of redefinitions as relationships outside of himself and of his control. These transformations become repetitive escalations, a series of lines of flight from one horror – the horror of death – to another, the worse, faceless horror of undeath.

Slavoj Žižek calls this novel 'perhaps the definitive novelization of "the return of the living dead"'.[24] In its relentlessly mythic pro-gression, *Pet Sematary* expresses a series of familiar Gothic concerns enacted around the trope of resurrection. Death is experienced as an impossible-to-bear loss that necessitates a compensatory return. The horror of the novel resides in the consequences of this failure to bear, which it conceives as a refusal to face up to the reality of death. Death lurks in the interstices between people, in secrecies, concealments, deceptions, illicit acts, in the performances and en-actments that constitute hidden texts within the family romance that opens the novel, revealing the fiction of that romance and the defining solitude of each family member. Death presents itself as something the protagonists come face to face with, something to be faced up to, and a place to be escaped from by both dead and living. Each aspect involves deception; death's falsity, a consequence of its Gothic conceptualisation, mirrors the falsities with which characters refuse death's truth, so that lying (to oneself, and to others) symbolically repeats the inaction of lying dead. *Pet Sematary* meditates on the demand to face up to the truth of one's actions, the ethical demands of experience. This facing up or facing the truth is also ultimately a demand to acknowledge the Gothic power of death, its 'mastery'. Within the novel's complex rhetoric, the place of death doubles death's face, envisaging mortality as a place from which unwonted and unwanted returns arrive.

Pet Sematary opens with the speculative viewing of a property, 'a big old New England Colonial' (*PS*, 10). Bought unseen by the family (but 'picked from photos' by Louis; it is 'the house that only he had seen up until now' (*PS*, 10)), the property is revealed to them and us for the first time in this opening. Louis watches their reactions; his wife Rachel's 'eyes sweeping the blank windows' (reprising the 'blank windows' of the Overlook hotel in *The Shining*), their daughter Ellie's eyes 'also surveying the house' (*PS*, 10). Seeing the house reterritorialises it from unseen mystery to a new symbolic space, the space of 'home'. Rachel, 'still looking at the house', defines it with the word 'Home', a word immediately imitated by their baby son Gage: 'Home' (*PS*, 11), his first word, defining as *heimlich* a space that the novel will soon render radically *unheimlich*. Seeing 'home' and saying 'home' are thus intimately bound in a logic of perception and definition, of representing perceptions in words, that *Pet Sematary* will gradually (and then rapidly) unravel. In this unravelling, 'home' will become *unheimlich* and seeing will become a refusal to see, to look (death, the truth, oneself) in the face. 'Home' and 'seeing' are also connected in the logic of faciality that structures the novel. *Pet Sematary* is a novel about facing up to realities or home truths, and also about the consequences of not facing these home truths down. The novel's drama concerns the necessity of facing the death of others and the possibility, within that necessity, of facing the death of the self. It demands of its protagonists a series of 'facings-off', of confrontations and repudiations, of narrations and expressions that revolve around saving and losing face.

Faces offer the novel's central images of Gothic monstrosity. As Louis Creed returns to the Micmac burial ground for the second time, to rebury the corpse of his son, he sees ahead of him a face:

> Suddenly the mist lost its light and Louis realised that a face was hanging in the air ahead of him, leering and gibbering. Its eyes, tilted up like the eyes in a classical Chinese painting, were a rich, yellowish-grey, sunken, gleaming. The mouth was drawn down in a rictus; the lower lip was turned inside out, revealing teeth stained blackish-brown and worn down almost to nubs. But what struck Louis were the ears, which were not ears at all, but curving horns [. . .] (*PS*, 324)

This manifestation is the novel's confrontation with an otherness born of transgression. Louis's movement into transgression is a movement 'beyond' that radically deterritorialises the novel's detailed descriptions of domestic circumstance (the Creed family and their neighbours the Crandalls) and internalised, negotiable personal trauma (Rachel's memories of her dead sister Zelda). The face in the mist is given a mythical and demonic identity, that of the Wendigo that apparently haunts the Micmac burial ground; but clearly, in the novel's relentless introversion into Louis's distorted world-view, it is more and less than this – 'if that was what it was and not just a shape made by the mist and his own mind' (*PS*, 324). It offers a reflection, too, of Louis's own face, an unwitting externalisation of the 'demonic self' that he has already learnt well to conceal. Its appearance reveals that concealment for what it is, an effacement of Louis's transformation (in a familiar King process) from doting father to possessed maniac. In response to this face, Louis imitates its 'tilted' eyes: 'Louis's wondering, terrified face tilted up and up, like a man following the trajectory of a launched rocket' (*PS*, 325). This movement is imitated again later by the burial ground itself: 'Here on top of this rock table, its face turned up to cold starlight and to the black distances between the stars, was a gigantic spiral' (*PS*, 327). The 'spiral' is the 'curlicue' of place in *Pet Sematary*, its written-ness as a 'face', investing it with the symbolic import necessary for its Gothic effect as manifestation of Louis's deepest repressions and of the novel's analysis of the face as a crucial site of Gothic monstrosity.

In *Pet Sematary* characters' faces function semiotically, as if they were written in close-up, tight to the image of the human (and inhuman) face, encoding a vestige of monstrosity in even the most familiar faces. Patricia MacCormack describes the face as 'the very mechanism of signification'.[25] King's writing makes full use of this 'mechanism', of the descriptive potential of the face as a signifier comprised of signifiers, an assemblage of signs that works to reveal and conceal emotions, thoughts, opinions, memories, desires. Faces appear everywhere in the novel's deep domesticity, in acts of communication, in secret glances, looks and gazes, and in moments of concealment. Faces communicate and conceal, functioning within a social signifying system as prominent if not primary media of (dis) information. They work at and beyond the fringes of that social system to include or exclude according to a facialised definition of what constitutes the human. Faces are the portals of insight into the other and into death, suggesting that *Pet Sematary's* scrutiny of death is closely connected to its scrutiny of how people interact facially. The novel insistently locates the effects of death in the human face's response to or rejection of it. We read of 'Ellie's suddenly anxious face' (*PS*, 53); consoled by a bereaved Jud, we see how she 'gazed at him, wide-eyed, at a loss for words'. Moments later, 'her face was still tense and set and tearful' (*PS*, 187). Rachel 'reads' her sister Zelda's face as a register of malicious deceit ('she'd say it was an accident, but you could *see* the smile in her eyes, Louis'), and Zelda's death involves her 'face [...] turned sideways, turned into the pillows' and 'gone *black*' (*PS*, 180–2; italics in original). Faces thus sometimes signify death and death's inhumanity. Church presents in death 'the mouth, so small and bloody, filled with needle-sharp cat's teeth [...] frozen in a shooter's snarl', with 'dead eyes' that 'seemed furious' (*PS*, 108). Resurrected, the cat comes face to face with Louis: 'He opened his eyes and stared into Church's greenish-yellow eyes. They were less than four inches from his own' (*PS*, 160). Here the syntax bounces back and forth as each face mirrors the other. Faces represent and reflect such close encounters with otherness and embody Gothic's concern with the otherness implicit within a notion of the self.

Faces are constantly read and misread. Louis misreads, and then rereads, Victor Pascow's ghostly face: 'A look was on his face which Louis at first mistook for compassion', which was 'really a kind of dreadful patience' (*PS*, 75) (Pascow, the car-crash victim whose death initiates the narrative was, of course, Louis's first, 'dreadful' patient). Louis, returning to work the day after this apparent nightmare, 'ducked into the bathroom, believing that he must look like hell. He was a little hollow under the eyes [...]' (*PS*, 80); the self's face also reveals and conceals the self's otherness to itself. Norma Crandall, suffering a cardiac arrest on her kitchen floor, looks at Louis: 'There had been some pain in her eyes, but not agony' (*PS*, 95). Faces conceal and reveal because they make available the possibility, but also suggest the difficulty, of interpreting the other. Faces are, furthermore, markers of the novel's embedded concern with colonial American history.[26] Jud Crandall relates going to bury his dead dog with Stanny B., who, he imagined, would 'turn around, all grinning and black-eyed, his face streaked up with that stinking paint they made from bear-fat' (*PS*, 41). Pascow returns as a ghost, with 'blood [which] had dried on his face in maroon stripes like Indian war-paint' (*PS*, 72). Pascow's face defines his 'presence' in the narrative; 'His bloody lips were wrinkled back from his teeth and his healthy road-crew tan in the moon's bony light had become overlaid with the white of a corpse about to be sewn into its winding shroud' (*PS*, 74). As Louis faints, 'Pascow's face, leaning down, filled the sky' (*PS*, 75).

Jud, the neighbour who leads Louis astray (but also a demonic father-figure) possesses the face which particularly reveals the remark-able diversity of facial significance in the novel, offering Louis a conflicting variety of potential readings. Leading Louis to bury the dead cat, Jud's face shifts in meaning to accommodate 'an odd, dancing light in his eyes' and 'stark terror' (*PS*, 116–17); later, 'Jud smiled – or at least, his lips slanted' (*PS*, 120). Jud displays the truth of facial meaning and its deceptive force – face as revelation, face as (dis)simulation. At the end of this episode he looks at Louis 'from his inscrutable old man's eyes' (*PS*, 124). Confessing his earlier use of the Micmac burial ground, he breaks down: 'Abruptly, almost shockingly, Jud covered his face with his hands' (*PS*, 147). What the face reveals can be regulated by its concealment and exposure; he 'took his hands away from his face and looked at Louis with eyes that seemed incredibly ancient, incredibly haggard' (*PS*, 148). This is the face as pure medium, its signifying mechanism revealed and revelatory, opened but undirected, simply available to be read. It is the face of death evoked, in *Pet Sematary*, in Louis's imagining of Norma Crandall's corpse 'on a stone slab in a Mount Hope crypt; by now the white cotton the mortician would have used to stuff her cheeks would be turning black' (*PS*, 192). It is also Louis's face as he exhumes Gage's corpse, 'his face a horrible livid colour, his eyes black holes, his mouth drawn down in a trembling bow of horror and pity and sorrow' (*PS*, 306).

Crossings

Early in *Pet Sematary* the fatal/facial logic of the narrative is set in motion by the death of a cat. Jud's discovery of this death inculcates in Louis the desire and repetition-compulsion that drives the novel, narrated in a key passage:

> It was about five-thirty. Twilight was ending. The landscape had a strange dead look. The remainder of sunset was a strange orange line on the horizon across the river. The wind howled straight down Route 15, numbing Louis's cheeks and whipping away the white plume of his breath. He shuddered, but not from the cold. It was a feeling of aloneness that made him shudder. It was strong and persuasive. There seemed no way to concretize it with a metaphor. It was faceless. He just felt by himself, untouched and untouching.
>
> He saw Jud across the road, bundled up in his big green duffle-coat, his face lost in the shadow cast by the fur-fringed hood. Standing on his frozen lawn, he looked like a piece of statuary, just another dead thing in this twilit landscape where no bird sang.
>
> Louis started across, and then Jud moved – waved him back. Shouted something Louis could not make out over the pervasive whine of the wind. He stepped back, realizing that the wind's whine had deepened and sharpened. A moment later an air-horn blatted and an Orinco truck roared past close enough to make his pants and jacket flap. Damned if he hadn't almost walked right out in front of the thing.
>
> This time he checked both ways before crossing. There was only the tanker's tail lights [*sic*], dwindling into the twilight. (*PS*, 107)

Prefatory to Louis's encounter with the doubled monstrous others of death and resurrection, the self-conscious imagery and repetitions of this passage frame another encounter, that with the neighbour who figures a domesticated version of that otherness. All the key themes of King's Gothic are embedded here in a moment of fatal hesitation that internalises horror within Louis, the prelude to a series of choices that condemn him to the novel's mythic narrative of repetitive death and resurrection, the primal narrative of Gothic's parody of Christian myth. As this passage implies, otherness and the liminal, forbidden spaces it inhabits structure *Pet Sematary*. Here, they coalesce in the activity of crossing, emphasising the crucial status of these paragraphs in the novel.

Louis, facing the demand to cross the road (an encounter with death, figured in the near-miss of the Orinco lorry, one of the vehicles probably responsible for the death of his cat and certainly for the death of his son) confronts also a choice. By crossing he also opens the space of possibility around which the novel's drama revolves, the possibility offered by Jud's knowledge of the Micmac burial ground of not facing death or of facing it down. Louis's choice is inextricably linked to the novel's analysis of social relations and their demands. Crossing the road prefigures the crossing of the boundary between life and death, between the *heimlich* domestic world and the abject horror to come. The crossing, connected to the choices Louis must make, is also a crossing into a particular relation with Jud, 'another dead thing' who is both figure of the paternal Law (Louis thinks of him as a 'father', a word repeated three times in the novel's opening sentence) – and a 'friend' (*PS*, 9), a word laden with Frankensteinian import: 'I greatly need a friend, Margaret', announces Walton, early in Shelley's novel.[27] Mary Ferguson Pharr has noted the debt of *Pet Sematary* to *Frankenstein*, the way it 'amplif[ies] the cultural echo [Shelley] set in motion',[28] although King's novel clearly owes its basic narrative structure more to W. W. Jacobs's short story 'The Monkey's Paw'.

'Strangeness', the 'horizon' and the 'dead look' combine in this passage to Gothic effect: later, 'the fading light' and 'the whole setting' appear 'eerie and gothic' (*PS*, 109). 'Facelessness' here implies anonymity, featurelessness, indistinctness, a lack of identity or presence. It suggests a threatening non-identity, an indeterminacy of time and place that disorients, displaces and dislocates. Facelessness here echoes other moments of faceless horror in King's writing, like Wendy Torrance's momentary horror at her son's birth, '*He has no face!*' (*S*, 54; italics in original), or the 'no face' of *It* (*It*, 998). It counterpoints its apparent opposite, faciality or the possession of facial features, oscillating throughout this sequence of *Pet Sematary*. Church, the cat, is dead but 'in no way mangled or disfigured'. Instead, its corpse is recognisable, its eyes 'half open, as glazed as green marbles' and its mouth 'also open' (*PS*, 108). Faciality marks the cat's corpse – 'Now, in death, he looked to Louis like the old Church' (*PS*, 108) – investing it with a residual identity that differentiates it from and simultaneously connects it to the 'dead', 'faceless' landscape and the faceless 'dead thing' that seems to be Jud. In a world and a time of death (death of the day and of the year, at Thanksgiving), this death is different, pre-empted in Louis's internal monologue, on hearing of Church's death, that his own *'family's supposed to be different*. Church wasn't supposed to get killed because he was inside the magic circle of the family' (*PS*, 106; italics in original). The difference of death is revealed in this logic to be akin to the 'difference' of one's own family and of what one owns. Ownership, family, property and death circulate in an inexorable, destructive logic inscribed in the faces of this text.

King's language here encodes these choices and crossings and their connection to death in the image, seen 'across the river', of 'The remainder of sunset', echoing 'the remains of the Micmac Indian tribe' (*PS*, 10), whose legacy the novel ostensibly redresses in its concern with burial rites and respect for the dead. Louis sees Jud across the road, which he 'crosses' after 'look[ing] both ways'. These crossings and re-crossings, linked to the acts of looking that structure social relations and with which the novel opens, mark also the novel's concern with movement between life, death and undeath. Louis is forbidden by Pascow's ghost to cross the barrier beyond the 'Pet Cemetery': 'The barrier was not made to be broken' (*PS*, 75). Žižek, reading *Pet Sematary* as 'a perverted *Antigone*', in which Louis 'deliberately sabotages normal burial' by imposing 'a perverted burial rite', 'his monstrous act', argues that 'he is willing to risk eternal damnation, to have his son return as a murderous monster, just to have him back', that is, to cross the 'barrier'.[29] *Antigone*, as Jacques Lacan notes, is concerned in part with 'a life that is about to turn into certain death, a death lived by anticipation, a death that crosses over into the sphere of life, a life that moves into the realm of death'.[30]

His 'aloneness' at this moment of crossing causes Louis to 'shudder', echoing the name 'Jud', his surrogate father, neighbour and friend. Jud personifies the demand of the social to which Louis must respond, a demand relentlessly posited in this passage through its encoding of the landscape and that which it contains as faceless. Louis's actions in the novel repeatedly reject the demands of friendship: Pascow, returning in Louis's dreams as a ghost, announces himself: 'I come as a friend' (*PS*, 75). But Louis refuses this word: 'but was *friend* actually the word Pascow had used? It was as if Pascow had spoken in a foreign language which Louis could understand through some dream magic' (*PS*, 75). The word Louis's mind refuses is, presumably, *fiend*. Louis's 'aloneness', experienced as he contemplates the liminal world at the edge of 'twilight' (another borderline word reiterated three times in the passage above), separates him from social bonds and from the family to which he has hitherto been devoted. He ultimately 'crosses' into a new space, that of the solitude of death.

'Aloneness' establishes a course of action: separation, secrecy and individual choices will henceforth determine Louis's actions in the novel. This 'aloneness' is furthermore inexpressible, abstract and impossible 'to concretize [. . .] with a metaphor' (*PS*, 107). It is effectively literal and thus beyond metaphorisation, an encounter with solitude that the novel then characterises through the figure of facelessness that resonates throughout King's works: 'It was faceless'. The 'facelessness' of 'it' (here referring to the feeling of 'aloneness' but carrying again the trace of the ungendered monstrosity, the 'horrible neutrality' of the monstrous) is also the horror of 'It', the horror that facelessness engenders intermittently through King's works. It internalises an echo of the 'strange dead look' of the landscape and of Jud's own 'facelessness', his reduction in this passage to a Deleuzian 'monstrous hood', 'his face lost in the shadow cast by the fur-fringed hood'. Louis crosses the road towards him, but 'Even this close, Louis couldn't see Jud's face, and the uncomfortable feeling persisted that this could have been anyone' (*PS*, 107). Throughout, Louis looks (he 'knelt down to look at the cat'), but does not see.

If 'facelessness' encodes the monstrous failure of social and family bonds in Louis's 'crossings' or transgressions, the real faces of monstrosity in *Pet Sematary* are, of course, the novel's resurrected corpses, disfigured figures of the abjection of death. Louis is unable to resist resurrecting these corpses. His transgression of American rites of burial culminates, in terms of the novel's 'gross-out' horror, in his illegal exhumation of his son's corpse and his reinterring it in the Micmac burial ground. In this grotesque sequence (the most extreme encounter with the abject in all of King's writing and the novel's most violent transgression of social conventions of acceptability), Gage's face is initially hidden: 'Gently, he used his handkerchief to wipe away the damp moss that was growing on Gage's skin – moss so dark that he had been momentarily fooled into thinking Gage's whole head was gone' (*PS*, 304). The language used here emphasises the abjection of both the corpse and the activity Louis undertakes. The 'scum' of 'moss', a 'light slime of growth', product of 'the fetid dampness' of the grave, signifies death's horror, the novel's central version of the horror of the faceless other. Gage's face, revealed, is a composite, a shattered version of the 'white screen/black holes' models of the face, 'like looking at a badly made doll. [...] His eyes had sunken deep behind closed lids. Something white protruded from his mouth like an albino tongue' (*PS*, 304–5).

The novel completes its Gothic redefinition of the nuclear family by closing with the return of Rachel's corpse, murdered by her resurrected son. Louis doesn't face this return: 'He did not turn around but only looked at his cards as the slow, gritting footsteps approached' (*PS*, 367). The scene is resurrected from an earlier King text, *'Salem's Lot*, where Corey Bryant returns to kill her abusive husband: '"Darling", she said. Reggie screamed' (*SL*, 421). It echoes, too, the unfaced resurrected corpse of 'The Monkey's Paw', and is borrowed by King directly from Richard Matheson's *I am Legend*, in which the returning vampire wife, also unfaced, utters the name of her horrified husband.[31] In a crucial clue to the centrality of gender to King's conceptions of monstrosity, Rachel's voice, speaking the last uttered word of *Pet Sematary*, 'Darling' (*PS*, 367), becomes in this final sentence a disembodied *it* ('"Darling", it said'), signifying her reduction by the abjection of monstrosity from woman to resurrected corpse. In this reduction subjectivity is displaced from the body and erased, leaving only the neutered voice as an expression of the 'horrible neutrality' signified in King's Gothic by the word 'It'. *Pet Sematary* thus enacts a reversal of the gender-shift of 'it' to 'she' in *It*. Where *It* can only imagine 'It' as a 'she', *Pet Sematary*'s closing figure of the monstrous presents a 'she' as an 'it', collapsing the key tropes of King's versions of Gothic monstrosity – death, the abjection of the corpse and the feminine – into a single, faceless but female entity. Louis, playing solitaire at this moment, embodies in this closing scene the final solitude of the masculine hero who, by not turning round at the novel's end (but turning, instead, the card he is playing), refuses to face a monstrously abject, feminised death for which he is wholly responsible. This is his experience of the solitude King defines as a product of 'the emotions which drive wedges between us' (*DM*, 26–7). In order to emphasise the solitude of this closing encounter King revised this ending from an earlier draft of the novel, in which Louis is playing 'cribbage' with his colleague Steve Masterton, who has previously assisted him with burying Rachel's corpse.[32] It is, however, a solitude deferred by King's Gothic writing into intertextuality, a 'final' moment (insofar as anything is 'final' in this novel of non-finalities) of derivation that deflects the self's encounter with the monstrously feminised and abject other, leaving it incomplete, unfaced and faceless, a persistent, revenant product of Gothic texts and traditions and of the demand placed upon the writer to face them.

9

Conclusion: King's Gothic Endings

'And it always, in the end, came round to the same place again.' (*St*, 1007)

Pet Sematary ends with Rachel's return from the dead and Louis's refusal to turn to face this return. It is a return that that also embeds the novel's reliance on the return of other gothic precursor texts like 'The Monkey's Paw' and *I am Legend*. As a moment of closure such an ending remains incomplete, suspended, like the novel's deaths, in the intertextual spaces to which it defers. In effect, it enacts in textual form the incorrect burials with which the novel has been concerned, repeating at textual and generic levels their symbolic consequences: uncanny return, unwanted resurrection, the misery of entrapment and repetition within inescapable cycles, a faceless but feminised horror, all versions of the key tropes of King's Gothic. 'The Langoliers' ends with another kind of return, that of the survivors from the rapidly disappearing past into the present. *The Tommyknockers* ends with the return of David Brown from the non-time/non-place of his unwitting banishment to Altair-4. The final pages of *Misery* are, as we have seen, haunted by fears of and desires for different kinds of resurrection and return. At their most destructively extreme, King's endings are conventionally apocalyptic, often (as in *The Stand*, as this chapter's epigraph indicates) self-consciously drawing on mythic notions of cyclical return. More frequently, they tap more subtly into the ways Gothic endings deploy such returns as forms of perpetuation, resisting conventional closure and inviting instead deferral and extension, suspending the ambiguous relationship between individual transgression and social conformity that defines the ideological territory with which the texts are concerned. As we have seen in earlier chapters, King's Gothic structures its themes and generic characteristics around such recurrent tropes, which are also wholly characteristic of Gothic writing more generally: repetition, doubling and allusion, secrecy and concealment, the writer and the text, specific uncanny features of time and place, resurrection and its hazards, degeneration, abjection and monstrosity.

Clôture/closing tradition

Chapter 3 addressed King's 'Note' to 'Secret Window, Secret Garden' as a key statement of his writerly aesthetic and an important text in terms of understanding King's comprehension of writing's Gothic potentials. This chapter will initially return to this 'Note' in order to discuss some of the mechanisms of closure to be found in King's narratives. In reading those mechanisms, it will also consider some recent critical responses to King as extensions of or closures to particular ways of reading his work. King discusses in this 'Note' his belief in a suggestively machinic conception of the universe as an 'abstract image of life', 'a series of cycles' with 'some finite, repeating function' (*FPM*, 305). Repetition as cyclical order is thus established as one of the ideological tenets guiding King's fiction, but King goes on to argue, of his own texts on writers and writing, that cycles 'end' in a process which he describes by the 'parliamentary term [. . .] cloture', a term, he points out, adapted by 'psychologists' (*FPM*, 305). 'Clôture' (which King uses without the circumflex), a French word signifying closure, suggests the ways in which, in parliamentary or legal process, debates are concluded with a view to their textual continuation in the conclusive issuing of bills or other legal and political documentation. It is, King argues, 'as apparent in my work as anywhere else' (*FPM*, 305). He describes 'Secret Window, Secret

Garden' as 'the [that is, his] last story about writers and writing and the strange no-man's-land that exists between what's real and what's make-believe' (*FPM*, 305). 'Secret Window, Secret Garden' signifies for King then an anticipated moment of 'clôture' or closure, an 'end' (in 1990) to his hitherto repetitive thematic concern with 'writers and writing'. It is a 'closure' which is, of course, also a continuation into subsequent narratives (the textual issuing of further documents after clôture) of this central concern, which has been explored earlier through the sequence of texts including *Misery* and *The Dark Half* (and in those texts, earlier still, that feature writer-protagonists, like *The Shining*, *'Salem's Lot*, and, as we have seen, *Carrie*). It subsequently continues, despite its ostensible closure at the end of this novella, resurrected later in his career in writer-texts like *Bag of Bones* and *Lisey's Story* (2006) and in the transmutation of the writer-hero into a painter-hero in *Duma Key* (2008).

The word 'clôture' invites, furthermore, the specific kind of reading identified by Simon Critchley as 'clôtural', a reading that encounters and elaborates the doubleness of the text being read, its working both within the tradition it resists and against it. Critchley's 'clôtural' reading seeks to enable and sustain a flexible and ambivalent comprehension of the complex relations of Derridean deconstruction to the tradition of Heideggerian philosophy, which deconstruction seeks both to supersede and to accommodate itself within. It affords a way of thinking about King's writing in terms of moments of the 'transgression and restoration of closure', in which 'two irreconcilable lines of thought open up within a text'.[1] These conflicting 'lines of thought' are traceable in the contradictory location and function of 'Secret Window, Secret Garden' in King's oeuvre: a closure text that, in closing them, also continues and extends its themes; a discrete text that yet (self-consciously) repeats and reworks the concerns of its precursor, upon which it depends; a novella belatedly doubling a novel, extending and compressing that novel's concerns, establishing in this movement of extension/compression a strange economy – closure/disclosure, ending/continuing – of theme in its relation with its precursor. This novella in turn becomes symptomatic of the kind of dialectic of ending and not-ending that King's narratives repeatedly establish. Extensive intratextual references trigger in turn micro-sequences of wordplay, such as, for example, the allusion to

The Dead Zone in *Cujo*, as George Bannerman, being killed by the rabid dog, remembers Frank Dodd, the serial killer of the earlier novel; trying to 'dodge' the 'dog', he thinks of 'Dodd' (*Cu*, 308–9) in a bizarrely Gothic lexical game culminating in the 'God' appealed to as George realises the horror of what is happening to him (a particularly dramatic clôture in King's writing): '*What's he done to me down there? Oh my God, what's he done?*' (*Cu*, 310; italics in original). Further levels of inter-generic binding and other forms of imposed coherence, traced at different points in the discussions above, suggest an oeuvre deeply concerned with its own self-dependent continuities and perpetuations, its own need to sustain narrative lines of flight from and filiation to its generic sources.

Reading King clôturally opens spaces for considering the double movements of ending and perpetuating that structure his versions of Gothic in their oscillation between transgression (Louis at the Micmac burial ground, Bobbie excavating the Tommyknockers' spaceship, Mark Petrie entering the Marsten House) and the kinds of restoration of social and civic order that the narratives subsequently seek (and sometimes fail) to establish or impose. Critchley argues, in relation to Derrida's reading of Heidegger, that 'The movements of transgression and restoration cannot be separated. Their ir-reducibly double gesture provides the rhythm of deconstructive, or *clôtural*, reading' (italics in original).[2] This is also the 'rhythm' of Stephen King's Gothic, a 'rhythm' of transgressive movements that promise double resolutions of momentary liberation from and restorative return to social order, enactments of King's conservative 'double' sense of Gothic as both 'expressing our faith and belief in the norm' and (*pace* John Wyndham) 'watching for the mutant' (*DM*, 56), its movements both of 'disestablishment and disintegration' and of returning to 'a more stable and constructive state again' (*DM*, 27). The endings of King's fictions exemplify the ideological double-bind that his Gothic establishes in its general repudiation of other forms of excess than the excesses of violence, of the 'gross-out' levels of horror he momentarily achieves and of the social orthodoxies towards which King's versions of Gothic inexorably drive.

Conclusion

Critical/clôtural readings

We will return at the end to two examples of the questions raised by the concept of ending (of narratives, of texts, of symbolic concerns and of generic dependencies) that preoccupy King's fiction. This chapter will first extend our discussion of King's Gothic by suggesting ways in which his texts, in their double movements beyond and back across the limits that preoccupy Gothic writing, generate the potential for contemporary critical readings, particularly those inspired by identity studies and the burgeoning critical engagements with ecological issues. In much of King's writing, closure completes the principal ideological trajectory, embedded in all his writing, of a return from drastic, monstrous crisis to some kind of status quo, the closing achievement of a conventional ordering of individual and social desires that seeks to accommodate both. King's notorious interpretation early in his career of horror fiction (rather than specifically Gothic fiction) as a conservative genre tends to be confirmed at these points: 'The writer of horror fiction is neither more nor less than an agent of the status quo', he argues in *Danse Macabre* (*DM*, 56). Furthermore, he argues that 'The purpose of horror fiction is not only to explore taboo lands but to confirm our own good feelings about the status quo by showing us extravagant visions of what the alternative might be' (*DM*, 316), a cathartic vision that, as we have seen, enables the writer 'to bring things back to a more stable and constructive state again' (*DM*, 27). Despite frequently addressing such issues through the subversive or counter-cultural positions and utterances of specific characters (Gard, in *The Tommyknockers*, is a notable example), King offers little space for genuine consideration of the possibility that horror fiction might, through its forms and themes and through generic and other forms of innovation, challenge the status quo (or, indeed, that the status quo might *need* challenging). Yarbro's noting of the 'disheartening' conventionality of King's treatment of femininity, explored in the previous chapter, is a pressing case in point.[3] Differentiating and defining the clearly Gothic elements of King's works and relating them to Gothic and Gothic-influenced or influencing traditions of popular fiction suggests one method of distancing his texts and their effects from this conservative impulse. In Gothic, 'returning' is rarely to a 'constructive or more stable state'; Gothic texts render such reassurances problematic and the Gothic elements of King's writings, specifically their concern with the logics and processes of *writing itself*, tend to resist such cosy closures.

King's ostensible concern with what he calls above 'the alternative' provides a ground for considering 'alternative' critical approaches to his writing, approaches different from the concerns of most of his critics with sociological, myth-critical, psychoanalytic, genre-based and other related modes of critical analysis and engagement. King's writing suggests a wider range of potential critical readings through its relentless currency, its deep embedding in and yet intermittent scepticism towards the discourses and symbolisms of contemporary culture. While his nods to contemporary history are, as we have seen, for the most part cosmetic or, more potently, legitimating elements of his realism, his language and his repeated resorting to generically familiar formal solutions to ideological problems are clearly products of a deeper conflict. This conflict may be initially understandable as that between the written text and those technologies that promise to supersede it, a conflict King's writing offers at times as a version of other, grander or more historically urgent transformations. In *Cell* (2006), a novel ostensibly addressing the hazards of postmodern communications technology, King also makes his clearest gesture towards a post-9/11 American social consciousness, suggesting, as the novel's speculative argument elaborates, that the two are linked in his comprehension of current affairs. Drawing heavily on the horror iconography characteristic of George A. Romero's films (and dedicated to Romero and Richard Matheson), *Cell* represents an America decimated by something that may have been a terrorist attack. A signal transmitted down cell-phones has deranged vast sections of the population, reducing them to a zombie-like existence and destroying the social fabric. Post-9/11 iconography is evident from early in the novel, when a plane crashes into buildings on Charles Street in Boston (*Ce*, 28). 'If this was an act of terrorism', thinks hero Clayton Riddell, 'it was like none he had seen or read about' (*Ce*, 17).

Formally structured by the familiar King and Hollywood-narrative conventions of the small group of survivors and their individual acts of heroism and self-sacrifice, *Cell* offers a restricted vision of the potentials of contemporary Gothic for an engagement with the post-9/11 world and seems concerned more obviously with the consumerism its title homonymically implies. Indeed, the novel's opening is structured around a series of exchanges and transactions, expressed in verbs like 'affording', 'receiving', 'buying', 'paying for', that establish the conventional capitalist reality soon to be destroyed by the 'Pulse' (*Ce*, 3–7). The key phrase that links this transactional logic to King's deeper ideological concerns is offered in the action of 'engaging in a small bit of commerce with a total stranger' (*Ce*, 5). 'Total strangers' effectively describes the whole of the society of *Cell*. Critics have commented extensively elsewhere on the marked absence of black, Asian, Muslim or other non-white or non-Western characters from King's texts and on their treatment of homosexuals, women and other identities that differ from the gender, religion, sexuality, race and class of the author. *Cell*'s one real concession to identity diversity, the gay character Tom, is unconvincing, little more than a superficially updated version of *The Shining*'s Stuart Ullman, suggesting that King's varieties of Gothic are still historically bound to the late twentieth-century socio-historical contexts in which they developed and to prejudices that belong in those contexts.

As we have seen, Steven Bruhm's analysis of homophobia and constructions of sexual difference in King's novels has explored this territory in some detail.[4] Sean Eads has recently extended this route of enquiry in his detailed and insightful analysis of homosexuality in *'Salem's Lot* and its relations to a more general sense of a 'potentially monstrous sexuality'[5] that we have seen elsewhere, in King's feminisations of the monstrous. Strengell's absolute refusal of such a reading, emphatically imposed by her citation of King's own refusal – 'Case closed', she asserts in a premature act of critical clôture[6] – fails to quell the potential spaces King's writings repeatedly, sometimes unwittingly, open for queer and other sexually organised readings of Gothic, which King himself invites in texts like *Gerald's Game*. That text's subjecting of its heroine to relentless, unwarranted suffering is reprised in analogous but radically different form in *The Girl Who Loved Tom Gordon* (1998), a novel that invites different critical approaches related to ecocriticism and recent turns to green politics. Such approaches are also suggested by the repeated use in King's novels of notions of empty territory, such as *Pet Sematary*'s 'woods that went on damn near forever' (*PS*, 10), or the 'miles of wilderness owned by the New England Paper Company' (*T*, 4) in *The Tommyknockers*. Such territories are always initial and provisional, placed at the openings of texts and then (as in *The Girl Who Loved Tom Gordon*) populated, filled in by King's symbolic and social imagination, as the narratives work (in good American Gothic style) to domesticate and familiarise them.

'The woods themselves are real', King warns us in the 'Author's Postscript' at the end of *The Girl Who Loved Tom Gordon*; 'If you should visit them on your vacation, bring a compass, bring good maps . . . and try to stay on the path' (*GL*, 292). The novel itself finishes with the words 'Game over' (*GL*, 290), an ending that enacts the text's coded desire for closure, expressed throughout in Trisha MacFarland's desire to learn (in the novel's celebration of American football) *'the secret of closing'* (*GL*, 116, 236; italics in original). Trisha, lost, like Gretel, in the New England woods, is forced to learn new ways of reading her environment and its potential hostilities. Like the survivors in 'The Langoliers', she is also lost in a kind of 'post', finding different 'posts' that may be 'signposts', 'gateposts' or just 'posts': 'How can I know anything from it when it's a post, not a signpost?' (*GL*, 237) she asks, an Alice lost in her own Gothic Wonderland. This novel is concerned with a particular kind of survival and its dependency on reading signs and closing narratives. From the initial, homely and emphatically inscribed domesticity signified by Tom Gordon's autograph, written in 'broad black felt-tip strokes' (*GL*, 12) on her Boston Red Sox cap, to the 'dead tree that split halfway up and became a black letter Y against the declining sun' ('Why bother?' is Trisha's reading of it; it repeats the forking paths of the woods, 'forked in a Y' (*GL*, 23), where Trisha initially loses her way) (*GL*, 137), Trisha is cruelly and repeatedly forced to learn to read her environment anew. She also learns in the process of how that once familiar space can rapidly become other, just as her body's allergic and physical reaction to it becomes 'radically different' (*GL*, 213). Such moments of identification indicate the novel's potential collapsing of the monstrously hostile environment with the female body, a covert rhetorical move familiar in King's works and arguably endemic to Gothic writing.

The Girl Who Loved Tom Gordon demonstrates a potential new intensity in King's writing, a new level of isolated individual suffering (Trisha is more alone even than Paul Sheldon), a new kind of Gothic torment structured around absolute forms of alienation, but couched in the familiar rhetorical tropes of reading and writing as processes for negotiating the horror of the real and its relentless intrusions into the mundanities of King's social worlds. Trisha's 'desperate' desire is that 'there is no *thing*' (*GL*, 109; italics in original). Echoing the elusive 'real thing' of 'Secret Window, Secret Garden', it is, of course, futile in the narrative's Gothic logic. 'There was *something*' (*GL*, 111; italics in original) the narrative replies, establishing another kind of Gothic rhythm, that of denial and menacing admission, to sustain its tensions. *The Girl Who Loved Tom Gordon* then establishes its own version of the repetition that organises King's Gothic in its reprise of the degree of isolation and suffering King establishes in earlier texts like *Misery* and *Gerald's Game*. Its concern with the 'game' (echoing 'play' in *The Shining*) and its metaphor of 'closing' derived from that concern balances the emphasis these texts place on the real, pressing desire in these narratives for 'survival' (Jessie Burlingame, in *Gerald's Game*, thinks that 'Survival was not a matter for politeness or apology' (*GG*, 71)). This balance invites a clôtural reading of irresolvable tensions between competing drives towards closure and continuity in King's Gothic. The remainder of this chapter will address examples of this tension through readings of the endings (or, at least, the concluding pages) of two of King's novels, offering a double closure to this discussion, in keeping with the deferrals and delays characteristic of King's works.

Endings 1: Needful Things *and the economy of desire*

'Once things really get rolling, they can rarely be stopped . . .' (*NT*, 441)

Needful Things, published early in George Bush senior's presidential term and thus at the belated end of the Reaganite period of American politics, offers King's most extended and forceful allegory of consumerism as the misdirection and corruption of desire. The novel is a kind of Faustian parable firmly located in the extensive and detailed domestic realism familiar from novels like *'Salem's Lot* (and deriving, as we have seen, from *Peyton Place*, which is mentioned early in the novel (*NT*, 14)). It presents as its Gothic monster shop-keeper Leland Gaunt, a merchant of desirable objects, whose shop, 'Needful Things', opens in the town of Castle Rock and quickly, and apparently miraculously, provides the text's central characters with the things they covet most, the true objects of their desires. Dramatic social and familial disruption ensues, as the symbolic debts incurred for ostensible ownership of these coveted objects are repaid through escalating acts of destruction, meanness and cruelty in a rapidly proliferating system of jealousies, misunderstandings and acts of revenge, through which the novel progresses towards the collapse of its whole social world. Redemption comes in the form of Sheriff Alan Pangborn (also a central character in *The Dark Half*), whose apparent exemption from the social circuits of desire and greed afford him a critical and salvational position that redeems the town and the narrative. The novel centres on a critique of Leland Gaunt's conventional capitalist philosophy ('Everything is for sale' (*NT*, 404)), which is also an overt analysis of desire in capitalism, its combination of deceptive satisfaction and unquestioned ideological faith. 'I believe I have something that's going to make you very happy' (*NT*, 39), Gaunt tells one character in the novel.

As in the opening pages of *Cell* and implicitly in the '*closing*' metaphor of *The Girl Who Loved Tom Gordon* ('Always Be Closing' being the 'ABC' of American salesmen), the language of transaction and exchange permeates the novel's rhetoric and particularly its representations of the relationships between the police officers in the text, so that even the offer of a cup of coffee from his clerical assistant stimulates an auctioneer-like response from Pangborn: 'Sold' (*NT*, 110), while the police-station noticeboard features informal records (accounts) of small financial debts between officers (*NT*, 99). Corresponding to this rhetoric and its prominence is the logic of choice and consequences: 'every choice has consequences' (*NT*, 437), Norris Ridgewick (another police officer) learns. This fiscal-moral language (a version of the Reaganite economics of choice) is balanced by a coded critique of economics as mere trickery, the deceitful replacement of one thing with another. Alan Pangborn is, among other things, an amateur magician, able to perform sleight-of-hand tricks as a means of establishing relationships with child witnesses. But this magician's tricks are paralleled by the con-tricks and deceits of Leland Gaunt, a different kind of magician whose deceptions play on individuals' desires to know and to own, desires that destructure the novel. Brian Rusk's early adolescent dreams, which lead him eventually to commit suicide, are dreams of dark knowledge that he unconsciously relates, through the image of the magician, to both Gaunt and Pangborn: 'but what makes me unhappy are the things I know now. It's like knowing how the magician does his tricks' (*NT*, 472).

'Unhappiness' consequent on the burden of unwanted knowledge (for Brian, the knowledge is closely related to the familiar King trope of becoming adult) is thus central to the sleight-of-hand trick the novel itself plays. This involves the establishment of the conventional figure of patriarchal authority – the Sheriff – at the moral and ethical centre of a text ostensibly critiquing, through its analysis of capitalism, precisely this authority structure and the social and economic systems upon which it rests. The relation between Pangborn and Gaunt is ultimately, of course, that of reader and writer. The narrative Gaunt forcibly inscribes into Castle Rock, in books like that apparently found in Gaunt's shop by Ace Merrill (*NT*, 351–5) and unreadable to everyone else, is subject to extended and unwanted critical scrutiny by Pangborn's detective/readerly skills, while Gaunt himself, exploiting the connections between faces and otherness noted earlier, interprets Pangborn's face as that of a critical reader, and thus as a threat: 'He was even better at reading faces than remembering them, and the words on this one were large and somehow dangerous' (*NT*, 216). The two communicate in these opening exchanges through notes and notices, 'a hand-lettered sign' and a 'scribbled [. . .] message' (*NT*, 217), of which Gaunt 'read both sides carefully' (*NT*, 218). Reading and writing thus mediate the initial stages of an ideological conflict between two narratives: Gaunt's transgressive and destructive liberation of the people of Castle Rock to become parodically anti-Oedipal 'desiring-machines' driven by the logic of consumerism and Pangborn's restorative narrative of social order and the rule of Law, or the contest between newly emergent, ruthless market forces and an older, superficially benevolent patriarchal authority. While it is Alan's partner Polly who provides, towards the novel's end, the ultimate insight into the disastrous, Gothic consequences of Gaunt's economy – '*He makes you buy back your own sickness, and he makes you pay double!*' (*NT*, 677; italics in original) – Alan Pangborn is the novel's principal vehicle of redemption.

American community in *Needful Things* is thus presented as fractured, riven at fundamental levels by conflicting, irresolvable desires which yet drive it, open to enthralment by an ideology of debt and repayment wholly out of proportion to the ostensible logics of 'need' and 'cost' (or 'defining worth by need', as Gaunt puts it (*NT*, 56)). The interplay of 'need', greed' and 'deed' (*NT*, 94–5) concerns the text. The word 'thing' circulates through this economy, accruing (as it does in relation to monstrosity in *It*) a range of uncanny significances. 'Things' variously names objects and actions and people, so that 'Needful Things' names both Gaunt's shop (with its 'false front' (*NT*, 687)) and its customers, as well as the 'things' they buy and the 'lousy things' (*NT*, 689) they must do to pay for them. Eventually Gaunt is named as a 'thing' himself, 'the Gaunt-thing' (*NT*, 689). Objects like the 'snake-in-the-can-of-nuts' trick that belonged to his dead son Todd and that Alan finds in his car become '*thing*[*s*]', 'the damned thing' (*NT*, 65–6; italics in original), persistent mementoes (in this case) of bereavement and loss, but also crucial elements of the economy of trickery and deception the novel sets in motion and of its eventual resolution. So many of Gaunt's 'things' rely on nostalgic recollection and childhood desire for their effects that they also become vehicles for the relentless, cynical game of the commodification of desire as nostalgia, the fraudulent 'gift' (*NT*, 436) of Gaunt's version of consumerism that lies at the heart of the intricate 'soap-opera history' (*NT*, 130) of *Needful Things*.

The novel's concluding redemption comes (as it does in *The Tommyknockers* and elsewhere in King) in the form of state authority, offered as a kind of palliative magic that counters the bad perpetrated by Leland Gaunt. 'Todd's last joke', the 'snake-in-the-can', is the means of reparation, a transformation of the Edenic snake that, in King's narrative, bites the Devil (*NT*, 684). Alan's magician skills are linked in the novel's syntax to America's Puritan heritage ('*Listen to you, Mr Amateur Magician, sounding like a Puritan*' (*NT*, 65; italics in original)) and thus to its Gothic literary lineage, while Leland Gaunt, bitten in the end by a paper snake and thus a victim of an amateur trickery that balances his own, 'looked like a woodcut of Ichabod Crane' (*NT*, 684) as Alan dispossesses him finally of what he 'owns': '*Give it to me – it's mine*' (*NT*, 685; italics in original).The final contest over Gaunt's valise, with its cargo of the town's souls, lays bare the novel's ideological project and its historical context of 1980s post-modern capitalism:'Don't you believe in free trade, Sheriff Pangborn? What are you, some sort of Communist?' (*NT*, 686). Within this Gothic economy, surplus value – the excess of desire and the excessive destruction this brings to Castle Rock – is suddenly, at this conclusion, codified in textual terms as the return (as in the conclusion of *Pet Sematary*) of versions of other King narratives. Pangborn, performing a deceptive shadow-play, a 'miracle of transmutation' (*NT*, 688) with his hands, creates a 'projected shadow-bird' and cites *The Dark Half* ('The sparrows are flying again'). He then creates 'a large shadow-dog – perhaps a St Bernard', citing *Cujo* (*NT*, 687). The game of exchange draws here on its own place within the tradition of King's works, deploying intertextual references to those works to dispossess and disinherit Gaunt, pretender to the ownership of Castle Rock. Alan, too, is ultimately dispossessed of the town by these events:'*My town*, he thought. *It was my town. But not anymore. Not ever again*' (*NT*, 693; italics in original).

The real owner of Castle Rock and of its narratives, asserted through this concluding intertextual authority and gestured towards in the novel's intermittent writerly metaphors, is, of course, Stephen King.The author's name insists throughout (and nearly rhymes with) *Needful Things* in other intertextual allusions to (for example) the novella 'The Body' via the character Ace Merrill, who also learns in *Needful Things* 'that he was not a king and Castle Rock was not his kingdom', in contrast with the 'bigshot writer' Gordon LaChance (that is, King himself?) 'living in another part of the state' (*NT*, 606). King inscribes himself many times into this novel: Cora Rusk believes, wearing her Elvis sunglasses, that she has '*a date with The King*' (*NT*, 576; italics in original); Polly Chalmers sings 'Iko Iko' to herself: 'Look at my king, all dressed in green' (*NT*, 383).This self-reflexivity asserts a final level of authorial ownership, an imprinting of writerly possessiveness upon the text that muddies further its ostensible critique of the abuses of power and desire that ownership might entail and sets in motion the rhyming, repetitive interplay of 'King' and 'thing' that drives the narrative. Unsurprisingly, *Needful Things* opens and closes with further, formal repetition: 'You've Been Here Before' (*NT*, 9, 693) names both opening and closing sections, indicating the reader's return to this Gothic place. At the end the narrative, too, returns as a new shop, 'ANSWERED PRAYERS', opening in another small town. The threat of repetition, echoing the ending of *Carrie*, thus perpetuates *Needful Things*. Alluding to Ecclesiastes on its final page, the novel invokes the Old Testament assertion that 'there ain't nothing new under the sun' (*NT*, 698), a proverb that might, of course, equally apply to many of King's own interventions in the Gothic mode.

Endings 2: Duma Key's 'painted words'

'*Know when you are finished, and when you are, put your pencil or your paintbrush down. All the rest is only life.*' (*DK*, 581; italics in original)

If the author becomes in many of King's works a driving metaphor or guarantee of possessive power within his own writing, then so too does that writing provide a key resource for its own prolongation as it enters into the Gothic tradition to which it contributes and on which it draws. The (im-)possibility of narrative and textual conclusion within this tradition, the difficulties that closure presents and its tendency to contradict the requirements of a Gothic structured around repetition and return, embody the recurrent ideological tension at the centre of King's Gothic. Narrative closure, too, often corresponds to an ideological indeterminacy and irresolution, the individual text unable to close out and instead reworking or simply repeating its relation to the intertextual, collective field. Reworking in ostensibly different media the haunted-writer narrative of *Bag of Bones* and incorporating another version of that novel's attention to America's racial history (one hampered, as we have seen, by a similar structural misogyny), the final pages of *Duma Key* enact a similar extension of the narrative into other intertextual fields. These pages offer a restorative perpetuation and repetition in response to a series of transgressions, indicating again the Gothic difficulty of ending.

Somewhat superficially, *Duma Key* shifts attention from the writer to the painter. Edgar Freemantle, disabled by a freak accident, relocates to the Florida island of Duma Key, renting a Poe-like house there ('Like the House of Usher', we are told (*DK*, 36)). He discovers an ability to paint of which he was previously unaware, producing pictures of such quality and impact that his opening show is a sell-out. These paintings, the novel reveals, affect reality in disturbing ways and threaten the lives of those who own them. It transpires that they are inspired by the ghost of a drowned woman, 'Perse' (an abbreviation of 'Persephone'). The novel's plot, again hampered by some brutally misogynistic passages early on as Edgar vents his fury against, it seems, all things feminine, derives in part, as we have seen, from Coleridge's 'Rime of the Ancient Mariner', with elements of Wilde's *The Picture of Dorian Gray* (1891) (which is mentioned in the novel (*DK*, 250)) and Henry James's *The Aspern Papers* (1888). It owes something, too, to Margaret Atwood's *Cat's Eye* (1988), echoing that novel's descriptions of paintings and their uncanny effects. King's shift from writing to painting is authenticated in the novel by the revelation that Duma Key was a holiday resort for generations of twentieth-century artists, including, in a notably populist gesture towards academic credibility, Salvador Dalí. It offers another space for an analysis of artistic (ostensibly differentiated from writerly) creativity in which King again both draws on and repudiates the influence of tradition. Freemantle is presented as 'a true American primitive' (*DK*, 159) in the novel's rejection of 'schools of art' and '*ism*' (*DK*, 162; italics in original). Edgar is, indeed, King's most recent version of the individual 'talented' (*DK*, 162) artist working outside and apparently uninfluenced by tradition (but nevertheless able to describe in the novel's final paragraphs his ability to produce 'the perfect surreal touch' (*DK*, 578)). This ambivalent rejection of and dependence upon tradition is crucial to *Duma Key* and to grasping its position in relation to the Gothic tropes King has now repeatedly deployed across a thirty-six-year writing career. The novel constructs the artistic tradition as a space outside its ideological remit, populated and defined not by 'primitive' artists, but by art dealers, 'art mavens' and 'motherfucking *professors*' (*DK*, 297; italics in original). This is an extreme example of the tendency, identified by Sherry R. Truffin, of King's writings to dismiss education as an exercise in the abuse of power.[7] Its effect, however, is paradoxically to enable different kinds of tradition to enter its textual frames. Most obviously, Freemantle's paintings depend upon the tradition implied by the novel's theory of artistic inspiration as a form of possession by the dead, reinforcing the Gothic comprehension of tradition that we have noted elsewhere in King.

One of the novel's central images involves drowned twin girls, clearly alluding to *The Shining* as a major precursor haunted-house novel (and *Duma Key*, less effective as a novel of Gothic place, nevertheless draws on devices and methods similar to the earlier novel). It alludes (again) to Shakespeare and T. S. Eliot ('the empty, pupil-less pearls that were her eyes' (*DK*, 438)), amongst dozens of other literary allusions, and involves also another version of the telepathy that preoccupies King (the character Wireman's 'empathy got raised to telepathy' (*DK*, 382), we are told). Suppressing artistic tradition, but drawing instead on key features of the tradition of texts by the same author to which it belongs, *Duma Key* also uses imagery of writing to describe Freemantle's painting. Frequently incorporating words into the images, he calls his paintings 'scribbles'. The word means 'to write carelessly or hastily' and derives from Latin *scribere*, 'to write'.[8] It is etymologically linked to written 'description' and 'describing', in which forms all the paintings in this novel exist. He notes 'The scribbled afterglow [that] had a sullen, furnacey quality', 'The casual scribble of light on the water', and describes Dalí's sketches as 'These not-quite-offhand scribbles' (*DK*, 44, 84, 136). Dalí himself is, rather oddly, confused early in the novel with the writer Salman Rushdie (*DK*, 58). Painting itself resembles writerly inscription: 'I had caught her BRILLIANTLY in just a few harsh strokes of black that were almost like Chinese ideograms', Edgar thinks of one image (*DK*, 105; emphasis in original), and another character asks him, 'can ghosts write on canvas?' (*DK*, 404). 'I copied it out of a book' (*DK*, 17), Freemantle admits of his early effort. In another familiar metaphor early on, he dismisses his art: 'Each sunset was only a pencilled piece of shit' (*DK*, 55).

Such rhetoric implies that the turn to painting in *Duma Key* marks not a shift away from, but a covert movement back towards, or reiteration of, writing as the principal vehicle of King's Gothic.

Edgar Freemantle is clearly another version of King's writer-heroes, masquerading now as a painter. The final paragraphs of the novel invite analysis in these terms, as Edgar returns, after the novel's climactic action, to 'the house on Aster lane' (*DK*, 578) and to painting. His new picture, 'rendered so realistically', yet with that 'perfect surreal touch' (*DK*, 578), is of his old house on Duma Key, with its 'pilings' and 'two red-headed dolls' (*DK*, 578). The 'pilings' at the end of this text echo the 'pilings' of Revere beach imagined by Paul Sheldon (*M*, 4) in his initial agony in *Misery*, and the ending of *Duma Key* is effectively a reprise of *Misery* as, just as Paul's writerly creativity returns, so Edgar's 'remembered sensation of power' (*DK*, 578) also returns, enabling him (in further echoes of *Misery*) to 'see my picture almost with the eye of a god . . . or goddess' (*DK*, 579). The final return of *Duma Key* is to the imagery and resurrected creativity of *Misery*, just as the novel itself has reprised other key moments in King's oeuvre. Early on in the novel Edgar dismisses one aspect of its detailed back-story: 'That's just too gothic' (*DK*, 126). *Duma Key*'s repetitions, resurrections and returns are ultimately the keys to its own place as a key text of Gothic excess in the excessively Gothic canon of King's writings, a canon to which (as its title indicates) it aspires, ultimately, to be the 'key'. But *Duma Key* also ends with another reprise, that of the clôture King asserted back in 1990 in the 'Note' to 'Secret Window, Secret Garden', as Edgar describes his 'last painting' when he also takes up his brushes again:

> I painted awhile, then put the brush aside. I mixed brown and yellow together with the ball of my thumb, then skimmed it over the painted beach . . . oh so lightly . . . and a haze of sand lifted, as if on the first hesitant puff of air. (*DK*, 578–9)

This time is also a repetition of the new that is, also, old: 'last' and 'first' operate in a complex relationship here that delineates the concern of King's Gothic with a creativity that derives from its own previous productivity and from the traditions it denies. This closure or clôture is also continuation, the double assertion of a beginning in an end, the suspension of ending in beginning-again that perpetuates the Gothic.

Duma Key's apparent return to *Misery* suggests that the two texts are closely linked by their structural and Gothic misogyny and by a concern with the disabled artist, another insistent King trope, inviting contemporary critical analysis through the theoretical lenses of disability studies. This suggests in turn that one of many aspects of King's Gothic can be seen in the image of the writer-artist disabled by creativity, subject to draconian laws of productivity that restrict ('hobble', as it is put in *Misery*) other kinds of freedom. The final sentences of *Duma Key*, cited as the epigraph of this section, complete the novel's exercise in aesthetics, its instructions to the would-be artist. The closing assertion that 'All the rest is only life' implies finally the priority of the artwork over the 'only life', an inverted echo of the 'not life' that King defines (returning again to *Misery*) as 'writing' in 'An Evening with Stephen King': 'In *Misery* and *Bag of Bones*, I think that I was trying to say that writing is not life' (*SW*, 398). This relation between the 'only life' and the 'not life' of King's Gothic, another rhythm that structures its narratives, repeatedly returns in his endings to enforce and repudiate with recurrent insistence the (im-)possibility of Gothic ending.

Notes

1: Rereading Stephen King's Gothic

1. David Punter, 'Problems of recollection and construction: Stephen King', in Victor Sage and Allan Lloyd Smith (eds), *Modern Gothic: A Reader* (Manchester: Manchester University Press, 1996), pp. 121–140 (p. 122).

2. Jacques Derrida, *The Truth in Painting* (Chicago and London: University of Chicago Press, 1987), p. 215.

3. John Frow, *Genre* (Abingdon: Routledge, 2006), p. 66.

4. Fred Botting, *Gothic* (London: Routledge, 1996), p. 180.

5. Ken Gelder, *Popular Fiction: The Logics and Practices of a Literary Field* (Abingdon: Routledge, 2004), p. 19.

6. Tim Underwood and Chuck Miller (eds), *Bare Bones: Conversations on Terror with Stephen King* (Sevenoaks: Hodder & Stoughton), p. 61.

7. Michael R. Collings, cited in Heidi Strengell, *Stephen King: Monsters Live in Ordinary People* (London: Duckworth, 2007), p. 258.

8. Jacques Derrida, 'The Law of genre', in *Acts of Literature* (London: Routledge, 1992), pp. 221–52 (p. 223).

9. Strengell, *Stephen King*, p. 255.

10. Frow, *Genre*, p. 139.

11. Daniela Caselli, *Beckett's Dantes: Intertextuality in the Fiction and Criticism* (Manchester: Manchester University Press, 2005), p. 6.

12. Tony Magistrale, *Landscape of Fear: Stephen King's American Gothic* (Madison, WI: The Popular Press, 1988), p. 2.

13. Ibid., p. 107.

14   Harold Bloom (ed.), *Stephen King: Bloom's Modern Critical Views* (New York: Chelsea House, 2007), p. 208.

15   Gelder, *Popular Fiction*, p. 96.

16   Fred Botting, *Limits of Horror: Technology, Bodies, Gothic* (Manchester: Manchester University Press, 2008), p. 122.

17   Clare Hanson 'Stephen King: powers of horror', in Brian Docherty (ed.), *American Horror Fiction: From Brockden Brown to Stephen King* (Basingstoke: Macmillan, 1990), pp. 135–54.

18   Natalie Schroeder, 'Stephen King's *Misery*: Freudian sexual symbolism and the battle of the sexes', *Journal of Popular Culture*, 30: 2 (1996), pp. 137–48.

19   Anne Williams, *Art of Darkness: A Poetics of Gothic* (Chicago: University of Chicago Press, 1995), p. 50.

20   Jerrold E. Hogle (ed.), *The Cambridge Companion to Gothic Fiction* (Cambridge: Cambridge University Press, 2002), p. 1.

21   Catherine Spooner, *Contemporary Gothic* (London: Reaktion Books, 2006), p. 32.

22   Jerrold E. Hogle, 'The gothic ghost of the counterfeit and the progress of abjection', in David Punter (ed.), *A Companion to the Gothic* (Oxford: Blackwell, 2001), pp. 293–304 (p. 294).

23   Hanson, 'Stephen King', p. 135.

24   Jodey Castricano, *Cryptomimesis: The Gothic and Jacques Derrida's Ghost Writing* (Montreal: McGill-Queen's University Press, 2001), p. 56.

25   Jacques Derrida, *Specters of Marx* (London: Routledge, 1994), p. 10.

26   Castricano, *Cryptomimesis*, p. 57.

27   Punter, 'Problems of recollection and construction', p. 122.

28   Fred Botting, 'Aftergothic: consumption, machines, and black holes', in Hogle, *The Cambridge Companion*, pp. 277–300 (p. 288).

29   Alan Ryan, 'The Marsten House in *'Salem's Lot*', in Tim Underwood and Chuck Miller (eds), *Fear Itself: The Horror Fiction of Stephen King* (New York: Signet/New American Library, 1985), pp. 191–204 (pp. 194–5).

30   George Seferis, *Complete Poems* (London: Anvil Press Poetry, 1995), pp. 113–14.

31   Richard Matheson, *Hell House* (New York: TOR Books, 1999), p. 23.

32   Underwood and Miller (eds), *Bare Bones*, p. 56.

33   Strengell, *Stephen King*, pp. 157–60.

34   Botting, *Limits of Horror*, p. 4.

2: Carrie's *Gothic Script*

1   Shirley Jackson, *The Haunting of Hill House* (London: Robinson, 1987), p. 7.
2   Neil Cornwell, *The Literary Fantastic: From Gothic to Postmodernism* (London: Harvester Wheatsheaf, 1990), p. 107.
3   Strengell, *Stephen King*, p. 162.
4   Hermann Melville, *Moby-Dick, or, The Whale* (London: Penguin Books, 1987), p. 287.
5   Hanson, 'Stephen King', pp. 140–4.
6   Ibid., pp. 142, 141.
7   Chelsea Quinn Yarbro, 'Cinderella's revenge; twists on fairy tales and mythic themes in the work of Stephen King', in Underwood and Miller, *Fear Itself*, pp. 61–74 (p. 63); Linda Badley, 'The sin eater: orality, post-literacy and the early Stephen King', in Bloom, *Stephen King*, pp. 95–124 (p. 104).
8   Douglas E. Winter, *The Art of Darkness: The Life and Fiction of Stephen King* (Sevenoaks: Hodder & Stoughton, 1989), p. 39.
9   Strengell, *Stephen King*, p. 162.
10 James Egan, 'Sacral parody in the fiction of Stephen King', *Journal of Popular Culture*, 23:3 (1989), 125–41 (139); Anne E. Alexander, 'Stephen King's *Carrie*: a universal fairytale', *Journal of Popular Culture*, 13:2 (1979), 282–8 (283).
11 Jackson, *Haunting*, pp. 10–11.
12 Underwood and Miller, *Bare Bones*, p. 17.
13 Winter, *The Art of Darkness*, p. 33.
14 Tony Magistrale, *Hollywood's Stephen King* (Basingstoke: Palgrave Macmillan, 2003), p. 26.
15 Williams, *Art of Darkness*, p. 102.
16 Tom Newhouse, 'A blind date with disaster: adolescent revolt in the fiction of Stephen King', in Garry Hoppenstand and Ray B. Browne (eds), *The Gothic World of Stephen King: Landscape of Nightmares* (Bowling Green, OH: Bowling Green State University Press, 1987), pp. 49–55 (pp. 51–2).
17 Brian McHale, *Postmodernist Fiction* (London and New York: Methuen, 1987), p. 11.
18 Fredric Jameson, *The Geopolitical Aesthetic: Cinema and Space in the World System* (Bloomington: Indiana University Press, 1992), p. 68.
19 Botting, *Limits of Horror*, pp. 15–77.
20 Nicholas Royle, *The Uncanny* (Manchester: Manchester University Press, 2003), p. 12.

21 Alexander, 'Stephen King's *Carrie*', pp. 282–8.
22 Underwood and Miller, *Bare Bones*, p. 204.
23 Royle, *The Uncanny*, p. 271.
24 Ibid., p. 272.
25 Nicholas Royle, *Telepathy and Literature: Essays on the Reading Mind* (Oxford: Blackwell, 1991), p. 7.
26 Royle, *The Uncanny*, p. 261.
27 Valentine Cunningham, *Reading after Theory* (Oxford: Blackwell, 2001), p. 164.
28 Edgar Allan Poe, 'The Purloined Letter' (1845), in J. P. Muller and W. J. Richardson (eds), *The Purloined Poe: Lacan, Derrida, and Psychoanalytic Reading* (Baltimore and London: The Johns Hopkins University Press, 1988), pp. 3–28 (p. 8).
29 Ibid.
30 Jacques Lacan, 'Seminar on *The Purloined Letter*', in Muller and Richardson (eds), *The Purloined Poe*, pp. 28–54 (p. 35).
31 Jacques Derrida, 'The purveyor of truth', in Muller and Richardson, *The Purloined Poe*, pp. 173–212 (p. 198).
32 Hanson, 'Stephen King', p. 142.
33 Ibid., p. 144.
34 Maurice Blanchot, *The Space of Literature* (Lincoln and London: University of Nebraska Press, 1985), p. 22.
35 Derrida, 'The purveyor of truth', pp. 199, 203.
36 Jacques Derrida, 'Telepathy', in Martin McQuillan (ed.), *Deconstruction: A Reader* (Edinburgh: Edinburgh University Press, 1999), pp. 496–526 (p. 521).
37 Derrida, *Specters of Marx*, p. 172.

3: Disinterring, Doubling: King and Traditions

1 Jacques Derrida, *Dissemination* (London: The Athlone Press, 1981), p. 91.
2 Henry James, 'The real thing', in *Collected Stories*, vol. 2 (London: Everyman's Library/Random House, 1999), p. 40.
3 Roger Luckhurst, 'The uncanny after Freud: the contemporary trauma subject and the fiction of Stephen King', in Jo Collins and John Jervis (eds), *Uncanny Modernity* (Basingstoke: Palgrave Macmillan, 2008), pp. 128–45 (p. 136).
4 Bloom, *Stephen King*, p. 61.

[5]   Marshall Brown, *The Gothic Text* (Stanford: Stanford University Press, 2005), p. 128.

[6]   Slavoj Žižek, *Looking Awry: An Introduction to Jacques Lacan through Popular Culture* (Cambridge, MA: MIT Press, 1991), p. 22.

[7]   Bloom, *Stephen King*, p. 207.

[8]   Gelder, *Popular Fiction*, pp. 9–100.

[9]   Andrew Smith and Jeff Wallace (eds), *Gothic Modernisms* (Basingstoke: Palgrave, 2001), pp. 1, 3.

[10] Jane Goldman, *Modernism, 1910–1945: Image to Apocalypse* (Basingstoke: Palgrave Macmillan, 2004); Giovanni Cianci and Jason Harding (eds), *T. S. Eliot and the Idea of Tradition* (Cambridge: Cambridge University Press, 2007).

[11] Goldman, *Modernism*, pp. 87–8.

[12] T. E. Hulme, *Selected Writings* (Manchester: Carcanet, 1998), pp. 61, 66.

[13] Robyn Furth, *Stephen King's The Dark Tower: A Concordance*, vol. II (London: Hodder & Stoughton, 2005), p. 656.

[14] Underwood and Miller, *Bare Bones*, p. 123.

[15] See M. R. Collings, *Stephen King as Richard Bachman* (Mercer Island, WA: Starmont House, 1985).

[16] See Hogle, 'The gothic ghost of the counterfeit'.

[17] Ibid., p. 293.

[18] Ibid.

[19] Ibid., p. 295.

[20] Ibid.

[21] Ibid., p. 298.

[22] Simon Critchley, 'Black Socrates: questioning the philosophical tradition', in Martin McQuillan, *Deconstruction*, pp. 143–153 (p. 149).

[23] Leslie Moran, 'Law and the Gothic imagination', in Fred Botting (ed), *Gothic* (London: D. S. Brewer, 2001), pp. 87–110 (p. 91).

[24] Bloom, *Stephen King*, p. 208.

[25] Punter, *A Companion to the Gothic*, p. x.

[26] Carol Lawson, 'Behind the best-sellers – Stephen King', *New York Times*, 23 September 1979.

[27] T. F. Hoad, *The Oxford Concise Dictionary of Etymology* (Oxford: Oxford University Press, 1996), p. 426.

[28] Jacques Derrida, *Paper Machine* (Stanford: Stanford University Press, 2005), p. 162.

[29] Sigmund Freud, *The Uncanny* (New York and London: Penguin Books, 2003), pp. 141–2.

[30] Royle, *The Uncanny*, p. 16.

31 Sigmund Freud, *The Pelican Freud Library Vol. 11: On Metapsychology – The Theory of Psychoanalysis* (London: Penguin Books, 1984), pp. 283ff.
32 Botting, *Limits of Horror*, p. 185.
33 Fred Botting, *Gothic* (London: Routledge, 1996), p. 174.
34 James, 'The real thing', p. 59.

4: Genre's Gothic Machinery

1 Jacques Derrida, 'Living on: borderlines', in Harold Bloom (ed.), *Deconstruction and Criticism* (London and Henley: Routledge and Kegan Paul, 1979), pp. 62–142 (p. 107).
2 Ben P. Indick, 'King and the literary tradition of horror and the supernatural', in Underwood and Miller, *Fear Itself*, pp. 175–190 (p. 175).
3 Don Herron, 'Horror springs in the fiction of Stephen King', in Underwood and Miller, *Fear Itself*, pp. 75–102 (p. 88).
4 Indick, 'King and the literary tradition', p. 177.
5 Derrida, 'The Law of genre', p. 223.
6 Gelder, *Popular Fiction*, p. 96.
7 Attridge, in Derrida, *Acts of Literature*, p. 221.
8 Frow, *Genre*, p. 102.
9 Ibid., p. 135.
10 Noel Carroll, *The Philosophy of Horror, or Paradoxes of the Heart* (London: Routledge, 1990), pp. 31–2.
11 Derrida, 'The Law of genre', pp. 224–5.
12 Thomas O. Beebee, *The Ideology of Genre: A Comparative Study of Generic Instability* (Pennsylvania: Pennsylvania State University Press, 1994), pp. 249–50.
13 Fredric Jameson, *The Political Unconscious: Narrative as Socially Symbolic Act* (London: Methuen and Co., 1981), p. 107.
14 Ibid., p. 108.
15 Barbara Creed, *The Monstrous-Feminine* (London: Routledge, 1993), pp. 16–30.
16 Strengell, *Stephen King*, p. 239.
17 H. P. Lovecraft, 'The colour out of space', in *The Call of Cthulhu and other Weird Stories* (London: Penguin Books, 2002), pp. 170–199 (p. 181).
18 Ibid., p. 171.
19 Angela Carter, 'Lovecraft and Landscape', in George Hay (ed.), *The Necronomicon: The Book of Dead Names* (London: Corgi Books, 1980), pp. 171–182 (p. 175).

[20]   Roger Luckhurst, *Science Fiction* (Cambridge: Polity, 2005), p. 15; Fredric Jameson, *Archaeologies of the Future: The Desire Called Utopia and other Science Fictions* (London: Verso, 2005), p. 284.

[21]   Fredric Jameson, *Postmodernism, or, The Cultural Logic of Late Capitalism* (London: Verso, 1991), p. 17.

[22]   Strengell, *Stephen King*, p. 238.

[23]   Winter, *The Art of Darkness*, p. 203.

[24]   Strengell, *Stephen King*, p. 240.

[25]   Gilles Deleuze and Felix Guattari, *Anti-Oedipus – Capitalism and Schizophrenia* (London: The Athlone Press, 1984), p. 109.

[26]   Bruce Baugh, 'How Deleuze can help us make literature work', in Ian Buchanan and John Marks (eds), *Deleuze and Literature* (Edinburgh: Edinburgh University Press, 2000), pp. 34–56 (pp. 34, 35).

[27]   Gilles Deleuze and Felix Guattari, *A Thousand Plateaux: Capitalism and Schizophrenia* (London and New York: Continuum, 1988), p. 4.

[28]   Ibid.

[29]   Franz Kafka, *Metamorphosis and Other Stories* (London: Penguin Books, 2007), pp. 147–80.

[30]   Deleuze and Guattari, *A Thousand Plateaux*, pp. 232–309.

[31]   Deleuze and Guattari, *Anti-Oedipus*, p. 8.

[32]   Anna Powell, *Deleuze and Horror Film* (Edinburgh: Edinburgh University Press, 2005), p. 93.

[33]   D. H. Lawrence, *Psychoanalysis and the Unconscious* and *Fantasia of the Unconscious*, in *The Cambridge Edition of the Works of D. H Lawrence* (Cambridge: Cambridge University Press, 2004), p. 12.

[34]   Brian Massumi, *A User's Guide to Capitalism and Schizophrenia: Deviations from Deleuze and Guattari* (Cambridge, MA and London: MIT Press, 1992), p. 30.

[35]   Deleuze and Guattari, *Anti-Oedipus*, p. 1.

[36]   Derrida, 'The Law of genre', p. 221.

[37]   Powell, *Deleuze and Horror Film*, p. 88.

[38]   Derrida, 'The Law of genre', p. 227–8.

5: Misery's Gothic Tropes

[1]   Mary Shelley (1818), *Frankenstein* (Oxford: Oxford World's Classics, 1998), p. 195.

[2]   Ibid.

[3]   Hanson, 'Stephen King', p. 149.

4   C.T. Onions (ed.), *The Shorter Oxford English Dictionary* (Oxford: Oxford University Press, 1975), p. 1334.
5   Shelley, *Frankenstein*, p. 15.
6   Bram Stoker (1897), *Dracula* (Oxford: Oxford University Press, 1996), pp. 301, 308.
7   Edgar Allan Poe, *Tales of Mystery and Imagination* (Leicester: Galley Press, 1987), p. 348.
8   Magistrale, *Landscape of Fear*, p. 16.
9   Strengell, *Stephen King*, p. 103.
10 Poe, *Tales of Mystery and Imagination*, p. 348.
11 Royle, *The Uncanny*, p. 47.
12 Ibid., p. 156.
13 Ibid., p. 143.
14 Freud, *The Uncanny*, p. 124.
15 Ibid., p. 132.
16 Ibid., p. 150.
17 Hoad, *Oxford Concise Dictionary*, p. 295.
18 Samuel Beckett, *The Beckett Trilogy: Molloy, Malone Dies, The Unnameable* (London: Picador, 1979), p. 382.
19 Samuel Beckett, *Endgame* (London: Faber and Faber, 1985), p. 12.
20 Poe, *Tales of Mystery and Imagination*, p. 348.
21 Chris Baldick, *In Frankenstein's Shadow: Myth, Monstrosity and Nineteenth-Century Writing* (Oxford: Oxford University Press, 1987), p. 13.
22 John Fowles, *The French Lieutenant's Woman* ([1967] London: Vintage Books, 2004), p. 390.
23 John Fowles, *The Collector* ([1963] London: Triad Granada, 1982), p. 274.
24 Ibid., pp. 126, 143.
25 See Amit Marcus, 'Narrative ethics and incommensurate discourses: Lyotard's *The Differend* and John Fowles's *The Collector*', *Mosaic*, December 2008.
26 Hanson, 'Stephen King', p. 150.
27 Fowles, *The Collector*, p. 31.
28 Ibid., p. 199.
29 Ibid., pp. 147, 159, 142.
30 Ibid., p. 129.
31 Ibid., p. 271.
32 Badley, 'The sin eater', p. 112.
33 Friedrich Nietzsche, *Beyond Good and Evil* (Harmondsworth: Penguin Books, 1973), p. 84.
34 Kathleen Margaret Lant, 'The rape of constant reader: Stephen King's

construction of the female reader and violation of the female body in
Misery', in Bloom, *Stephen King*, pp. 141–166 (p. 153).

35 Fowles, *The Collector*, p. 167.
36 T. S. Eliot, *Collected Poems and Plays* (London: Faber & Faber, 1969),
    p. 174.
37 Fowles, *The Collector*, p. 132.
38 George Landow, cited in Sean Burke, *The Death and Return of the Author:
    Criticism and Subjectivity in Barthes, Foucault and Derrida* (Edinburgh:
    Edinburgh University Press, 1998), p. 200.
39 See typescript in Box 2303, Stephen King Papers, Fogler Library Col-
    lection.
40 Roland Barthes, 'The death of the author', in *Image-Music-Text* (London:
    Fontana, 1977), pp. 142–8.
41 Underwood and Miller, *Bare Bones*, p. 121.
42 Barthes, 'The death of the author', p. 148.
43 Ibid., p. 144.

6: Gothic Time in 'The Langoliers'

1   H. G. Wells (1895), *The Time Machine* (London: Dent, 2002), p. 47.
2   Emmanuel Levinas, *Time and the Other* (Pittsburgh: Duquesne University
    Press, 1987), p. 52.
3   Kelly Hurley, 'British Gothic fiction 1885–1930', in Hogle, *The Cam-
    bridge Companion to Gothic Fiction*, pp. 189–208 (p. 197).
4   Luckhurst, *Science Fiction*, p. 35.
5   Wells, *The Time Machine*, p. 66.
6   Ibid., p. 46.
7   Ibid., p. 11.
8   Ibid., p. 9.
9   Ibid., p. 95.
10 Ibid., pp. 14–15.
11 Luckhurst, *Science Fiction*, p. 39.
12 Wells, *The Time Machine*, p. 30.
13 Derrida, *Specters of Marx*, p. 38.
14 Jacques Derrida, *The Politics of Friendship* (London: Verso, 2005), p. 76.
15 Ibid., p. 76.
16 Jacques Derrida, 'Violence and metaphysics: an essay on the thought
    of Emmanuel Levinas', in *Writing and Difference* (London, Melbourne
    and Henley: Routledge and Kegan Paul, 1978), pp. 97–192.

17 Derrida, *The Politics of Friendship*, p. 77.
18 Wells, *The Time Machine*, p. 44.
19 Jacques Derrida, *Margins of Philosophy* (Brighton: The Harvester Press, 1982), p. 4.
20 Derrida, *Specters of Marx*, p. 18.
21 Gilles Deleuze, *The Logic of Sense* (London and New York: Continuum, 1990), p. 73.
22 Ibid.
23 David Glover, 'The spectrality effect in early modernism', in Smith and Wallace, *Gothic Modernisms*, pp. 29–43 (pp. 31–2).
24 Kurt Vonnegut, *Slaughterhouse-5* (St Albans: Triad/Granada, 1979), p. 23.
25 Jacques Derrida, 'Of an apocalyptic tone recently adopted in philosophy', *Oxford Literary Review*, 6:2 (1984), 3–37 (27–8).
26 Jacques Derrida, 'No apocalypse, not now (full speed ahead, seven missiles, seven missives)', in *Psyche: Inventions of the Other Vol. 1* (Stanford: Stanford University Press, 2007), pp. 387–409 (pp. 404–5).
27 Jacques Derrida, *Of Grammatology* (Baltimore and London: The Johns Hopkins University Press, 1976), pp. lxxxix–lc.
28 Jacques Derrida, *The Truth in Painting* (Chicago and London: The University of Chicago Press, 1987), p. 108.
29 William Shakespeare, *Macbeth* (Stratford: The Arden Shakespeare, 2001), V. viii. 16, p. 159.
30 Derrida, *Specters of Marx*, p. 3.
31 Maurice Blanchot, *The Writing of the Disaster* (Lincoln and London: University of Nebraska Press, 1995), p. 28.
32 Jacques Derrida, *Writing and Difference*, p. 225.
33 Derrida, *Margins of Philosophy*, p. 8.
34 Derrida, *Specters of Marx*, p. 37.
35 Derrida, *The Truth in Painting*, p. 223.

7. 'This Inhuman Place': King's Gothic Places

1 Alasdair Patterson, *Topiary* (Durham: Pig Press, 1982), p. 17.
2 See Stephen King Special Papers, Fogler Library Collections, Box 1014, File 1, MS 278.
3 Slavoj Žižek, *In Defence of Lost Causes* (London: Verso, 2008), p. 16.
4 Fredric Jameson, *Signatures of the Visible* (London: Routledge 1992), p. 93.

Notes

5   Hoppenstand and Brown, *The Gothic World of Stephen King*, p. 6.
6   Rebecca Janicker, 'The horrors of Maine: space, place and regionalism in Stephen King's *Pet Sematary*', *U. S. Studies Online*, vol. 11 (Autumn 2007), n.p.
7   Tony Magistrale, 'Stephen King's *Pet Sematary*: Hawthorne's woods revisited', in Hoppenstand and Browne, *The Gothic World of Stephen King*, pp. 126–134 (p. 127).
8   Carter, 'Lovecraft and landscape', p. 173.
9   Magistrale, *Landscape of Fear*, p. 25.
10 Eve Kosofsky Sedgwick, *The Coherence of Gothic Conventions* (London: Methuen and Co., 1986), p. 9.
11 Brown, *The Gothic Text*, pp. 28, 190.
12 Gaston Bachelard, *The Poetics of Space* (Boston, MA: Beacon Press, 1994), p. 8.
13 Williams, *Art of Darkness*, p. 39.
14 Ibid., p. 39.
15 Castricano, *Cryptomimesis*, p. 61.
16 Jean-François Lyotard, *The Inhuman: Reflections on Time* (Oxford: Polity Press, 1991), p. 2.
17 Ibid., p. 50.
18 Royle, *The Uncanny*, p. 257.
19 Mark Wigley, *The Architecture of Deconstruction: Derrida's Haunt* (Cambridge, MA: MIT Press, 1993), pp. 107–8.
20 Botting, *Gothic*, p. 3.
21 Poe, *Tales of Mystery and Imagination*, p. 388.
22 Eliot, *Collected Poems and Plays*, pp. 71, 61, 72.
23 See for example Valdine Clemens, *The Return of the Repressed: Gothic Horror from* The Castle of Otranto *to* Alien (Albany: State University of New York Press, 1999), p. 187.
24 Hanson, 'Stephen King', p. 148.
25 Clemens, *The Return of the Repressed*, pp. 187, 190.
26 Linda Holland-Toll, 'Bakhtin's carnival reversed – King's *The Shining* as dark carnival', *Journal of Popular Culture*, 33;2 (1999), 131–46 (133.)
27 Strengell, *Stephen King*, p. 96.
28 Ibid., pp. 87–8.
29 Joseph Grixti, *Terrors of Uncertainty: The Cultural Contexts of Horror Fiction* (London: Routledge, 1989), p. 59.
30 Hanson, 'Stephen King', p. 148.
31 Steven Bruhm, 'Picture this: Stephen King's queer gothic', in Punter, *A Companion to the Gothic*, pp. 269–280 (pp. 269–70).

32 Michel Foucault, 'Of other spaces', *Diacritics*, 16:1 (Spring 1986), 22–7 (24).
33 Fred Botting, 'In gothic darkly: heterotopia, history, culture', in Punter, *A Companion to the Gothic*, pp. 3–14 (p. 9).
34 Bruhm, 'Picture this', p. 271.
35 Freud, *The Uncanny*, p. 141.
36 Hoad, *Oxford Concise Dictionary*, p. 498.
37 Ibid., p. 299.

8. Facing Gothic Monstrosity

1 Underwood and Miller, *Bare Bones*, p. 197.
2 Rainer Maria Rilke, *The Notebooks of Malte Laurids Brigge* (London: Penguin Books, 2009), p. 6.
3 Michel Foucault, *Abnormal: Lectures at the College de France 1974–1975* (London: Verso, 2003), p. 56.
4 Creed, *The Monstrous-Feminine*, p. 10.
5 Jacques Lacan, *The Ethics of Psychoanalysis: The Seminar of Jacques Lacan Book VII* (London: Routledge, 1992), p. 52.
6 See Freud, *On Metapsychology*.
7 Douglas Keesey, 'The face of Mr Flip: homophobia in the horror of Stephen King', in Bloom, *Stephen King*, pp. 67–82 (p. 67).
8 Jacques Lacan, *Écrits: A Selection* (London: Tavistock, 1977), p. 147.
9 Sigmund Freud, *The Pelican Freud Library Vol. 2: New Introductory Lectures on Psychoanalysis* (Harmondsworth: Penguin Books, 1973), pp. 104, 107.
10 Ibid., p. 112.
11 Strengell, *Stephen King*, p. 178.
12 Lars Iyer, *The Critique of Everyday Life* (weblog; 2005).
13 Yarbro, 'Cinderella's revenge', p. 65; see also Hanson, 'Stephen King'; Lant, 'The rape of constant reader'; Luckhurst, 'The uncanny after Freud'.
14 William Wordsworth and Samuel T. Coleridge, *Lyrical Ballads* (London: Routledge, 2005), p. 60.
15 Lyotard, *The Inhuman*, pp. 184–5.
16 Deleuze and Guattari, *A Thousand Plateaux*, pp. 168, 190.
17 Underwood and Miller, *Bare Bones*, p. 94.
18 Deleuze and Guattari, *A Thousand Plateaux*, pp. 167–8.
19 Richard Rushton, 'What can a face do?', *Cultural Critique*, 51 (2002), 219–37 (225).
20 Deleuze and Guattari, *A Thousand Plateaux*, p. 167.

21   Gilles Deleuze, *Cinema 1: The Movement Image* (London: The Athlone Press, 1992), p. 87.

22   Deleuze and Guattari, *A Thousand Plateaux*, p. 167.

23   W. W. Jacobs, *The Monkey's Paw and Other Stories* ([1902] Harmondsworth: Penguin Books, 1962), p. 65.

24   Žižek, *Looking Awry*, p. 25.

25   Patricia MacCormack, 'Pleasure, perversion, death: three lines of flight for the viewing body', section 3.1, 'A brief introduction to psychoanalytic death' (2009), n.p.

26   See Castricano, *Cryptomimesis*, pp. 54–82.

27   Shelley, *Frankenstein*, p. 9.

28   Mary Ferguson Pharr, 'A dream of new life: Stephen King's *Pet Sematary* as a variant of *Frankenstein*', in Hoppenstand and Brown, *The Gothic World of Stephen King*, pp. 115–125 (p. 120).

29   Žižek, *Looking Awry*, p. 26.

30   Lacan, *The Ethics of Psychoanalysis*, p. 248.

31   Richard Matheson, *I am Legend* ([1956] London: Victor Gollancz, 2006), p. 66.

32   See Stephen King Special Papers, Box 1014, edited TS, entitled *The Pet Sematary*, dated 24 September 1979, p. 186.

Conclusion: King's Gothic Endings

1   Simon Critchley, *The Ethics of Deconstruction* (Edinburgh: Edinburgh University Press, 1999), pp. 88–9.

2   Ibid., p. 81.

3   Yarbro, 'Cinderella's revenge', p. 65.

4   Bruhm, 'Picture this', pp. 269–80.

5   Sean Eads, 'The vampire George Middler: selling the monstrous in *'Salem's Lot*', *Journal of Popular Culture*, 43:1 (2010), 78–96 (83).

6   Strengell, *Stephen King*, p. 44.

7   Sherry R. Truffin, "Screaming while school was in session': the construction of monstrosity in Stephen King's schoolhouse gothic', in Ruth Anolik and Douglas L. Howard (eds), *The Gothic Other: Racial and Social Constructions in the Literary Imagination* (Jefferson, NC: MacFarland and Co., 2004), pp. 236–48.

8   Hoad, *Oxford Concise Dictionary*, p. 424.

Bibliography

Primary sources

Stephen Edwin King Papers, Special Collections, Raymond H. Fogler Library, University of Maine:

Box 718 *Carrie*
Box 1008 *The Shining*
Box 1014 *The Pet Sematary*
Box 1016 *Skeleton Crew*
Box 1019 *The Dark Half*
Box 2293 *Four Past Midnight*
Box 2303 *Misery*
Box 2314 *The Tommyknockers*
Box 2702 *Articles, Synopses and Editorials*
Box 2703 *Books about King*

Secondary sources

Alexander, A. E. (1979). 'Stephen King's *Carrie*: a universal fairytale', *Journal of Popular Culture*, 13: 2, 282–8.
Anolik, R. B. and Howard, D. L. (eds) (2004). *The Gothic Other: Racial and Social Constructions in the Literary Imagination* (Jefferson, NC: McFarland and Company).

Bachelard, G. (1994). *The Poetics of Space*, trans. Maria Jolas (Boston, MA: Beacon Press).

Badley, L. (2007). 'The sin eater: orality, post-literacy and the early Stephen King' in Bloom (ed.) (2007), pp. 95–124.

Baldick, C. (1987). *In Frankenstein's Shadow: Myth, Monstrosity, and Nineteenth-century Writing* (Oxford: Oxford University Press).

Barthes, R. (1977). 'The death of the author', in *Image-Music-Text*, ed. and trans. Stephen Heath (London: Fontana).

Baugh, B. (2000). 'How Deleuze can help us make literature work', in Buchanan, I. and Marks, J. (eds) (2000), pp. 34–56.

Beahm, G. (ed.) (1989). *The Stephen King Companion* (London: Macdonald and Co.).

Beckett, S. (1979). *The Beckett Trilogy: Molloy, Malone Dies, The Unnameable* (London: Picador).

Beckett, S. (1985). *Endgame* (London: Faber & Faber).

Beebee, T. O. (1994). *The Ideology of Genre: A Comparative Study of Generic Instability* (Pennsylvania: Pennsylvania State University Press).

Blanchot, M. (1985). *The Space of Literature*, trans. Ann Smock (Lincoln and London: University of Nebraska Press).

Blanchot, M. (1995). *The Writing of the Disaster*, trans. Ann Smock (Lincoln and London: University of Nebraska Press).

Bloom, H. (ed.) (1979). *Deconstruction and Criticism* (London and Henley: Routledge and Kegan Paul).

Bloom, H. (ed.) (2007). *Stephen King: Bloom's Modern Critical Views* (New York: Chelsea House.

Botting, F. (1996). *Gothic* (London: Routledge).

Botting, F. (2001). *The Gothic: Essays and Studies 2001* (Cambridge: D. S. Brewer).

Botting, F. (2002). 'Aftergothic: consumption, machines, and black holes', in Hogle, J. E. (2002), pp. 277–300.

Botting, F. (2008a). *Limits of Horror: Technology, Bodies, Gothic* (Manchester: Manchester University Press).

Botting, F. (2008b). *Gothic Romanced: Consumption, Gender and Technology in Contemporary Fiction* (Abingdon: Routledge).

Boundas, C.V. and Olkowski, D. (eds) (1994). *Gilles Deleuze and the Theater of Philosophy* (London: Routledge).

Brannigan, J., Robbins, R. and Wolfreys, J. (eds) (1996). *Applying: To Derrida* (Basingstoke: Macmillan).

Brown, M. (2005). *The Gothic Text* (Stanford: Stanford University Press).

Bruhm, S. (2001). 'Picture this: Stephen King's queer Gothic', in Punter (ed.) (2001), pp. 269–80.

Buchanan, I. and Marks, J. (eds) (2000). *Deleuze and Literature* (Edinburgh: Edinburgh University Press).

Burke, S. (1998). *The Death and Return of the Author: Criticism and Subjectivity in Barthes, Foucault and Derrida* (2nd edn) (Edinburgh: Edinburgh University Press).

Carroll, N. (1990). *The Philosophy of Horror, or Paradoxes of the Heart* (London: Routledge).

Carter, A. (1980). 'Lovecraft and landscape', in Hay, G. (ed.) (1980), pp. 171–82.

Caselli, D. (2005). *Beckett's Dantes: Intertextuality in the Fiction and Criticism* (Manchester: Manchester University Press).

Castricano, J. (2001). *Cryptomimesis: The Gothic and Jacques Derrida's Ghost Writing* (Montreal: McGill-Queen's University Press).

Cianci, G. and Harding, J. (eds) (2007). *T. S. Eliot and the Idea of Tradition* (Cambridge: Cambridge University Press).

Clemens, V. (1999). *The Return of the Repressed: Gothic Horror from The Castle of Otranto to Alien* (Albany: State University of New York Press).

Collins, J. and Jervis, J. (eds) (2008). *Uncanny Modernity: Cultural Theories, Modern Anxieties* (Basingstoke: Palgrave Macmillan).

Collings, M. R. (1985). *Stephen King as Richard Bachman* (Mercer Island, WA: Starmont House).

Cornwell, N. (1990). *The Literary Fantastic: From Gothic to Postmodernism* (London: Harvester Wheatsheaf).

Creed, B. (1993). *The Monstrous-Feminine: Film, Feminism, Psychoanalysis* (London: Routledge).

Critchley, S. (1999). *The Ethics of Deconstruction* (2nd edn) (Edinburgh: Edinburgh University Press).

Critchley, S. (1999). 'Black Socrates: questioning the philosophical tradition', in McQuillan, M. (ed.) (1999), pp. 143–53.

Cunningham, V. (2001). *Reading After Theory* (Oxford: Blackwell).

Davidson, H. (ed.) (1999). *T. S. Eliot* (London: Longman).

Deleuze, G. and Guattari, F. (1984). *Anti-Oedipus: Capitalism and Schizophrenia*, ed. and trans. Brian Massumi (London: The Athlone Press).

Deleuze, G. and Guattari, F. (1988). *A Thousand Plateaux: Capitalism and Schizophrenia*, trans. Brian Massumi (London and New York: Continuum).

Deleuze, G. (1990). *The Logic of Sense*, trans. Mark Lester with Charles Stivale (London and New York: Continuum).

Deleuze, G. (1992). *Cinema I: The Movement Image*, trans. Hugh Tomlinson and Barbara Habberjam (London: The Athlone Press).

Derrida, J. (1976). *Of Grammatology*, trans. Gayatri Chakravorty Spivak (Baltimore and London: The Johns Hopkins University Press).

Derrida, J. (1978). *Writing and Difference*, trans. Alan Bass (London, Melbourne and Henley: Routledge and Kegan Paul).

Derrida, J. (1979). 'Living on: borderlines', in Bloom, H. (ed.) (1979), pp. 62–142.

Derrida, J. (1981). *Dissemination*, trans. Barbara Johnson (London: The Athlone Press).

Derrida, J. (1982). *Margins of Philosophy*, trans. Alan Bass (Brighton: The Harvester Press).

Derrida, J. (1984). 'Of an apocalyptic tone recently adopted in philosophy', trans. John P. Leavey, Jr., *Oxford Literary Review*, 6: 2, 3–37.

Derrida, J. (1987a). *The Truth in Painting*, trans. Geoff Bennington and Ian McLeod (Chicago and London: The University of Chicago Press).

Derrida, J. (1987b). 'Geschlecht II: Heidegger's hand', trans. John P. Leavey, Jr., in Sallis, J. (ed.) (1987), pp. 161–96.

Derrida, J. (1988). 'The purveyor of truth', in Muller, J. P. and Richardson W. J. (eds) (1988), pp. 173–212.

Derrida, J. (1992). *Acts of Literature*, ed. Derek Attridge (London: Routledge).

Derrida, J. (1994). *Specters of Marx*, trans. Peggy Kamuf (London: Routledge).

Derrida, J. (1999). 'Telepathy', in McQuillan, M. (ed.) (1999), pp. 496–526.

Derrida, J. (2005a). *The Politics of Friendship*, trans. George Collins (London: Verso).

Derrida, J. (2005b). *Paper Machine*, trans. Rachel Bowlby (Stanford: Stanford University Press).

Derrida, J. (2007). *Psyche: Inventions of the Other Vol. 1*, ed. Peggy Kamuf and Elisabeth Rothenburg (Stanford: Stanford University Press).

Docherty, B. (ed.) (1990). *American Horror Fiction: From Brockden Brown to Stephen King* (Basingstoke: Macmillan).

Eads, S. (2010). 'The vampire George Middler: selling the monstrous in '*Salem's Lot*', *Journal of Popular Culture*, 43: 1, 78–96.

Egan, J. (1989). 'Sacral parody in the fiction of Stephen King', *Journal of Popular Culture*, 23: 3, 125–41.

Eliot, T. S. (1969). *The Complete Poems and Plays of T. S. Eliot* (London: Faber & Faber).

Fantastic Fiction Ltd. Available online at *http://www.fantasticfiction.co.uk/s/shane-stevens/dead-city.htm* [accessed 1 February 2010].

Fischer, W. A. (2002). 'Stephen King and the publishing industry's worst nightmare', *Business Strategy Review*, 13: 2, 1–10.

Foucault, M. (1986). 'Of other spaces', trans. Jay Miskowiec, *Diacritics*, 6: 1 (Spring), 22–7.

Foucault, M. (2003). *Abnormal: Lectures at the Collège de France 1974–1975*, ed.Valerio Marchetti and Antonella Salomoni, trans. Graham Burchell (London:Verso).

Fowles, J. (1982). *The Collector* (London:Triad/Granada).

Fowles, J. (2004). *The French Lieutenant's Woman* (London: Vintage Books).

Freud, S. (1973). *The Pelican Freud Library Vol. 2: New Introductory Lectures on Psychoanalysis*, ed. and trans. James Strachey (Harmondsworth: Penguin Books).

Freud, S. (1984). *The Pelican Freud Library Vol. 11: On Metapsychology – The Theory of Psychoanalysis*, ed. Angela Richards, trans. James Strachey (London: Penguin Books).

Freud, S. (2003). *The Uncanny*, trans. David McClintock (New York and London: Penguin Books).

Frow, J. (2006). *Genre* (Abingdon: Routledge).

Furth, R. (2005). *Stephen King's* The Dark Tower*: A Concordance*, vol. II (London: Hodder & Stoughton).

Gelder, K. (2004). *Popular Fiction:The Logics and Practices of a Literary Field* (Abingdon: Routledge).

Glover, D. (2001). 'The spectrality effect in early modernism', in Smith, A. and Wallace, J. (eds) (2001), pp. 29–43.

Goldman, J. (2004). *Modernism, 1910–1945:Image toApocalypse* (Basingstoke: Palgrave Macmillan).

Grixti, J. (1989). *Terrors of Uncertainty:The Cultural Contexts of Horror Fiction* (London: Routledge).

Grunenberg, C. (1997). *Gothic: Transmutations of Horror in Late Twentieth Century Art* (Boston, MA: ICA and Cambridge, MA: MIT Press).

Hanson, C. (1990). 'Stephen King: powers of horror', in Docherty, B. (ed.) (1990), pp. 135–54.

Hay, G. (ed.) 1980. *The Necronomicon: The Book of Dead Names* (London: Corgi Books).

Herron, D. (1985). 'Horror springs in the fiction of Stephen King', in Underwood,T. and Miller, C. (eds) (1985), pp. 75–102.

Hoad,T. F. (ed.) (1996). *The Oxford Concise Dictionary of English Etymology* (Oxford: Oxford University Press).

Hogle, J. E., 'The Gothic ghost of the counterfeit and the progress of abjection', in Punter, D. (ed.) (2001), pp. 293–304.

Hogle, J. E. (ed.) (2002). *The Cambridge Companion to Gothic Fiction* (Cambridge: Cambridge University Press).

Hohne, K. A. (1994). 'The power of the spoken word in the works of Stephen King', *Journal of Popular Culture*, 28: 2, 93–103.

Holland-Toll, L. (1999). 'Bakhtin's carnival reversed: King's *The Shining* as dark carnival', Journal of Popular Culture, 33: 2, 131–46.

Holmgren-Troy, M. and Wennö, E. (eds) (2008). *Space, Haunting, Discourse* (Cambridge: Cambridge Scholars Publishing).

Hoppenstand, G. and Browne, R. B. (eds) (1987). *The Gothic World of Stephen King: Landscape of Nightmares* (Bowling Green, OH: Bowling Green State University Press).

Hulme, T. E. (1998). *Selected Writings*, ed. Patrick McGuinness (Manchester: Carcanet).

Hurley, K. (1996). *The Gothic Body: Sexuality, Materialism and Degeneration at the* fin de siècle (Cambridge: Cambridge University Press).

Hurley, K. (2002). 'British Gothic fiction 1885–1930', in Hogle, J. E. (ed.) (2002), pp. 189–208.

Indick, B. P. (1985). 'King and the literary tradition of horror and the supernatural', in Underwood, T. and Miller, C. (eds) (1985), pp. 175–90.

Iyer, L. (2005). *The Critique of Everyday Life* (weblog). Available online at *http://spurious.typepad.com/spurious/(2005)/03/the_everyday_1.html* [accessed 13 December 2009].

Jacobs, W.W. (1962). *The Monkey's Paw and Other Stories* (Harmondsworth: Penguin Books).

Jackson, S. (1987). *The Haunting of Hill House* (London: Robinson).

James, H. (1999). *Collected Stories*, vol. 2, sel. John Bayley (London: Everyman's Library/Random House).

Jameson, F. (1981). *The Political Unconscious: Narrative as Socially Symbolic Act* (London: Methuen and Co.).

Jameson, F. (1991). *Postmodernism Or, The Cultural Logic of Late Capitalism* (London and New York: Verso).

Jameson, F. (1992a). *The Geopolitical Aesthetic: Cinema and Space in the World System* (Bloomington: Indiana University Press).

Jameson, F. (1992b). *Signatures of the Visible* (London: Routledge).

Jameson, F. (2005). *Archaeologies of the Future: The Desire Called Utopia and Other Science Fictions* (London: Verso).

Janicker, R. (2007). 'The horrors of Maine: space, place and regionalism in Stephen King's *Pet Sematary*', U.S. Studies Online (11, Autumn 2007). Available online at *http://www.baas.ac.uk/index.php?option=com_content &view=article&id=157%3Aissue-11-autumn-2007-article-2&catid=15&Itemid=11* [accessed 10 June 2010].

Jones, S. (ed.) (1992). *James Herbert: By Horror Haunted* (Sevenoaks: New English Library).

Kafka, F. (2007). *Metamorphosis and Other Stories*, trans. Michael Hofmann (London: Penguin Books).

Keesey, D. (2007). 'The face of Mr Flip: homophobia in the horror of Stephen King', in Bloom, H. (ed.) (2007), pp. 67–82.

Kosofsky Sedgwick, E. (1986). *The Coherence of Gothic Conventions* (London: Methuen and Co.).

Kristeva, J. (1982). *Powers of Horror: An Essay on Abjection*, trans. Leon S. Roudiez (New York: Columbia University Press).

Lacan, J. (1977). *Écrits: A Selection*, ed. and trans. Alan Sheridan (London: Tavistock).

Lacan, J. (1988). 'Seminar on *The Purloined Letter*', in Muller, J. P. and Richardson, W. J. (eds) (1988), pp. 28–54.

Lacan, J. (1992). *The Ethics of Psychoanalysis: The Seminar of Jacques Lacan Book VII, 1959–1960*, ed. Jacques-Alain Miller, trans. Dennis Porter (London: Routledge).

Lant, K. M. (2007). 'The rape of constant reader: Stephen King's construction of the female reader and violation of the female body in *Misery*', in Bloom, H. (ed.) (2007), pp. 141–66.

Lawrence, D. H. (2004). *Psychoanalysis and the Unconscious and Fantasia of the Unconscious*, in *The Cambridge Edition of the Works of D. H. Lawrence*, ed. Bruce Steele (Cambridge: Cambridge University Press).

Lawson, C. (1979). 'Behind the best-sellers – Stephen King', New York Times, 23 September. Available online at *http://www.nytimes.com/books/97/03/09/lifetimes/kin-v-behind.html* [accessed 1 March 2010].

Levinas, E. (1987). *Time and the Other [and Additional Essays]*, trans. Richard A. Cohen (Pittsburgh: Duquesne University Press).

Levinas, E. (1996). *Proper Names*, trans. Michael B. Smith (London: The Athlone Press).

Levinas, E. (2001). *Existence and Existents*, trans. Alphonso Lingis (Pittsburgh: Duquesne University Press).

Levinas, E. (2003). *Totality and Infinity: An Essay on Exteriority*, trans. Alphonso Lingis (Pittsburgh: Duquesne University Press).

Lovecraft, H. P. (1973). *Supernatural Horror in Literature* (New York: Dover Publications).

Lovecraft, H. P. (2002). *The Call of Cthulhu and Other Weird Stories*, ed. S. T. Joshi (London: Penguin Books).

Lovecraft, H. P. (2002). 'The Colour Out of Space', in Lovecraft (2002), pp. 170–99.

Luckhurst, R. (2005). *Science Fiction* (Cambridge: Polity).

Luckhurst, R. (2008). 'The Uncanny after Freud: the contemporary trauma subject and the fiction of Stephen King', in Collins, J. and Jervis, J. (eds) (2008), pp. 128–45.

Lyotard, J.-F. (1991). *The Inhuman: Reflections on Time*, trans. Geoffrey Bennington and Rachel Bowlby (Oxford: Polity Press).

MacCormack, P. (2009). 'Pleasure, perversion and death: three lines of flight for the viewing body', section 3.1, 'A brief introduction to psychoanalytic death'. Available online at *http://www.cinestatic.com/trans-mat/MacCormack/PPD3-5.htm* [accessed 28 January 2009].

McHale, B. (1987). *Postmodernist Fiction* (London and New York: Methuen).

McQuillan, M. (ed.) (1999). *Deconstruction: A Reader* (Edinburgh: Edinburgh University Press).

Magistrale, T. (1987). 'Stephen King's *Pet Sematary*: Hawthorne's woods revisited', in Hoppenstand, G. and Browne, R. (eds) (1987), pp. 126–34.

Magistrale, T. (1988). *Landscape of Fear: Stephen King's American Gothic* (Madison, WI: The Popular Press).

Magistrale, T. (2003). *Hollywood's Stephen King* (Basingstoke: Palgrave Macmillan).

Marcus, A. (2008). 'Narrative ethics and incommensurable discourses: Lyotard's *The Differend* and John Fowles's *The Collector*', Mosaic (December).

Massumi, B. (1992). *A User's Guide to Capitalism and Schizophrenia: Deviations from Deleuze and Guattari* (Cambridge, MA and London: MIT Press).

Matheson, R. (1999). *Hell House* (New York: TOR Books).

Matheson, R. (2006). *I am Legend* (London: Victor Gollancz).

Melville, H. (1987). *Moby-Dick, or, The Whale*, ed. Harold Beaver (London: Penguin Books).

Mighall, R. (1989). *A Geography of Victorian Gothic Fiction: Mapping History's Nightmares* (Oxford: Oxford University Press).

Moran, L. (2001). 'Law and the Gothic imagination', in Botting, F. (ed.) (2001), pp. 87–110.

Morgan, J. (1998). 'Toward an organic theory of the Gothic: conceptualizing horror', *Journal of Popular Culture*, 32: 3, 59–80.

Morrison, T. (1992). *Playing in the Dark: Whiteness and the Literary Imagination* (London: Picador).

Muller, J. P. and Richardson, W. J. (eds) (1988). *The Purloined Poe: Lacan, Derrida, and Psychoanalytic Reading* (Baltimore and London: The Johns Hopkins University Press).

Myrone, M. (ed.) (2006). *The Gothic Reader: A Critical Anthology* (London: Tate Publishing).

Nash, J. W. (1997). 'Postmodern Gothic: Stephen King's Pet Sematary', *Journal of Popular Culture*, 30: 4, 151–60.

Nietzsche, F. (1973). *Beyond Good and Evil*, trans. R. J. Hollingdale (Harmondsworth: Penguin Books).

Onions, C. T. (ed.) (1975). *The Shorter Oxford English Dictionary* (2 vols) (Oxford: Oxford University Press).

Paterson, A. (1982). *Topiary* (Durham: Pig Press).

Pharr, M. P. (1987). 'A dream of new life: Stephen King's *Pet Sematary* as a variant of *Frankenstein*', in Hoppenstand, G. and Brown, R. (eds) (1987), pp. 115–25.

Poe, E. A. (1987). *Tales of Mystery and Imagination* (Leicester: Galley Press).

Poe, E. A. (1988). 'The Purloined Letter', in Muller, J. P. and Richardson, W. J. (eds) (1988), pp. 3–28.

Pourteau, C. (1993). 'The individual and society: narrative structure and thematic unity in Stephen King's Rage', *Journal of Popular Culture*, 27: 1, 171–8.

Powell, A. (2005). *Deleuze and Horror Film* (Edinburgh: Edinburgh University Press).

Punter, D. (1996). 'Problems of recollection and construction: Stephen King', in Sage, V. and Lloyd Smith, A. (eds) (1996), pp. 121–40.

Punter, D. (ed.) (2001). *A Companion to the Gothic* (Oxford: Blackwell).

Rilke, R. M. (2009). *The Notebooks of Malte Laurids Brigge*, trans. Michael Hulse (London: Penguin Books).

Riquelme, J. P. (ed.) (2008). *Gothic Modernism: Essaying Dark Literary Modernity* (Baltimore: The Johns Hopkins University Press).

Robbins, R. and Wolfreys, J. (eds) (2000). *Victorian Gothic: Literary and Cultural Manifestations in the Nineteenth Century* (Basingstoke: Palgrave).

Royle, N. (2003). *The Uncanny* (Manchester: Manchester University Press).

Royle, N. (1991). *Telepathy and Literature: Essays on the Reading Mind* (Oxford: Basil Blackwell).

Rushton, R. (2002). 'What can a face do?', *Cultural Critique*, 51, 219–37.

Ryan, A. (1985). 'The Marsten House in *'Salem's Lot*', in Underwood, T. and Miller, C. (eds) (1985), pp. 191–204.

Sage, V. and Lloyd Smith, A. (eds) (1996). *Modern Gothic: A Reader* (Manchester: Manchester University Press).

Sallis, J. (ed.) (1987). *Deconstruction and Philosophy: The Texts of Jacques Derrida* (Chicago: The University of Chicago Press).

Schroeder, N. (1996). 'Stephen King's *Misery*: Freudian sexual symbolism and the battle of the sexes', *Journal of Popular Culture*, 30: 2, 137–48.

Seferis, G. (1995). *Complete Poems*, trans. and ed. Edmund Keeley and Philip Sherrard (London: Anvil Press Poetry).

Shakespeare, W. (2001). *Macbeth*, ed. Kenneth Muir (Stratford: The Arden Shakespeare).

Shelley, M. (1998). *Frankenstein*, ed. Marilyn Butler (Oxford: Oxford World's Classics).

Smith, A. and Wallace, J. (eds) (2001). *Gothic Modernisms* (Basingstoke: Palgrave).

Spooner, C. (2006). *Contemporary Gothic* (London: Reaktion Books).

Stevenson, R. L. (1979). *Dr Jekyll and Mr Hyde and other stories*, ed. Jenni Calder (London: Penguin Books).

Stoker, B. (1996). *Dracula*, ed. Maud Ellmann (Oxford: Oxford University Press).

Strengell, H. (2007). *Stephen King: Monsters Live in Ordinary People* (London: Duckworth).

Truffin, S. R. (2004). "'Screaming while school was in session': The construction of monstrosity in Stephen King's schoolhouse Gothic', in Anolik, R. and Howard, D. L. (eds) (2004), pp. 236–48.

Underwood, T. and Miller, C. (eds) (1985). *Fear Itself: The Horror Fiction of Stephen King* (New York: Signet/New American Library).

Underwood, T. and Miller, C. (eds) (1986). *Kingdom of Fear: The World of Stephen King* (New York: New English Library/Hodder & Stoughton).

Underwood, T. and Miller, C. (eds) (1989). *Bare Bones: Conversations on Terror with Stephen King* (Sevenoaks: Hodder & Stoughton).

Vidler, A. (1992). *The Architectural Uncanny: Essays in the Modern Unhomely* (Cambridge, MA and London: MIT Press).

Vonnegut, K. (1979). *Slaughterhouse-5* (St Albans: Triad/Granada).

Wells, H. G. (2002). *The Time Machine* (London: J. M. Dent/Everyman's Library).

Wigley, M. (1993). *The Architecture of Deconstruction: Derrida's Haunt* (Cambridge, MA: MIT Press).

Williams, A. (1995). *Art of Darkness: A Poetics of Gothic* (Chicago: University of Chicago Press).

Winter, D. E. (1989). *The Art of Darkness: The Life and Fiction of Stephen King* (Sevenoaks: Hodder & Stoughton).

Wordsworth, W. and Coleridge, S. T. (2005). *Lyrical Ballads*, ed. R. L. Brett and A. R. Jones (London: Routledge).

Yarbro, C. Q. (1985). 'Cinderella's revenge; twists on fairy tales and mythic themes in the work of Stephen King', in Underwood, T. and Miller, C. (eds) (1985), pp. 61–74.

Žižek, S. (1991). *Looking Awry: An Introduction to Jacques Lacan through Popular Culture* (Cambridge, MA: MIT Press).

Žižek, S. (2008). *In Defence of Lost Causes* (London: Verso).

Index

Index